D1665715

LIGHT FOR OUR WORLD

Log cabin, Perry County, 1839

LIGHT FOR OUR WORLD

Essays Commemorating the
150th Anniversary of
Concordia Seminary,
St. Louis, Missouri

Edited by
JOHN W. KLOTZ

1989
CONCORDIA SEMINARY
ST. LOUIS

Concordia Seminary, St. Louis, Missouri 63105

© 1989 Concordia Seminary

ISBN 0-911770-57-7

Printed in the United States of America
By The Ovid Bell Press, Inc., Fulton, Missouri

Foreword

When the 150th Anniversary Committee of Concordia Seminary, St. Louis began its work in preparation for marking the sesquicentennial of the seminary, a variety of suggestions were considered. It was decided that some should be considered which would have a relatively immediate effect and that others should be planned which would have a more lasting effect. Among the latter was the *Festschrift* which is herewith dedicated to the glory of God and to the honor of His name in preserving our heritage of Lutheran confessional theology for these one hundred and fifty years.

The *Festschrift* is a collection of articles which cover a variety of topics, all of them theological in their orientation. Most have been prepared by members of the faculty of Concordia Seminary. Others have been prepared by theologians at our sister seminaries throughout the world. Two alumni have contributed, one who has served in the parish ministry and another who has served on a secular campus. We are honored to have an article by Dr. Ralph A. Bohlmann, President of Synod and who also served as the Seventh President of Concordia Seminary.

The choice of the topics has been left to the authors. The variety of articles is a fitting reflection of the varied interests of those associated with Concordia Seminary; all are oriented, though, to the Scriptures and the Lutheran Confessions and are presented as a mark of gratitude to God for His preserving this institution from its very humble beginnings to its present status as a widely recognized citadel of confessional theology.

A special word of thanks is due to Dr. Quentin F. Wesselschmidt and the staff of *Concordia Journal*, David Kuhfal, Steve Niermann, Steve Smith, James Waddell, and Todd Wilken, for their careful editorial work on the manuscripts. We also acknowledge the important contributions of Dr. August R. Suelflow, who served as Chairman of the 150th Anniversary Committee, to Dr. Karl L. Barth, President of Concordia Seminary, for his encouragement and support in this project, and to the members of the 150th Anniversary

---

JOHN W. KLOTZ is Professor Emeritus of Concordia Seminary, St. Louis.

Academic Planning Subcommittee, who were responsible for organizing and overseeing this project, namely, Professor Andrew H. Bartelt, Dr. John F. Johnson, Dr. John W. Klotz, Dr. J. A. O. Preus III, Professor Leroy E. Vogel, and Dr. Quentin F. Wesselschmidt, Chairman. The Ovid Bell Press, Inc. is also to be thanked for their efforts in producing the *Festschrift*. Thanks are also due The Rev. Roy A. Ledbetter for his translation work.

To Him alone, Father, Son, and Holy Spirit, be the honor and glory!

John W. Klotz, Editor

Table of Contents

South Jefferson Seminary, 1883

LIGHT FOR OUR WORLD

Clayton Seminary, 1926

Introduction

A seminary, by definition, is a "seed plot"—a place where seed is planted and nurtured to enable it to grow, develop, and produce fruit.

For one hundred and fifty years, Concordia Seminary has been a very special kind of "seed plot." There the seed has consciously and consistently been the Word of God, in all its truth, purity, and power—not the notions of men.

There that seed has been planted and nurtured first and foremost in the hearts of men who will be sowers of that same seed as pastors, missionaries, and educators of The Lutheran Church—Missouri Synod.

There the conviction has remained strong that our efforts to nurture the planted seed must be characterized by professionalism and excellence, but with the awareness that only God can give the increase.

There the commitment to "Concordia"—the unified confession of God's truth drawn from the Word of God and set forth in the creeds and Confessions of Lutheranism—has remained steadfast and clear.

Words cannot adequately express the place that Concordia Seminary has occupied in the life and work of The Lutheran Church—Missouri Synod. Thousands of its graduates have served millions of people with the Word of God in the parishes, schools, offices, and mission fields of the Synod. Its professors have been major providers of the books, articles, and other materials that have shaped the theological and pastoral direction of the Synod throughout its history. Three of its presidents have also served as presidents of the Synod, and hundreds of its professors and graduates have served in key synodical leadership positions at various times and places. So close has been the relationship between Concordia Seminary and the Synod that it is virtually impossible to describe one without the other.

But nothing greater can be said about Concordia Seminary than

---

RALPH A. BOHLMANN is President of The Lutheran Church—Missouri Synod. He served as President of Concordia Seminary from 1975 until 1981.

that God's Spirit has used it mightily to bring hundreds of thousands of men and women from the darkness of sin to the light of their salvation in Jesus Christ. "Light is from above," proclaims the seminary motto. Indeed it is—not only in terms of the knowledge of God's will and way for mankind known only from His Word, but also in terms of the faith in Him and His redemptive work that dispels the darkness of sin and evil.

May this volume of essays serve not only to celebrate one hundred and fifty years of God's blessings upon Concordia Seminary, but to signal the seminary's continuing commitment to being a "seed plot" for sowers of God's true, powerful, and saving Word so that His saving light will continue to shine into the darkness of this world.

Ralph A. Bohlmann

Concordia Seminary:
A Theological Seminary of
The Lutheran Church —
Missouri Synod

KARL L. BARTH

> The higher schools are either the foremost arenas of the Holy Spirit for the upbuilding of the church, or they are the foremost arenas of the devil for tearing down the church, either wide open portals of paradise, or, if God's pure Word does not reign in them, as Luther once said of them, "great gates of hell."[1]

By God's grace, Concordia Seminary, celebrating the 150th anniversary of its founding on December 9, 1839, has been an arena where the Spirit of God has been at work to build the church.

This is not to say that the school has not experienced difficult, even turbulent times. Certainly its beginning was anything but auspicious, and its future frequently hung in the balance during the first ten years. The poverty, occasioned in part by the settlers' lack of practicality and evidenced by the fact that some of them had to live without a roof over their heads, was not the great problem. Nor was the "fever" and subsequent heavy death toll among the immigrants the most difficult turmoil. Within a short time all four founders—Brohm, Buenger, Fuerbringer, and Walther—were gone, yet the school survived.

Worst of all was the spiritual turmoil. The deposition of the colony's leader, the Rev. Martin Stephan, was only the prelude to a "witch's caldron of confusion, uncertainty, remorse ... anathema ..."[2] that characterized the conflict, ultimately settled by Walther's victory in the Altenburg Debate of April 1841. Carl S. Meyer ap-

---

KARL. L. BARTH is the Eighth President of Concordia Seminary, St. Louis.

propriately titled the first chapter of his *Log Cabin to Luther Tower* as "Poverty Its Birthright."

There were other periods of trouble and even controversy. The Civil War (which prompted the closing of the school for a short time) and the combining of the two seminaries for a period of years, the *Gnadenwahlstreit* and the disruption of the Synodical Conference, the suspension of the President and the subsequent "walk-out" in 1974 are all a part of the history of Concordia Seminary.

However, in spite of various times of trial, it has been an arena of the Spirit by which God's people have been built. More than 10,000 graduates have gone out to serve in some three dozen countries of the world. The seminary has been a blessing to other Lutherans of this country in a very direct way, at one time serving many students from the Norwegian and Wisconsin Synods.[3] Its faculty has provided strong theological leadership to our Synod throughout its history. The library is visited by scholars from all parts of the world and is acknowledged for its excellence, especially in the fields of Reformation research and Biblical studies. The graduate school, as we shall observe again later, has given strong direction to theologians of varying confessions. These are but a few of the blessings that might be listed under the caption: *Soli Deo Gloria*.

This is Concordia Seminary. Yet, if we were to select one characteristic of this school throughout its history, we should point to its confessional character, that is, its character as an institution confessing as church the doctrine derived from Holy Scripture, that "pure and clear fountain of Israel."[4] Every part—almost every word— of the title of this essay has to do with the seminary's confessional character.

Concordia Seminary is a *theological* seminary. Its "business" is theology. And what is theology? Our father in Christ, Francis Pieper, reminds us that theology is λόγος περὶ τοῦ θεοῦ, and that objectively speaking, theology refers to the doctrine of God.[5] The doctrine of God in turn is embraced in His twofold message of Law and Gospel. In short, Concordia Seminary sees as its task inculcating the doctrine which God has revealed to His creation in His Law and His Gospel.

The Law is a message of directives, prohibitions, threats, curses, death and damnation. "Thou shalt" and "Thou shalt not" is what the Law is all about. It demands perfect obedience to the will of the Creator, a will inscribed in the heart of our first parents in creation and later reduced to writing on Mount Sinai. Indeed, it makes promises. But it makes promises of peace, joy, and eternal life only to those who keep it perfectly. To those who break that Law in even the slightest degree it threatens hell and damnation. Paul's message in Galatians 3:10, "Cursed is everyone who does not continue in all things which are written in the book of the law, to do them," is simply an echoing, as the apostle himself affirms, of what God Himself had told His people in Deuteronomy 27.

The Gospel, on the other hand, brings only good news. It promises, comforts, assures, offers and gives peace, joy, and everlasting life. "God so loved the world that He gave His only begotten Son, that whoever believes in Him should not perish but have everlasting life" (John 3:16). The Savior, promised already to our first parents immediately after their fall in the garden, came to "ransom and redeem" His people. The Lord "laid on Him the iniquity of us all" (Is. 53:6). He "was offered once to bear the sins of many" (Heb. 9:28). And the righteousness which God offers through the merits of this Savior comes "to all and on all who believe" (Rom. 3:22).

Of course, the task of theology and of the theologian is not over when he has simply identified Law and Gospel as the message (the doctrine) of God. The two must be properly distinguished, and that is why the first president of Concordia Seminary, Dr. C. F. W. Walther, delivered thirty-nine lectures over a period of more than a year on "The Proper Distinction Between Law and Gospel." The second of his twenty-five theses states, "Only he is an orthodox teacher who not only presents all the articles of faith in accordance with Scripture, but also rightly distinguishes from each other the Law and the Gospel."[6] And sprinkling his fifth lecture with numerous quotations from both Luther and Gerhard, Walther reminds us that where this distinction between Law and Gospel is not both defined and adhered to, the doctrine of justification ultimately must be lost; the treasures which our Savior has brought to us are obscured, and no abiding comfort can be brought to the sin-stricken conscience of the fallen human beings.

An entire article of the Formula of Concord is devoted to the same subject. "The distinction between Law and Gospel is an especially brilliant light which serves the purpose that the Word of God may be rightly divided and the writings of the holy prophets and apostles may be explained and understood correctly."[7] The article goes on to remind us that all the believers from the beginning of the world have properly distinguished Law and Gospel. So it must be also today. No false promises must be attached to God's stern message of Law. No conditions must be placed upon His sweet and comforting Gospel. Even today it is our prayer that:

... the proclamation of the law and its threats will terrify the hearts of the unrepentant and bring them to a knowledge of their sin and to repentance ... [and] the proclamation of the Gospel of our Lord Christ will once more comfort and strengthen them with the assurance that if they believe the Gospel God forgives them all their sins through Christ, accepts them for His sake as God's children, and out of pure grace, without any merit of their own, justifies and saves them.[8]

Of course, in all of the λόγος περὶ τοῦ θεοῦ, the Gospel, as Dr. Walther points out in his last thesis on *Law and Gospel,* must have predominance. It would be good for every pastor in our church body, every professor at our colleges and seminaries, every student, indeed, every last Christian, to read and re-read that thirty-ninth evening lecture of our sainted father. It is there that he makes his oft-quoted statement, "God grant that someday people may say about you that you are preaching well, but too sweetly!" It is there that he so eloquently urges the students not to stand in their pulpits with long and mournful faces as though they were inviting people to a funeral but like men announcing a wedding. It is there that he quotes from Luther's *Preface to the Epistle to the Galatians,* where Luther says, "In my heart there reigns and shall ever reign this one article, namely, faith in my dear Lord Jesus Christ, which is the sole beginning, middle and end of all spiritual and godly thoughts which I may have at any time, day or night."[9]

This theology, this doctrine of God, comes only from God's book, Holy Scripture. *Quod non est biblicum non est theologicum.* The fathers who produced the confessional writings of the Evangelical Lutheran Church were theological. They were true theologians. In the preface to *The Book of Concord,* they state, "We have in what follows purposed to commit ourselves exclusively and only, in accordance with the pure, infallible, and unalterable word of God."[10] Not only did they make plain their intention "that no other doctrine be treated and taught in our lands, territories, schools, and churches than that alone which is based on the Holy Scriptures of God ..." but they went on to say, "We desire particularly that the young men who are being trained for service in the church and for the holy ministry be faithfully and diligently instructed therein." Indeed, because Holy Scripture was for them the only source and norm of their theology, they could so confidently exclaim, "We are certain of our Christian confession and faith on the basis of the divine, prophetic, and apostolic Scriptures."[11]

In this confession they echoed the spirit of the great reformer, whose quotations on the inspiration, utter reliability, and all-sufficiency of Scripture are legend. Luther wastes no time in getting to his view of Scripture when he writes his preface to the Old Testament. His frequently-cited statement says it all:

> I beg and really caution every pious Christian not to be offended by the simplicity of the language and the stories frequently encountered there but fully realize that, however simple they may seem, these are the very words, works, judgments, and deeds of the majesty, power, and wisdom of the most high God.

And that Luther saw very clearly the close relationship of this view of Scripture to the message of the Gospel, he goes on to say just a few lines later, "Here you will find the swaddling clothes and the manger in which Christ lies, and to which the angel points the shepherds."[12]

And because these Scriptures bring us the words of God (not just the "word" in some undefined sense), Luther describes the attitude of the true theologian when he states, "The Holy Scriptures require a humble reader who shows reverence and fear toward the Word of God and constantly says, 'Teach me, teach me, teach me!'. . . . It's difficult for a man who has excellent gifts not to be arrogant."[13]

Contrast this attitude of Luther and those responsible for our Lutheran Confessions with the attitude of the practitioners of historical criticism. Edgar Krentz describes what took place during the nineteenth century in the area of Biblical interpretation.

> The Scriptures were, so to speak, secularized. The biblical books became historical documents, to be studied and questioned like any other ancient sources. The Bible was no longer the criterion for the writing of history; rather history had become the criterion for understanding the Bible. The variety in the Bible was high-lighted; its unity had to be discovered and could no longer be presumed. The history it reported was no longer assumed to be everywhere correct. The Bible stood before criticism as defendant before judge.[14]

And that the twentieth century has not brought a change for the better is evident when we read later, "The scriptures are *panta anthrôpina,* completely human. This basic recognition about the nature of the Bible entails the axiom that one interprets the Bible by the same methods and procedures used on any other book."[15]

Of course, not all practitioners of historical criticism take the method to what the more radical proponents consider its logical conclusion to be, namely, a denial of Christ's vicarious atonement and the resurrection of our Lord and Savior. Some simply nibble on the edges and question the historicity of the first few chapters of Genesis. Others limit their critical investigation to other stories in the Old Testament. Others deny or at least question some of the miracles of our Savior as well as many of His statements as recorded by the four evangelists. There is a broad spectrum.

However, as our students at Concordia Seminary are reminded in a course on historical criticism, the latter is to be condemned not because of where it *may lead,* but rather it is to be faulted for where it *begins.* When the Bible stands as "defendant before a judge," the moment one interprets the Bible by the same methods and procedures used on any other completely human book, one is engaged in an illicit adventure. The doctrine of the Gospel is not one that dares to float free without any moorings in that reliable Word that we have from our God in Holy Scripture.

Such a magisterial use of reason is a kind of theological "enthusiasm." But it is not the only kind of enthusiasm rampant in our day. There are those who, while they may not look to their own learning, look inward to their feelings. What experiences have they had? How deep is their commitment? What gifts do they have? The *extra nos* character of Lutheran theology is substituted for by an experiential theology that again fails to cling to the Word and clings instead to its own viscera. Nor should this surprise us. Luther reminds us in the Smalcald Articles:

> ... enthusiasm clings to Adam and his descendants from the beginning to the end of the world. It is a poison implanted and inoculated in man by the old dragon, and it is the source, strength and power of all heresy. ... Accordingly, we should and must constantly maintain that God will not deal with us except through His external Word and sacrament. Whatever is attributed to the Spirit apart from such Word and sacrament is of the devil.[16]

Objectively speaking, theology is doctrine. Theology also has its subjective sense and meaning. In its subjective sense, Pieper reminds us, it denotes "the knowledge of God and of divine matters."[17] He goes on to describe theology in its subjective sense as a spiritual aptitude which presupposes that the theologian is a child of God through faith in Jesus Christ. This spiritual aptitude is not something developed in a person by his innate powers or abilities but involves the supernatural working of the Spirit of God. Saint Paul makes that so evident when he writes to his friends in Corinth, "Not that we are sufficient of ourselves to think of anything as being from ourselves, but our sufficiency is from God, who also made us sufficient as ministers of the new covenant" (2 Cor. 3:5-6). He stresses the importance of "the genuine faith that is in you" when he writes to his friend Timothy (2 Tim. 1:5) and in the next chapter reminds the young preacher that "the hard working farmer must be first to partake of the crops" (2:6). And because it is God alone who can make the theologian sufficient, first of all by his conversion, Luther reminds us that popes and universities can make doctors of the arts but only the Holy Spirit can make doctors of the Scriptures.

True it is that a seminary must stress the academic pursuit, and we shall have more to say about that later. However, to define theology as a spiritual aptitude which presupposes a genuine faith in Jesus Christ as the Savior means that a theological seminary must also place great emphasis on the development of the spiritual life of those who will be entrusted with the care of the souls of people.

This is not to say that the efficacy of the means of grace depends upon the faith of those who dispense them. Our father confessors remind us that "the sacraments are efficacious even if the priests who administer them are wicked men."[18] Luther reminds us in the Large Catechism that "even though a knave should receive or administer it, it is the true Sacrament (that is, Christ's body and blood) just as truly as when one uses it most worthily. For it is not founded on the holiness of men but on the Word of God."[19] In other words, a person may be converted through the preaching of an unconverted preacher.

Yet what is happening on the ecclesiastical scene among ordained clergymen must both horrify and warn us. The name of God is blasphemed among the unbelievers through behavior of the clergy that is unseemly, that flaunts the will of God. Much has been written lately about the personal life of Paul Tillich and of other theological "giants." The scandals among television evangelists must have the devil rejoicing. We do not have to look that far away however. Divorce, once a rarity even among our lay people, now is all too common even among the clergy. Drunkenness, immorality, homosexual behavior, contentiousness, laziness, lack of dedication to the divine call, all remind us how important it is that we remember theology as a spiritual aptitude that presupposes faith and a corresponding walk in righteousness of life.

The development of this spiritual aptitude begins with a devotional study of the Word. The theologian is to join the psalmist and say, "How sweet are your words to my taste, sweeter than honey to my mouth!" (Ps. 119:103). He joins the prophet Jeremiah to exclaim, "Your words were found, and I ate them, and your Word was to me the joy and rejoicing of my heart" (Jer. 15:16). In such rejoicing over the Word of God there is the certainty and conviction that it is what it claims to be, the Word of God. And that conviction comes not because some seminary professor tells the student that this ought to be his attitude toward the Word. It comes from reading that Word, which is not only a devouring flame and a crushing hammer but also a live-giving "power of God to salvation" (Rom. 1:16).

The temptation, of course, is for the theologian to feel that he has done enough when he has used that Word in the preparation of his ministerial duties, and he does indeed derive benefit when he uses Scripture as a tool. Spiritual benefit comes to the searcher of the Word when he preaches textual sermons and gathers from other parts of Scripture supporting material for his sermons. The undershepherd does derive benefit when his Bible classes are more than "pooled ignorance" and involve on his part a mining of the treasures of God's Word. He does derive blessing when his topics to groups within the congregation consist of "meat and potatoes" from the rich banquet table that God gives us in His Word. Yet it is essential that he study this Word first of all for *himself* and for the development of that theological aptitude which only the Spirit of God can develop.

Also the prayer life of the pastor (or would-be pastor) is crucial to his development as a theologian. Prayer is not a means of grace. God creates saving faith through Word and Sacrament. "Through these, as through means, He gives the Holy Spirit, who works faith, when and where He pleases, in those who hear the Gospel."[20] Nevertheless, prayer is "the Christian's vital breath," his response by way of praise, thanksgiving, petition, and intercesssion for all that God in mercy has provided by His Spirit. How can one develop as a theologian and grow in the *habitus spiritualis supernaturalis* if he does not spend time each day on his knees in fervent prayer to the God who would use him as His instrument?

The seminary, if it is a theological seminary, must develop this spiritual life. Professors must model it. Lecturers must encourage it. The entire communal life of the seminary is in itself to be a spiritual experience in which we help one another "grow in grace and in the knowledge of our Lord and Savior Jesus Christ" (2 Pet. 3:18).

The emphasis of this essay is on the fact that Concordia Seminary is a *theological* seminary. However, a few things need to be said about the other words in the title, for they, too, bring a theological emphasis. For one thing, we are a *seminary*, not a Bible college. We offer more, and must offer more, than a course or two in doctrine and a few courses on various books of the Bible. Unfortunately, many of those who call continuously for more "real world" preparation seem willing to minimize academic discipline and the need for scholarship. A weekend course is seen as sufficient to equip lay people to preach. Parish evangelists, including those not theologically prepared, are advertised, after brief training in a non-seminary setting, to be available as preachers. Why this frenzy to have people perform ministerial duties without ministerial education and training? "We need results!" A pragmatic age looks for statistics which indicate growth, and there is always the temptation to act as though we want to say, "Hang the theology! Let's get the job done."

The "lamp of learning" which is etched into the stone on our Wyneken Hall is no mere empty symbol. There is in this place a continuing commitment to sound scholarship and to academic excellence on the part of both faculty and students. We are committed to being a seminary. Such a commitment involves also a working knowledge of the languages in which it pleased the Spirit of God to give us Holy Scriptures. In my inaugural address in 1982 I quoted father Luther's words to the mayors and aldermen of the cities of Germany on this subject. He wrote:

> "What God did not despise but chose before all others for His Word, we should likewise esteem above all others. . . . Let this be kept in mind *that we will not preserve the Gospel without the languages.* The languages are the scabbard in which the Word of God is sheathed. They are the casket in which this jewel is enshrined; the cask in which this wine is kept; the chamber in which this food is stored" (emphasis mine).

This is just another way of saying that those who graduate from this place are to have more than a pious heart, a zealous spirit and a jolly good disposition. The Lord reminds us in His Holy Word that preachers of the Word are to be craftsmen, "rightly dividing the Word of truth" (2 Tim. 2:15). They must be apt to teach and preach— so says the apostle in his first letter to Timothy. And this is why we emphasize that a seminary calls for education and not just for training. Our graduates are to be able to expound the Word. They are to be immersed in what our fathers have said and must be conversant with all the current shifting winds on the theological landscape. Such an emphasis on academic excellence is essential if the distinction between the universal priesthood of believers and the office of the public ministry, so badly blurred even among some in our circles today, is to be maintained.

We are talking about doctrine. Doctrine is practical. It is practical because its heart and center is the precious Gospel message, which we want to share with all the world. It is the *doctrine* that "God so loved the world that He gave His only begotten Son. . ." which cheers our souls. It is the *doctrine* that our Lord is even now in heaven preparing a place for us which stills the conscience of the elderly child of God. It is the *doctrine* that God chose us in Christ even before the world began that gives confidence to the middle-aged and teenager as well. To say that we are "theological" and to say that we are a "seminary" is, rightly understood, to make the same statement.

We would stop short, however, were we merely to distinguish a seminary from a Bible college. The other side of the coin is that a seminary, although it is engaged in vigorous study of the Word of God, is not a place where we can (or should expect to) prepare "instant experts." The very word "seminary" should rid us of any such delusion. It comes from the Latin stem *semen,* seed. A seminary, as Webster reminds us, is a "seed bed, nursery." It is "an environment in which something originates. . . ." The graduate is not one who has "finished" his theological task in the sense that he has mastered theology. He does not have all of his skills honed. He can never boast that his attitudes need no improving. He is not one who can simply turn to a certain page and find the answer to all of the things that will confront him when he leaves the nursery and begins his work in the harvest field of the Lord. Tragedy results when either the graduate or those whom he serves have a false expectation level of the pastor's abilities as a theologian.

It is significant that the bylaws of the Synod, in speaking of eligibility for individual membership, state that "a graduate of an authorized Synodical institution must be declared qualified for a first call and recommended by the faculty of the respective Synodical institution before the effective date of the first call to service in the church. . . ."[21] Note that he is declared qualified *for a first call.* He has not learned it all. The faculty is acutely aware of that fact, and in recent years has changed its resolution on endorsement of candidates. Prior to the 1986-87 year, the faculty resolutions regarding candidates stated that "the faculty endorse each of the following men for placement as a candidate and declare him to be qualified in every respect for the office of the ministry of Word and Sacrament in the church. . . ." "Qualified in every respect" is a rather ambitious description. The current resolution is worded this way: "the faculty express its satisfaction that each of the following men will meet all personal, professional, and theological requirements for the office of ordained minister, declare each of them qualified for a first call. . . ."

As an addendum to the above, it should be stated that Concordia Seminary trains generalists. It is our hope and prayer to give men that broad and basic education and training that will enable them to function in a proper way as theologians of the church, regardless of the ministry to which they should be called. Some specialized training is of course available, particularly in the area of ministry to the hearing impaired, for example. And we wish that we had the time to do it in many more areas. Indeed, we have suggested to the Synod through its Board for Mission Services and its Board for Higher Education Services that all graduates who are called to rather specialized ministries, such as the inner city, the rural parishes, campus ministries, multiple ministries as associates or assistants, be given post-M.Div. training for at least a period of one to four weeks, so that they can function more effectively and "land on their feet" when they arrive at their first calling.

Nevertheless, a seminary can provide only the basics, especially in a day when more and more of our students come to us from non-synodical educational backgrounds. More than time is involved. Interest is another consideration. Very frequently a student's interest in a particular ministry may not be generated until the time that he goes out to vicar and has his appetite whetted for some specific aspect of ministerial endeavor. It would hardly be practical then to devote the entire last year of his training to this particular phase, especially when there is no guarantee that he will be immediately called upon to serve in such a specialized ministry.

Furthermore, ministries change with the years. Recently I spent a weekend with a pastor who has served in four different parishes. He began in a small rural parish. He moved to the central city. He moved again to a suburban situation. Now he serves in a neighborhood that is gradually changing. Can a seminary provide training for all that is entailed in all these ministries? The answer is obvious.

Therefore when we talk about a seminary, we ought to avoid two extremes. On the one hand, we need more than minimal training for an office mandated by the Lord with very specific qualifications. The guidelines established by the Lord in Scripture dare not be sidestepped. On the other hand, a seminary is only a seed bed from which theologians are to grow and mature under the blessing of God.

Look again at the title of this essay. As a theological school and a seminary, we have taken the name *"Concordia."* This is the beautiful Latin word which means "harmony" or "concord." It is the name given to the confessional writings of the sixteenth century to which we subscribe. The very name bespeaks a confessional church. The congregational autonomy which we so much cherish and so zealously guard does not mean that each congregation is free to say and do "willy nilly" whatever it may choose. Article II of the Constitution of The Lutheran Church—Missouri Synod states that "the Synod and every member of the Synod accepts without reservation: 1) the Scriptures of the Old and New Testament as the written Word of God and the only rule and norm of faith and of practice; 2) all the symbolical Books of the Evangelical Lutheran Church as a true and unadulterated statement and exposition of the Word of God. . . ." We have a body of doctrine to which we hold. Our very first objective, under Scripture and the Lutheran Confessions, is according to that same Constitution to "conserve and promote the unity of the true faith (Eph. 4:3-6; 1 Cor. 1:10), work through its official structure toward fellowship with other church bodies, and provide a united defense against schism, sectarianism (Rom. 16:17) and heresy." With our name we accept that confessional basis, and we accept that objective.

Concordia Seminary shares the goal of the confessors, namely, that in such a confessional stance we might have *concordia,* that is, harmony and concord in doctrine. The confessors wrote, "The primary requirement for basic and permanent concord within the church is a summary formula and pattern, unanimously approved, in which the summarized doctrine commonly confessed by the churches of the pure Christian religion is drawn together out of the Word of God."[22] It was their intent to "persist in this confession until our blessed end and to appear before the judgment seat of our Lord Jesus Christ with joyful and fearless hearts and consciences."[23] Throughout its history Concordia has joined the confessors in their "goal that no other doctrine be treated and taught in our lands, territories, schools and churches than that alone which is based on the Holy Scriptures of God and is embodied in the Augsburg Confession and its Apology." And we too desire particularly that the young men who are being trained for service in the church and for the holy ministry be faithfully and diligently instructed therein, so that the pure teaching and confession of the faith may be preserved and perpetuated among our posterity through the help and assistance of the Holy Spirit until the glorious advent of our only Redeemer and Savior Jesus Christ.[24]

We are *Concordia* Seminary.

The manner in which the fathers expressed themselves indicates clearly that they understood the difference between the unity of faith to be found among all Christians and the harmony and concord in doctrine necessary for church fellowship. They recognized, as do we, that there are Christians in other denominations. However, the purpose of the confessional writings was to state clearly "the unanimously approved" doctrine, and nothing else was to be tolerated among those who claimed *concordia* with each other. False doctrine "we do not by any means intend to tolerate in our lands, churches and schools inasmuch as such teachings are contrary to the expressed Word of God and cannot coexist with it."[25] Again, they state that they are making their confession:

> so that the way may not be left free and open to restless, contentious individuals, who do not want to be bound to any certain formula of pure doctrine, to start scandalous controversies at will and to introduce and defend monstrous errors, the only possible consequence of which is that finally correct doctrine will be entirely obscured and lost and nothing beyond uncertain opinions and dubious, disputable imaginations and views will be transmitted to subsequent generations.[26]

May God keep Concordia Seminary, all its graduates, and all the congregations which they serve in such *concordia*.

Finally, it is significant that Concordia Seminary is described in our title as a seminary of *The Lutheran Church—Missouri Synod*. True it is that the Synod did not found the seminary. The founding of the seminary predates by some eight years the organization of the Synod in 1847. In fact, the existence of the little seminary had much to do with the reason for organizing the Synod, since one of the early purposes of our church body was to support the fledgling institution which, shortly after the organization of the Synod, was moved to St. Louis.

Nevertheless, Concordia Seminary is a seminary of the church.

The very first sentence in our Concordia Seminary catalog states, "Concordia Seminary's major function is to prepare men for the holy ministry of Word and Sacraments in The Lutheran Church—Missouri Synod." This statement corresponds with the very deed of transfer which turned the Perry County institution over to the Synod. Although young people who did not want to study theology were permitted to attend the *Gymnasium,* it was made very clear that "all legacies made to the institution and donations made to it shall be used exclusively for the benefit of such young men who are preparing themselves for service in The Lutheran Church. . . ."[27]

The close link between the seminary and the Synod has been there since the very beginning. Dr. C. F. W. Walther, the first president of the seminary, was also the first president of the Missouri Synod. Dr. Francis Pieper, who succeeded Dr. Walther as the president of the seminary, also served for twelve years as president of the Synod. The property is owned by the Synod. The school is financed in large part by the Synod. It operates under the bylaws of the Synod. Its Board of Regents is elected by the Synod.

We therefore make no apology for the fact that all of our candidates, prior to endorsement, are examined not only to see whether they can articulate in a clear and simple way their own faith and the faith which they would bring to others, but whether their doctrine is in complete harmony and concord with that of the church body which they hope to serve.

C. S. Lewis scored those clergymen in his own Anglican Church who felt that they could go beyond the lines of their own church doctrine and still remain priests within the Anglican fellowship. He stated:

> There is a danger here of the clergy developing a special professional conscience which obscures the very plain moral issue. Men who have passed beyond these boundary lines . . . are apt to protest that they have come by their unorthodox opinions honestly. . . . But this simply misses the point which so gravely scandalizes the layman. We never doubted that the unorthodox opinions were honestly held; what we complain of is your continuing your ministry after you have come to hold them. We always knew that a man who makes his living as a paid agent of the Conservative Party may honestly change his views and honestly become a Communist. What we deny is that he can honestly continue to be a Conservative

agent and to receive money from one party while he supports the policy of another.

We who serve at the seminary are pledged to maintain, under the blessing of God, the confessional unity and harmony which we as Lutheran Christians hold so dear. We are Concordia Seminary, a theological seminary of The Lutheran Church—Missouri Synod. Ours is a noble work. It has been richly blessed by our Lord. And for one hundred and fifty years of His gracious benediction, we can only say: *Soli Deo Gloria*.

Notes

[1] C. F. W. Walther, in his report to the 1874 Convention of The Synod, quoted in Carl S. Meyer, *Log Cabin To Luther Tower* (St. Louis: Concordia, 1965), p. 64.

[2] Walter Forster, *Zion On The Mississippi* (St. Louis: Concordia, 1953), p. 516.

[3] Meyer, p. 84, reports that in 1874-1875 one-third of the students came from those two bodies.

[4] FC, SD, Rule and Norm, 3.

[5] Francis Pieper, *Christian Dogmatics* (St. Louis: Concordia, 1950), vol. 1, p. 41.

[6] C. F. W. Walther, *The Proper Distinction Between Law And Gospel* (St. Louis: Concordia, 1929), p. 30.

[7] FC, SD, V, 1.

[8] FC, SD, V, 24, 25.

[9] Walther, pp. 401-413, from the thirty-ninth lecture.

[10] Preface to *The Book of Concord* (Tappert), p. 8.

[11] *Ibid.*, p. 12f.

[12] *Luther's Works*, Am. ed. (Philadelphia: Fortress), vol. 35, p. 236.

[13] *Ibid.*, vol. 54, p. 378.

[14] Edgar Krentz, *The Historical-Critical Method* (Philadelphia: Fortress, 1975), p. 30.

[15] *Ibid.*, p. 62.

[16] SA, III, VIII, 9-10.

[17] Pieper, p. 41.

[18] AC, VIII, 2.

[19] LC, V, 16. See Also Ap VII and VIII, 3, 19, 28, 47.

[20] AC, V, 2.

[21] *Synodical Handbook*, 1986, 2.09a.

[22] FC, SD, Rule and Norm, 1.

[23] Preface to *The Book of Concord*, p. 9.

[24] *Ibid.*, p. 9.

[25] *Ibid.*, p. 11.

[26] *Ibid.*, p. 13.

[27] Meyer, p. 18.

[28] C. S. Lewis, "On Living With The Times," *Christianity Today*, March 12, 1971, p. 4.

The Seminary Serves the Synod

AUGUST R. SUELFLOW

One of the great treasures of The Lutheran Church—Missouri Synod is Concordia Seminary, St. Louis, Missouri. It is an architectural gem with its unique Tudor Gothic architecture, located on a wooded seventy-two-acre campus in the heart of Clayton, Missouri, a fast-growing St. Louis suburb. It is also a real estate gem, located in the midst of other prominent educational institutions such as Washington University, Fontbonne College, and Christian Brothers College on each of three sides, and the world-renowned Forest Park to the east. Most of this property belonged to the ancient French De Mun family. The name is still embedded on the short street running along the eastern side of the Seminary, from which it derives its address.

The plot of ground on which the Seminary was constructed between 1924 and 1926 had been discovered early by the special Building Committee, which met for the first time on October 18, 1921. The resolution to build a new seminary had been adopted by The Lutheran Church—Missouri Synod at its convention in June 1920, backed up with a promise of one million dollars. The area was described:

> The site is undoubtedly one of the finest pieces of real estate in or around St. Louis. It is located in St. Louis County, within about five minute's walk of the western limits of the city of St. Louis, due west of the city's largest and finest park. Those who are acquainted in St. Louis will remember that Forest Park extends to the western limits of the city; that directly north of this end of the park is the entrance to Washington University. . . . The property in question is the so-called De Mun tract, which has been held by a St. Louis family for several hundred years, being a direct grant from the King of Spain. It has never since changed hands. Several years ago

---

AUGUST R. SUELFLOW is Director of Concordia Historical Institute, St. Louis and Chairman of the 150th Anniversary Committee at Concordia Seminary, St. Louis.

it was held at $4,000 an acre. The price agreed upon in the contract of sale was $2,600 per acre . . . (Theo. Graebner, *Concordia Seminary*, St. Louis, MO, Concordia Publishing House, 1926, p. 26).

The virgin wooded acreage described above appeared to be quite similar to that where the first log cabin seminary was constructed by the candidates of theology in the fall of 1839, in the now no-longer-existing community of Dresden in Perry County, Missouri.

But Concordia, St. Louis is also a unique synodical treasure in another way. It was established almost eight years prior to the organization of The Lutheran Church—Missouri Synod itself. In a sense it can be said that Concordia Seminary was largely responsible for organizing the Missouri Synod, because much of the initiative to form a synod and especially to establish its unique polity had come from its leading theological professor, C. F. W. Walther, who was elected its first president in April 1847. He remained the Synod's president until 1850, and also served a second term from 1864 to 1878. In fact, three of the Seminary's eight presidents have been intimately associated with the Synod. In addition to Walther, who served both as Seminary and Synod president for a total of seventeen years, Dr. Francis Pieper served in that same dual capacity from 1899-1911, a period of twelve years. However, after Dr. Pieper had completed his last term as synodical president the synodical Constitution was changed, no longer allowing the President of the Synod to hold office at the Seminary. Since then, Dr. Ralph A. Bohlmann, the first Seminary president after the internal turmoil of the 1970s was elected president of the Synod in 1981 and serves in that capacity today.

From 1839-1849 the Seminary depended almost exclusively upon the support from the Lutheran congregations in Perry County, Missouri and from Trinity, St. Louis. It virtually was an orphaned log cabin seminary at Dresden and later Altenburg, Missouri, barely able to remain alive. However, when The Lutheran Church—Missouri Synod formed in 1847, part of its agenda was to transfer responsibility of the institution to the Synod. Subsequently, the congregations which had supported the school transferred the adminstration and operation of the young institution to the Synod in 1849.

The greatest of all treasures produced by the Seminary over the course of years has been its more than ten thousand graduates. Symbolically we shall refer only to the first five graduates, Log Cabin

Seminary students and their illustrious career in helping build the people and Synod in their faith and life. Let them represent all other graduates as "first fruits" in this great one hundred and fiftieth Anniversary year.

It is most interesting to observe that the year the Synod was organized was also when the first Seminary "graduate" left the log cabin to serve in the Word and Sacrament ministry of the Synod. He was J. A. F. W. Mueller, who passed his examinations in October 1847. His pastorates included St. Louis County, Missouri; Chicago, Illinois; Pittsburgh and Jonesburg, Pennsylvania; and Chester, Illinois. He became a synodical leader, serving in various capacities, and was elected secretary of the Synod, a position which he held from 1860-1866.

The second graduate was Franz Julius Biltz, who at the age of thirteen was among the Saxon immigrants in 1838-39. He studied at the log cabin seminary from its beginning until March 1848, when he entered the parish ministry. He served in two states—Missouri and Maryland. It is chiefly in the parish at Concordia, Missouri, however, that he distinguished himself, founding St. Paul's College (today's high school) in 1884 and serving as fourth president of the Western District from 1875-1891, enduring severe hardships with his congregation during the Civil War.

C. H. Rudolf Lange graduated in 1848, together with F. J. Biltz, although the former had not received his entire training in the log cabin college. Lange served in St. Charles, Missouri, until 1858 when he was called back to the Seminary to teach English and philosophy. He served Concordia Seminary as a professor from 1858-1861, when he moved to Fort Wayne, Indiana, with the *Gymnasium,* and thereafter, with brief pastorates in Defiance, Ohio, and Immanuel, Chicago, he was called back to the professorship at the Seminary in 1878, where he served until the time of his death in 1892.

The class of 1849 consisted of two young men, Christian Heinrich Loeber and Heinrich Wunder. Both students were involved in the move with seven other students and teacher J. J. Goenner, when the institution was moved to St. Louis on December 16, 1849.

Loeber, called to Frohna, Missouri, only a few miles from the Altenburg log cabin seminary, was ordained and installed on January 13, 1850. Later he served congregations in Cooper's Grove, Illinois, and Milwaukee, Wisconsin. In 1885 he became the first president of Concordia College, Milwaukee, established in 1881. He resigned the presidency in 1893 and became chaplain at the Wartburg Hospital in Brooklyn, New York, until his death in 1897.

Wunder arrived in America in 1846 as a Loehe emissary and, after studying briefly at Fort Wayne, transferred to Altenburg. After one year, he completed his examination and was ordained at Millstadt, Illinois in December 1849. Later Wunder served St. Paul, Chicago, Illinois, for sixty-two years. Here he developed a special system of missionary expansion by establishing branch schools, most of which developed into separate congregations over the course of years. He was instrumental in establishing Concordia College, Milwaukee in 1881; and served as president of the Illinois District from 1870-1886. Of special interest is the fact that he was the first Missouri Synod pastor to receive an honorary doctorate from the Seminary, in 1909. The first doctorate ever went to P. L. Larsen of the Norwegian Synod in 1903.

These graduates were on the vanguard when the Seminary was small and have paved the way for all others to follow in going to the ends of the world to serve their Lord and His redeemed. The largest graduating class in 1958 saw one hundred and seventy-four receive their theological diplomas. What a magnificent treasure these "human resources" have been to the church throughout various generations! They are all symbolic of the graduates who have provided leadership in various positions in the Synod—as presidents and faculty members of its educational institutions, leadership on boards and commissions, and as executive secretaries of these boards and commissions. Their impact has been most remarkable and theologically unique. We shall now look at other areas where the Seminary, through its personnel, has rendered highly unique services to the Synod and its people.

Through Literature

Just as Martin Luther made extensive use of the printing press, so the faculty of Concordia Seminary established an outstanding record of contributing extensively and significantly to all ranges of theological literature, originally in German and later in English.

A great publication medium, *Der Lutheraner,* was established by C. F. W. Walther in 1844, three years before the Synod was organized. Walther continued as the sole editor of this popular publication until 1865. After that, it was edited by the Seminary faculty until 1964. An interesting story, attributed to F. C. D. Wyneken, pastor in Friedheim, Indiana, tells us that when he obtained a copy of this new publication he exclaimed, "Thank God there are other Lutherans in America!" The influence of *Der Lutheraner* provided not only widely-read news of important events within the Synod, but also served as the layman's "theological periodical" because of its innumerable instructive articles on doctrinal matters.

During the same time Walther edited *Der Lutheraner,* he also began in 1855 the publication of a separate theological journal entitled *Lehre und Wehre.* The journal was designed to meet the professional theological needs of the clergy and strongly supported confessional Lutherans at a time when this had come under considerable question by others. Walther continued as the single editor of this publication until 1860, when C. H. R. Lange became co-editor from 1861 to 1864. After that the editorship of the journal was turned over to the entire faculty until its merger with the *Theological Monthly* (1921-1929)—formerly the *Theological Quarterly* (1897-1920)—together with the *Homiletic Magazine* (1877-1929), to become the *Concordia Theological Monthly* (1929-1974). Each of these periodicals was edited by the faculty. The *Concordia Theological Monthly* became a distinguished theological journal until the traumatic days of the Seminary's internal difficulties in 1974, when it was discontinued. Immediately thereafter, however, the new faculty issued the *Concordia Journal,* first issued in January 1975.

For a long period of time, the one hundred and seven-year old *Lutheran Witness* was also edited by members of the Seminary's faculty. The *Lutheran Witness* originated in Zanesville, Ohio, in 1882 by Pastor Charles A. Frank, a graduate of St. Louis in 1868, as an English clarion call in support if the Missouri Synod's position in the controversy on conversion and election of grace. It was edited by various individuals until it became the English voice of the Missouri Synod in 1911. The co-editorship of Sommer and Graebner of the *Witness* began in 1914 and continued until 1949. This editorial partnership has been referred to as "one of the longest professional partnerships in American Lutheran Journalism" (*Lutheran Witness* January 1982, vol. 100, No. 1, p. 5). Faculty editing continued until 1952.

Faculty members have also made a most unique contribution to the worship life of the congregation and its hymnody. A major unifying factor in The Lutheran Church—Missouri Synod was its first hymnal, the *Kirchengesangbuch für Ev.—Luth. Gemeinden* prepared by C. F. W. Walther under the auspices of his congregation, Trinity, St. Louis in 1847. The Synod adopted this early hymnal as its own in the year it was organized. It was the standard hymnal throughout the Synod, revised occasionally, with numerous printings until 1927.

During the transition from German to English, several English hymnals were produced. Of note is a modest *Hymnal for Evangelical*

Lutheran Missions, edited by Professor F. Bente and published by Concordia Publishing House in 1905. Strangely enough, the *Evangelical Lutheran Hymn-book* of 1912 did not have any faculty representation in its production. However, its successor, *The Lutheran Hymnal,* produced in 1941 and still cherished by many congregations today, was produced under the chairmanship of Professor W. G. Polack. Other faculty members who assisted with its production at some time or other were Professors L. Fuerbringer, Walter Buszin, Richard W. Heintze, and Paul E. Kretzmann.

In 1942, Dr. Polack prepared the very popular *Handbook to the Lutheran Hymnal,* still considered a standard introduction to the history of the hymns in *The Lutheran Hymnal,* the original languages of the hymns, biographical sketches of the writers of the hymns, and the tunes, textual references, etc. Its value is seen in the fact that it has appeared in three editions.

Somewhat similarly, *Lutheran Worship,* prepared by the Commission on Worship of the LC—MS and published by Concordia Publishing House in 1982 enjoyed the input of individuals who today are serving on the Seminary faculty, namely, Drs. Norman E. Nagel and Alfred Fremder.

Very closely allied to the story of the production of hymnals under faculty assistance are the agendas and altar books which have been in use in the Synod during the course of its history. The first synodical agenda was issued by C. F. W. Walther and published in 1856. The agenda was based on the old Saxon agenda of the 1771. An English edition was prepared by Concordia Publishing House in 1881. The Walther agenda essentially remained in place until 1950 when a new one was prepared. The new Lutheran Worship Agenda (1984), Altar Book (1982) and Lectionary (1983) were produced in conjunction with *Lutheran Worship.* Faculty members, since the very beginning of the Synod, have also played a highly significant role in leading the Synod in its worship life, namely, in hymnology and liturgics.

Major and continuing contributions have also been made by faculty in pastoral theology, devotional, and homiletical literature. First and foremost among the literature produced in this area was Walther's *Americanisch-Lutherische Pastoraltheologie,* published in book form in 1872. Prior to that time, it had appeared serially in *Lehre und Wehre* between 1865 and 1872. The published volume came during the days of the developing Synod, while pastors were experiencing new circumstances on the American frontier. It provided resources for pastoral care, *Seelsorge* not generally available. Because of its popularity, Walther's pastoral theology was produced in four editions, the last one in 1890. It was Scripture-based and theologically-oriented.

In an abbreviated English version, John H. C. Fritz issued his *Pastoral Theology* in 1932. Fritz acknowledged his indebtedness to Walther in his Preface. It, too, experienced considerable popularity, requiring a second edition, issued in 1945. As recently as 1977 it was re-issued in the "Concordia Heritage" edition with a Preface by Professor Richard H. Warneck.

Richard Caemmerer edited a volume on pastoral theology and ethics, entitled *The Pastor at Work* (Concordia, 1960). Dr. Caemmerer's many contributions to pastoral theology and homiletics include *Preaching for the Church* (Concordia, 1959), *Feeding and Leading: On Witnessing and Proclaiming the Gospel* (Concordia, 1962), *Christ Builds His Church* (Concordia, 1963), *God's Great Plan for You* (Concordia, 1961), a series of Lenten sermons entitled *Jesus, Why?* (Concordia, 1970), a volume dealing with the sayings of Jesus, *Earth With Heaven* (Concordia, 1969), and *The Church in the World*, originally published in 1949 with a third printing in 1961.

In his own inimitable way, Professor William Gustav Polack, the multifaceted poet, novelist, hymnologist, and student of liturgics produced several popular devotional-sermonic materials, such as *Beside Still Waters* (Concordia, 1950), *Choice Morsels* (Rudolph Volkening, St. Louis, 1923), as well as several other popular volumes produced by Ernst Kaufmann of New York, such as *Hymns From the Harps of God,* 1940. His *Rainbow Over Calvary,* a series of Lenten sermons, was published by Augsburg Publishing House, Minneapolis, MN, in 1943.

A later popular author in this area was Professor Martin Franzmann who, in addition to his exegetical and isagogical contributions wrote *Ha, Ha Among the Trumpets: Biblical Insights Into the Sermon* (Concordia, 1966), devotional readings for the family in *The Courage for Daily Living* (Concordia, 1963) and a collection of prayers in contemporary poetic form, entitled *Pray For Joy* (Concordia, 1970). *Grace Under Pressure* (Concordia, 1966) projected him into the area of ecumenical relationships. Dr. Walter A. Maier, the popular Lutheran Hour speaker during its formative years, had most of his sermons published in annual editions.

The major faculty contributions to the literature of the church, however, are in the area of dogmatics, the study of doctrine, and on theological issues. While Walther contributed extensively to the theological literature of the Synod, he did not produce a dogmatics.

Instead, he addressed himself to the theological problems of the day, usually in thesis form, with a strong practical application. Much of his material in print today, available in English, appeared in the form of essays or lectures. He, as the most prolific essayist of the Synod, produced some fifty convention-essays alone. His three volumes on the church, begun in 1852, today are available in translation under the title of *Church and Ministry* (originally published as *Die Stimme unserer Kirche in der Frage von Kirche und Amt)*. The volume was translated by Professor John Theodore Mueller in the mid-1960s and published by Concordia Publishing House during the centennial year of Walther's death in 1987. The second presentation is *The Form of a Christian Congregation,* an address to the Western District of the LC—MS in 1862, published in book form in 1863 and enlarged in 1864. The original *Die rechte Gestalt einer vom Staat unabhangigen Ev. Luth. Ortsgemeinde* was translated by John Theodore Mueller and published by Concordia Publishing House in 1963. His third book on the church, *Die Ev. Luth. Kirche die Wahre sichtbare Kirche Gottes auf Erden* was published in St. Louis in 1867. This also was translated by J. T. Mueller under the title *The True Visible Church*, originally published by Concordia Publishing House in 1961. The latter two were republished in the "Concordia Heritage Series" in 1987.

The one volume of Walther's books which every student at Concordia Seminary reads at least once is *Law and Gospel.* This was originally published posthumously as *Die Rechte Unterscheidung von Gesetz und Evangelium*, by Concordia in 1897. The first English edition was translated by Professor W. H. T. Dau and came off the Concordia presses in 1929. This, too, was reprinted in 1986 with a foreword by a former Seminary faculty member, Jaroslav Pelikan.

In addition, a special six-volume edition of the translated works of Walther, including editorials from *Lehre und Wehre*, sermons, letters, law and gospel, selections from the books on the church and convention essays were edited by the undersigned and published by Concordia Publishing House in 1981. This handily provides a generous cross section of writings from the pen of Walther for the contemporary generation.

It is really quite unique that Walther never produced a dogmatics. The closest he ever came was his edition of the *Compendium Theologiae Positivae* of Johann Wilhelm Baier, which he edited selectively and published in three volumes in 1879. These volumes served as the textbook at the Seminary virtually until the time that Dr. Francis Pieper, Walther's successor as Seminary president from

1887-1931, produced his *Christliche Dogmatik* in three volumes between 1917 and 1924. A special index followed in 1928. This was superseded by *Christian Dogmatics*, by John Theodore Mueller in 1934, published by Concordia.

Closely identified with the field of systematic theology are the volumes produced in "comparative symbolics." Martin Guenther, an 1853 graduate of the Seminary and on its faculty from 1873-1893, is the "Father" of such an enterprise with the issuance of his *Populare Symbolik*, published by Louis Volkening of St. Louis in 1872. This pace-setter examined the doctrinal position of various denominations in America. Three editions edited by Ludwig Fuerbringer appeared in 1881, 1898 and 1913.

The first such English study appeared in 1934 in a volume entitled *Popular Symbolics*. Four faculty colleagues, namely, Theodore Engelder, William Arndt, Theodore Graebner and F. E. Mayer, the latter still on the faculty at Concordia Theological Seminary, Springfield, Illinois, at that time but later called to St. Louis, produced the new English version. In the Foreword, the collaborators expressed their indebtedness, among others "to Guenther's classical manual" *(Popular Symbolics,* St. Louis, MO: Concordia Publishing House, 1934, VI*)*. While the Guenther volume was developed according to doctrinal subjects, the English version was arranged according to denominational families, a pattern continued by Frederick E. Mayer in *The Religious Bodies of America* (Concordia, 1958). In a much more ambitious way, Arthur Carl Piepkorn, who served on the faculty from 1951 until the time of his death in 1973 produced *Profiles in Belief: The Religious Bodies of the United States and Canada* (Published in four volumes by Harper & Row Publishers, Inc.: New York, Hagerstown, San Francisco and London, 1977).

Not to be forgotten is the monumental production of the trilingual edition (German, Latin and English) of the Ecumenical Creeds and the historical Lutheran Confessions edited by Frederich Bente, Seminary professor from 1888-1904, in his *Concordia Triglotta* (Concordia, 1921). This still serves as a standard source of the critical texts of the Lutheran symbolical writings and was based upon the earliest German and Latin text. A colleague, Professor W. H. T. Dau, both an alumnus of the Seminary and a member of its faculty from 1905 until 1926, and later president of Valparaiso University, collaborated with Bente in this study of the Lutheran Confessions.

Also to be included in this category is Dr. August Lawrence Graebner's (faculty member from 1888-1904) *Outlines of Doctrinal Theology,* published by Concordia Publishing House in 1898 and reprinted in the "Concordia Heritage Series" in 1979 because of its continued value.

Dr. Robert D. Preus served on the faculty from 1957 until 1974 when he became president of our sister seminary in Fort Wayne, Indiana. He wrote *The Inspiration of Scripture* (published in Edinborough and London by Oliver & Boyd in 1957) and reprinted in the "Concordia Heritage Series" in 1981. This represents a study of the theology of the 17th century Lutheran dogmaticians. This was followed by two volumes entitled *The Theology of Post-Reformation Lutheranism*, both published by Concordia Publishing House, with Volume I appearing in 1970 and Volume II in 1972. These two volumes constitute the first thorough and definitive study of the orthodox Lutheran theologians in English.

One of the earliest professional historians on the faculty of Concordia Seminary was August Lawrence Graebner. He studied at the St. Louis Seminary and in 1887 was called to its faculty. Graebner's history of the Lutheran Church in Colonial America *(Geschichte Der Lutherischen Kirche in America),* published by Concordia Publishing House in 1892, had originally been planned as a two-volume edition. Regrettably, the manuscript of the second volume was never printed because it was in German. Graebner's extensive research, on location, was conducted along the eastern seaboard. Another contribution from the Graebner pen was a valuable biography entitled *Dr. M. Luther,* published in Milwaukee, Wisconsin by George Brumder in 1875. A second edition, demonstrating its popularity, was produced in 1883.

Perhaps somewhat in a similar vein, Friederich Bente (1858-1930), a St. Louis graduate of 1881 and professor at the Seminary from 1893 to 1926, writer of the historical introductions to the symbolical books of the Lutheran Church, produced an interesting English, two-volume history of *American Lutheranism* (Concordia, 1919) with the first volume dealing with the period of settlement up to the Tennessee Synod, and the second, published the same year, covered the history of the United Lutheran Church and its antecedent bodies.

One of the most prolific writers of semi-popular Reformation history was William Herman Theodore Dau, a graduate of St. Louis in 1886. He served on the faculty of Concordia College, Conover, North Carolina, and then became professor at Concordia Seminary in 1905, where he remained until 1926.

Dau's five books on the Lutheran Reformation present an outstanding contribution to the study of Martin Luther and his times.

The series began with *Luther Examined and Re-Examined* and *Four Hundred Years*, both published in 1917. This was followed by *The Leipzig Debate in 1519,* published in 1919, *The Great Renunciation* in 1920 and *At The Tribunal of Caesar* in 1921. All were produced by Concordia Publishing House, St. Louis, Missouri. Dau also edited one of the earliest anniversary histories of the LC—MS in 1922 when he produced *Ebenezer* (published by Concordia). The volume is valuable because Dau enlisted contributions from a great variety of authors who had actually been involved in much of the history they were helping to record.

In a more popular vein, W. G. Polack produced a valuable cursory history of Lutheranism in America with special references to the Missouri Synod, entitled *The Building of a Great Church.* The first edition, modest in size, was produced in 1926 by Concordia. A second, enlarged edition appeared in 1941 and for many years served as a textbook in Dr. Polack's courses in the history of Lutheranism in our country. A very fine and useful manual, titled *Into All The World* also written by Polack, became the textbook for the *History of Missions.* It was published by Concordia in 1930.

Encyclopedias were also produced. The first was edited by three faculty members—Ludwig Fuerbringer (a member of the St. Louis faculty from 1893-1947 and its president from 1931-1943); Theodore Engelder (a graduate of St. Louis who joined its faculty after having served the sister seminary in Springfield, Illinois for several years); and Dr. Paul E. Kretzmann, who served on the faculty from 1923-1946. This triumvirate produced *The Concordia Cyclopedia* (Concordia, 1927). It remained a valuable resource until the new *Lutheran Cyclopedia* (1954), edited by Dr. Erwin L. Lueker. This has now been superseded by a completely revised *Lutheran Cyclopedia,* also edited by Lueker and published by Concordia in 1975.

Perhaps this is also where one should refer to the valued St. Louis edition of Luther, sometimes referred to as *Walch 2.* The faculty long had a reputation for its profound interest in Luther. A special American Luther Society had been formed by the Lutherans in the Midwest in 1859. Their purpose was to produce a popular edition of Luther's Works in German. The edition, known as the *Luthers Volksbibliothek* was edited by Professor T. J. Brohm, with the first of 30 volumes appearing in 1859 and the last one in 1876. (Suelflow, *Heart of Missouri,* Concordia, 1954, p. 142).

The St. Louis edition of *Luther's Works* was largely conceived by C. F. W. Walther who, throughout his life, urged in editorials and presentations the great necessity that pastors of the Missouri Synod read Luther. When it became more difficult for some of the better editions of Luther to be purchased in America, several conferences suggested to the Synod that it sponsor a new edition of Luther's writings and that it be based upon the Walch edition of the early 1800s. Professor George Stoeckhardt, who served on the faculty from 1879 to 1913, served as the first editor. He produced one volume in 1880 and a second in 1881. The work was extremely slow and time-consuming until the Luther scholar, Rev. Albert F. Hoppe came to St. Louis in 1886 and completed the editing of the final volume in 1911. The St. Louis edition is still very much in use in Europe (Robert Kolb: "Luther For German Americans: The St. Louis Edition of Luther's Works" 1880-1910, *Concordia Historical Institute Quarterly,* vol. 56, Fall 1983, pp. 98-110).

Several of the volumes produced in the "Church in History" series issued by Concordia were produced by former faculty members. Carl A. Volz, who joined the faculty in 1964, produced *The Church of the Middle Ages* (Concordia 1970); and Roy A. Suelflow, who joined the faulty in 1974, *The Christian Churches in Recent Times* in 1980.

Carl S. Meyer edited a documentary history entitled *Moving Frontiers,* published by Concordia in 1964. Other faculty members contributed individual chapters. The volume has been so popular and useful that it has been reproduced in the "Concordia Heritage Series" in 1983 and as a separate paperback in 1986. Similarly, Meyer's *Log Cabin to Luther Tower: The 125 Year History of Concordia Seminary, St. Louis,* published by Concordia in 1965 is of special value during this anniversary year.

Most fascinating are the two autobiographical resources prepared by Ludwig Fuerbringer, a second generation immigrant who served on the Seminary faculty for fifty-four years. The first of the two autobiographies, *80 Eventful Years* appeared in 1944 and *Persons and Events* in 1947. Both volumes are charming and fascinating because of the places and the people which the author describes from his personal experiences.

A fascinating biography, *Dr. Bessie,* published by Concordia in 1963 was written by Alfred M. Rehwinkel. It is the story of his wife, who served as a pioneer medical doctor in Wyoming.

Two outstanding volumes from the pen of Dr. Arthur C. Repp, Sr., must be included. In the first, *Confirmation in the Lutheran Church* (Concordia, 1964) he traces confirmation practices since the Lutheran Reformation. The volume was reprinted in the "Concordia Heritage Series" in 1968. The second volume, actually a bibliography filled with such fascinating notes that it is history is entitled *Luther's*

Catechism Comes to America. It was published by the American Theological Library Association in Metuchen, New Jersey in 1982.

In the area of ethical and sociological resources Alfred M. Rehwinkel, who came to the Seminary from the presidency of St. John's College, Winfield, Kansas, in 1956, was most vocal. Among his contributions we see *Planned Parenthood* (Concordia, 1957) which was controversial at the time it appeared. Prior to that time he had issued his *Communism and the Church* (Concordia, 1948), and in 1956 *The Voice of Conscience* (also Concordia). Earlier, Walter A. Maier, the first Lutheran Hour speaker, who served on the faculty from 1922 until his untimely death in 1950, wrote a major volume on safeguarding the marriage vow, entitled *For Better and Not For Worse* published in 1935 by Concordia Publishing House.

Dr. John W. Klotz, who arrived on the campus in 1974, first as academic dean and later as Director of the Graduate School, published several books revealing his special knowledge in creation, evolution, biology and life sciences. Thus, he wrote his *Genes, Genesis and Evolution* in 1955. This was soon followed in 1961 by *Modern Science and the Christian Life.* In 1971, Concordia Publishing House issued his *The Ecology Crisis.*

With its historically strong emphasis on Biblical studies, the faculty of Concordia Seminary has served the church most admirably with the great variety of resources it has produced. There have been times when a certain caution was expressed in regard to publishing exegetical literature, lest these be viewed as the "official" exegesis. A church body accustomed to issuing "official" doctrinal statements takes great pains in approving hymnals and position papers on various theological issues, has at the same time regularly accepted the principle that there must be exegetical freedom, so that the richness of God's revelation may be searched and researched.

The record of the faculty working in isagogical, hermeneutical and exegetical literature nevertheless, is impressive. Many such studies frequently appeared in the Synod's journals in serial form. Books, however, were slower in development. One of the earliest commentaries produced on the entire Scriptures came from the pen of Paul E. Kretzmann, in his four-volume *Popular Commentary,* published between 1921 and 1923.

Dr. Martin Franzmann, a gifted writer who joined the faculty in 1946, produced an introduction to the New Testament by bringing all the weight of his scholarship on the origin, purpose and meaning of the New Testament in his *The Word of The Lord Grows* (Concordia, 1961). He also prepared a commentary on St. Matthew entitled *Fol-*

low Me: Discipleship According to St. Matthew, published by Concordia in 1961. This was followed with a commentary, *The Revelation to John*, (Concordia, 1976). In 1968 he produced a commentary on *Romans* (also Concordia). This may also be the time when we should comment on the many poetic contributions which Dr. Franzmann made to the church, and particularly the victorious and triumphant Seminary hymn which has been used at virtually every opening and closing service of the academic year since it was written in 1954, namely, "Thy Strong Word Did Cleave the Darkness."

One of the earliest publishers of exegetical materials was Dr. George Stoeckhardt, who served on the faculty from 1879-1913. Earlier he had rendered part-time service to the Seminary while pastor of Holy Cross, St. Louis. In addition to several volumes of sermons, Dr. Stoeckhardt produced two volumes of Bible history, one each on the Old and the New Testaments, entitled *Die Biblische Geschichte.* Both were published by Concordia Publishing House in 1906 and remained popular as long as there were those who could use the German language. His exegetical writings included the *Commentar uber den Propheten Jesaia,* (Concordia, 1902), *Commentar uber den Brief Pauli an die Epheser,* (Concordia, 1910), and finally *Commentar uber den Ersten Brief Petri* (Concordia, 1912). His commentary on Ephesians (translated by a faculty colleague, Martin S. Sommer, and titled *Commentary on St. Paul's Letter to the Ephesians*) was published in 1952 by Concordia and included in the "Concordia Heritage Series" in 1984.

Of continuing interest are the contributions of Dr. William F. Arndt, veteran faculty member, who served form 1921-1957. Arndt early developed his writing skills, as a member of the editorial committees of various journals. His earliest books include *Does The Bible Contradict Itself?*, (Concordia, 1926) with a second edition following in 1930. In a similar vein appeared his *Bible Difficulties* (Concordia, 1932). Both of these booklets were revised by Robert Hoerber, serving on the faculty since 1974, and Walter R. Roehrs, since 1944, under a new title, *Bible Difficulties and Seeming Contradictions*, published by Concordia in 1987. Dr. Arndt also provided the church with his mimeographed notes on the New Testament introduction (Concordia Seminary Mimeograph Co., 1940) and "The Life of St. Paul" (Concordia, 1944) as notable contributions to the study of the Scriptures. Demonstrating its great abiding value, Dr. Arndt's Bible commentary, *The Gospel According to St. Luke,* was originally published by Concordia in 1956 and reissued in the "Concordia Heritage Series" in 1981.

Dr. Horace Hummel has made outstanding literary contributions to Old Testament studies on its origin, purpose and meaning in his *The Word Becoming Flesh* (Concordia, 1979). Other Old Testament studies include the works of Ludwig Fuerbringer, who wrestled with Habakkuk in his *Eternal Why* (Concordia, 1947) and the two volumes dealing with the Old Testament prophets, *Jeremiah* (appearing from the Concordia presses in 1952) and *Minor Prophets* in 1956.

Not to be overlooked are *I and II Timothy, Titus and Philemon* (Concordia, 1970), which represent the joint venture of Professors Armin H. Moellering, who joined the faculty in 1979 and Victor Bartling, who came to the Seminary in 1950.

Of great value is the *Greek-English Lexicon of the New Testament*, which Arndt was privileged to collaborate with F. W. Gingrich in translating W. Bauer's *Griechisch-Deutsches Woterbuch* (published in Chicago: University of Chicago Press, 1957). Since then, it has again been revised by another former faculty member, Fredrick W. Danker. Helpful also in this study is F. W. Danker's *Multipurpose Tools for Bible Study*, (Concordia, 1970).

One of the standards still in the hermeneutical area is Dr. Ralph A. Bohlmann's *Principles of Biblical Interpretation in the Lutheran Confessions*. Dr. Bohlmann joined the faculty in 1960 and later served as Seminary and synodical president. The first edition was printed by Concordia Publishing House in 1968 and the revised edition published in 1983.

Finally, reference should also be made to two extremely popular volumes under the able editorship of Dr. Robert E. Hoerber, entitled *Reading the New Testament for Understanding* (Concordia, 1986), and *The Concordia Self-Study Bible,* (also Concordia, 1986).

What significant and far-reaching contributions have been made to the theological and historical literature written and edited by the members of the Seminary's faculty over the past one hundred and fifty years! Space limitations simply do not allow us to list everything. The above brief references have been chosen because of their enormous value to the Seminary classroom, the pastors and lay-people of the Synod over the past years. The Seminary has indeed served the Synod well!

In Special Capacities

Until the recent Bylaw changes, members of synodical colleges and seminaries were considered especially valuable members of synodical and district boards, committees, and commissions. Oftentimes they served as chairpersons or secretaries of such groups. Bylaw

3.69(h), which was adopted in 1981, specifically prohibited faculty members from such service. However, this Bylaw was rescinded at the Wichita Convention in July 1989 so that faculty members can again serve on the various boards, committees, and commissions.

When the Evangelical Lutheran Synodical Conference of North America was formed in 1872, the Seminary President Walther, was elected the first president. It virtually became traditional that professors from the St. Louis faculty serve on its mission board. One need only to think of the names of Professors Francis Pieper, Ludwig Fuerbringer, George Mezger, Theodore Graebner, John Theodore Mueller and Otto C. A. Boecler. Each served long terms with great distinction.

Generally, one can say that if synodical boards dealt with matters of theology, literature, church relations, missions, parish education, archives and history, doctrinal matters or inter-church relationships some faculty representation was always apparent. In fact, when the Board of Foreign Missions was greatly expanded in 1893, both Francis Pieper and August L. Graebner were elected to serve on it. Faculty members carried great responsibilities on such boards, including the Literature Board, the Committee on Lutheran Union, the Doctrinal Review Committee, the Commissions on Adjudication and Appeals, the Committee on Bible Versions and many others. Thus, the special expertise of theologians was put to practical use in the service of the Lord and His people.

Faculty members were also deeply involved in developing new work and service in the Synod. One such example is the founding of the Concordia Historical Institute, the Department of Archives and History of the Synod. Even though the Synod had established its archives at the time of its founding in 1847, this work was never really brought aggressively forward until the Concordia Historical Institute was established and incorporated in 1927. On its board at that time were four faculty members, namely Ludwig Fuerbringer, vice-president; W. G. Polack, secretary; R. W. Heintze, curator; and Theodore Graebner, board member. Arrangements such as this also included subsequent faculty members as Arthur C. Repp and Carl S. Meyer.

The establishment of radio station KFUO and The Lutheran Hour largely owe their existence to initiatives taken by faculty members. John H. C. Fritz was early involved in the work of the station, and Walter A. Maier, as speaker of The Lutheran Hour beginning with the first broadcast in 1930, put a very a special stamp on this radio ministry.

When the Sunday School Board was established, Paul E. Kretzmann served as one of the three members of the Board. Theodore
Graebner played an active role on the first Board for Young People's
Work, established in 1920. We need to record also the longtime
services of Theodore Graebner and Paul Bretscher, who served on
the Commission on Fraternal Organizations, established in 1926.
One may be emboldened to say that such special services and projects
as listed above probably would not have been established without
the vision and foresight of the faculty. Today, as a result, the Synod
is significantly richer in its mission and ministry.

The influence of the faculty, either corporately or individually
throughout the work of the Synod as servants on its boards and
commissions, as pastoral assistants in the parish and in many other
capacitites makes them particularly noteworthy.

Gutachten and Essays

During the days of the Synod's infancy, only little theological
literature was readily available. Salaries were low, and shipping
books from overseas was expensive. Besides, the young church body,
whose numbers were extremely small, did not always have the resources or the manpower available to produce position statements,
pamphlets and sermonic literature to meet the demands. Save for
certain books which the immigrants brought with them, the average
young pastor had access to a limited library. In the course of the
frontier ministry, however, there were many doctrinal and practical
questions which required answers. Where could a young pastor,
sometimes serving in isolation, turn for help? Obviously, he turned
to his local pastoral conference. But when, in the company of peers,
significant questions could not be answered, the conference addressed a letter to the Seminary faculty for an opinion, or *Gutachten*.

What a valuable study it would be to review existing *Gutachten,*
or opinions, issued by the Seminary on special problems. Unfortunately, not all opinions rendered have been preserved. From time
to time, some of the opinions were published, especially if they im-
pinged directly upon the life of the church, such as the one issued
by the faculty in 1949 stating that engagement was not necessarily
tantamount to marriage.

Without the distractions of television, telephones and telecom-
munications, the life together of the small faculty was far more
relaxed. Nevertheless, it was demanding because of the special literary projects in which each was engaged. Thus, when a request for
an opinion was received, a member of the faculty was selected to

provide the draft, and in both formal and informal gatherings of the faculty, the proposed draft was carefully reviewed before it was sent to the congregation or pastor who had raised the question.

A careful check of the Walther era indicates that between 1847 to 1886 (shortly before his death), a large number of opinions were produced, covering such subjects as the authority of a pastor, divorce and remarriage, membership in secret societies, marriage to an unbeliever, permitting separated couples to receive Holy Communion, marriage of a widower to his wife's sister, the second marriage of a husband whose wife refused to accompany him to America, issues relating to the "lesser ban," implications for permission to receive Holy Communion after a person had been married in a non-Lutheran church, and many others. Certainly all of these issues were not only valuable and significant to the clergy and their congregations, but usually helped solve the tension which had produced the questions. The call for such opinions decreased in ratio as synodical periodicals and other literature were produced.

When the Commission on Theology and Church Relations was formed in 1962 (*LC—MS Proceedings* 1962, pp. 123-24), much of the responsibility of rendering opinions on theological issues was transferred to the Commission and removed from both the Fort Wayne and St. Louis faculties. That which once had been traditionally the responsibility of the theological faculty, as was also the case for centuries in Europe, was now transformed to other areas of the synodical administration.

The Graduate School

Concordia Seminary granted its first Master of Sacred Theology degrees in 1923 to Erich M. Keller, Robert M. Schalm, and Ewald M. Plass. This serves as the starting point for outstanding and unique services rendered by the Seminary, not only to the Synod, but to the church throughout the world. From 1923 on, virtually each of the graduates performed outstanding and specialized services to the church, several of them returning to the Seminary as faculty members, or teaching at other synodical colleges and institutions. Their names read like an academic who's who of the Synod.

Among other S.T.M. candidates were O. P. Kretzmann, later president of Valparaiso University, Valparaiso, Indiana; and Seminary professors Arthur W. Klinck, Richard A. Jesse, Alfred O. Fuerbringer, Richard A. Caemmerer, Walter E. Buszin and Roy A. Suelflow, who also was the first to receive the degree of Doctor of Theology from the Seminary in 1946. Suelflow previously served as missionary in China, Japan and Taiwan, and also as president of the Lutheran Seminary in Chia Yi, Taiwan. Additional candidates who earned the S.T.M. and served on the faculty were Erich Kiehl, Henry W. Reimann, David S. Schuller, Horace D. Hummel, Arthur H. Strege, Martin A. Haendschke, Louis Brighton, L. Dean Hempelmann, John Johnson, Charles Knippel, Thomas Manteufel, Jacob A. O. Preus III, George S. Robbert, William J. Schmelder, and Paul Schrieber.

The vast majority of the more recent S.T.M. and Th.D. candidates have served with considerable distinction at other synodical schools, overseas seminaries of our sister and partner churches, and elsewhere, and through such services have extended the contributions and the influence of Concordia Seminary throughout the world by touching the life, theology and work in many respects.

Dr. Won Yong Ji, who received his S.T.M. in 1954 and his Doctor of Theology degree from our Seminary in 1957, taught for several years at the Lutheran Theological Academy in Seoul, Korea, was professor of the United Graduate School of Theology at Yonsei University in Seoul, and did a stint with the Lutheran World Federation in Geneva. But in addition to his academic contributions, Dr. Ji has translated the entire *Book of Concord* into his native Korean language, and has produced a new *History of Lutheranism in Korea*, published by the Seminary Press in 1988. In addition, he is serving as general editor and has translated several volumes of Luther's Works into Korean. He has been an Associate Professor of Systematic Theology in St. Louis since 1979.

Concordia Lutheran Seminary of Edmonton, Alberta, Canada, has four full-time faculty members, all of whom have received their Doctor of Theology degrees from our Seminary—President Milton Rudnick in 1963, Ronald Vahl in 1979, Norman J. Threinen in 1980 and Edward Kettner in 1985.

Our sister church, the Evangelical Lutheran Church of Brazil is generously represented by our former graduate students serving on the faculty of Seminario Concordia at Sao Leopoldo, Rio Grande Du Sol. Among them is Martim Karlos Warth, who earned his S.T.M. in 1966; Martin Walter Flor, S.T.M. in 1969; Paulo Flor, S.T.M. 1981, and Vilson Scholz, S.T.M. in 1981. Rudi Zimmer, president of the Escola Superior de Teologia at San Paolo in southern Brazil earned his Th.D. in 1980.

In the far East, we call attention to Henry Rowald, Synod's mission consultant in Asia, who received his S.T.M. in 1965. The president of Luther Seminary (Lutheran Church of Korea), at Seoul is Maynard Dorow, who received his S.T.M. in 1963. Also in South

Korea, serving at a Presbyterian seminary is Young Wah Na, a Th.D. recipient in 1988. Serving there with him is Pyeng Seh Oh, Th.D. 1961.

The President of the Lutheran Church of Nigeria is Rev. Nelson Unwene, who received his S.T.M. in 1974. In Ethiopa at Mekane Yesus Seminary in Addis Ababa is Professor Eshetu Abate, who received his S.T.M. in 1986 and Th.D. in 1988.

At Concordia Seminary, Nagercoil, India, an institution of our sister church, the India Evangelical Lutheran Church, is Victor Raj, who received his S.T.M. in 1976 and his Th.D. in 1981. Prior to that time, Herbert M. Zorn and Henry Otten, who labored in India for many years received their S.T.M. degrees in 1970. Also serving on the Nagercoil Seminary faculty is James Canjanam Gamaliel (S.T.M. 1975). A third member of that faculty is Arockiam Rajaian, who received his Th.D. in 1984.

The Lutheran Church-Hong Kong Synod operates Concordia Seminary, Kowloon, where Andrew Chiu (S.T.M. 1967, Th.D. 1973) serves as president. James Kam-Hung Ng (S.T.M. 1974) is serving a graduate school in Hong Kong. Andrew Ng (Th.D. 1986) serves as Dean of the China Graduate School of Theology in Hong Kong.

In Sumatra, Indonesia, a graduate of Concordia Seminary, Robinson Radjagukguk, with a 1973 S.T.M. is teaching at the seminary there. The Executive Director of the Asia Theological Association in Taiwan is Bon Rin Ro, a Th.D. recipient in 1969. He is a member of the Presbyterian Church of Taiwan.

The Lutheran Church in the Philippines has established a seminary in Baguio City. Its dean, Jose Babao Fuliga, received his S.T.M. in 1974 and Th.D. in 1982 from our Seminary.

Across the globe in Tokoyo, Japan, the Japan Lutheran Church Theological Training Program has Masao Shimodate (Th.D. 1985) serving as president. In addition, at the Kinki Evangelial Lutheran Church are several faculty members who have received graduate degrees from our Seminary, namely, Taizo Taniguchi (S.T.M. 1976)— teaching at the Lutheran Theological Seminary in Kobe—as is also Akio Hashimoto (S.T.M. 1983). The president of the Kobe Seminary is Dr. Gyoji Nabetani, who obtained his Th.D. in 1972. Recently, Dr. Nabetani summed up so well the Seminary's global influences on confessional and orthodox theology by reminding his students that even though our Seminary was not as well-known as either Harvard or Yale, our influences were indeed mighty throughout the world.

On this threshold of the Seminary's one hundred and fiftieth anniversary, we are aware of magnificent and enduring blessings

which our Heavenly Father has showered on us through both faculty
and students, and through them has touched the lives of countless
individuals around the world. We thank and praise His Holy Name
for the privilege of such service.

Concordia Seminary and Theological Education Today

JOHN F. JOHNSON

A quarter of a century ago, Luther Weigle, then Dean of Yale University Divinity School, wrote to Concordia Seminary President Alfred O. Fuerbringer, "You have one of the outstanding theological seminaries of this country and of the world. . . . Your institution is integrated into the life of your Church, serves the Church, and is supported by the Church to a degree that is notable among theological seminaries." Referring to Richard Niebuhr's description of a theological school as "the intellectual center of the Church's life," Weigle added, "I know of no theological seminary which better lives up to that definition in relation to the life of the Church of which it is a part."[1]

These comments typify the esteem in which Concordia Seminary has been held by theological educators and scholars since its founding in 1839. While experiencing the same vicissitudes endured by many other Protestant seminaries in America over the years—changing patterns of enrollment, variations in financial well-being, new perceptions of public ministry, and even ecclesiastical controversy—Concordia Seminary has been consistently recognized for its classical, decidedly academic program of pastoral training.

The Traditional Curriculum

For more than one hundred years after the establishment of the first seminary for the preparation of ministers in the United States, the curricular approach differed very little among existing institutions.[2] There was a required core curriculum embracing four divisions of theological study each of which was dependent upon and related to the other: 1) exegetical theology; 2) systematic theology; 3) historical theology; and 4) practical theology.

The conceptual underpinnings of this view of proper pastoral

JOHN F. JOHNSON served as Dean of Instruction at Concordia Seminary until July, 1989. He is serving presently as President of Concordia College, St. Paul, Minnesota.

preparation lay historically in two fundamental convictions. One was that in the Holy Scriptures of the Old and New Testaments God had given humankind an authoritative revelation and that the manner of gaining access to the real meaning of this revelation was a mastery of the Scriptures in their original languages. The other basic conviction was that the Biblical writings conveyed a consistent doctrinal framework covering what one should believe about God and His relationship to human creatures. The traditional lines of the seminary curriculum followed rather naturally from these convictions.[3]

In a formal sense, this same pattern has been employed at Concordia Seminary for generations. However, these four areas of study have been significantly shaped by the theological distinctives of confessional Lutheranism. The Augsburg Confession identifies the church as "the assembly of all believers among whom the Gospel is preached in its purity and the holy sacraments are administered according to the Gospel" (AC, VII). In other words, the purpose of the church is to be the institutional agency for the assurance of the forgiveness of sins. This Lutheran insight has shaped the seminary curriculum in several important ways—such themes as the distinction between Law and Gospel, the "two kingdoms," *simul iustus et peccator*, etc., have persisted. However, perhaps the greatest impact of the Lutheran understanding of the Church has been on the nature of the ministry itself.

Ultimately, of course, there is a ministry because of the ministry of Jesus Christ, who brought the Word of God into human life through His own life, death, and resurrection. It is His Spirit which creates and maintains the church. The primary task of the ministry, therefore, is to proclaim the Word and administer the Sacraments because it is through these means that people are enabled to live under grace in a world of sin. Since the source of the authority and the norm of the function of the ministry are in Christ and His Gospel, the Word which mediates Christ stands as the central concern of a seminary in the Lutheran tradition. It is the Word which informs the direction taken in the study of the four classical areas of theology.

I. The study of the Word, first of all, entails reading, interpreting, and applying the Scriptures in the languages in which they were originally written. This is the aim of exegetical theology. Conrad Bergendoff has noted that Lutheran theological seminaries

> agree that there is a function of theological education which involves a transmission of something once given. There is a work and word of God revealed in Scripture which carries

with it a certainty quite different from the hypotheses of secular learning. Secular learning often describes itself as a search for truth but can never agree what that truth is. The Christian, too, seeks truth, but knows one who is the Truth, and in His light finds truth.[4]

Consequently, the student studies the total area of Biblical theology—hermeneutics, isagogics, and exegesis.

II. The study of systematic theology seeks to structure the teachings of the Word in an ordered coherent way so that the content of the Church's *kerygma* may be set forth in the modern world. It is both an intellectual and a spiritual activity which includes the analysis, formulation, and pertinent application of the Word of God in terms of itself. To be sure, systematic theology employs all applicable tools and materials from other disciplines (e.g., history, psychology, philosophy, the social sciences) for the achievement of its task. However, the Lutheran theologian will carefully refuse to allow any instrument to determine the conclusions of theology. Systematic theology is not simply the exposition of a system of timeless ideas, comparable to the philosophy of Plato or some other form of idealism. Rather, it proceeds from a commitment to the Gospel as the center of all theology, to Scripture as the inspired Word of God and the only infallible rule of faith and life, and to the Lutheran Confessions as the correct exposition of the doctrines of Scripture. Systematic theology endeavors to proclaim the Gospel to all sorts and conditions of people in the most comprehensive and orderly way possible and with appropriate attention to the contextual problems of those to whom the Gospel is addressed.

III. The transmission of the Word has inevitably led to the growth and spread of the church. Thus, historical theology is concerned with the story of the church's development both institutionally and theologically over the centuries. Each age has prompted a new context for the Gospel and has illumined the failures as well as the success of the church. The study of historical theology also isolates the differing interpretations of the Word in a given historical situation and the divisions in the church which have resulted from varieties of reactions to the Gospel.

IV. Practical theology concerns itself with the application of the Word of God to the practical circumstances confronted within the context of a Lutheran parish. Areas of study in practical theology include preaching and worship, pastoral care and counseling, mission outreach, evangelism, and Christian education.

This aspect of the seminary curriculum, in particular, has been the subject of spirited debate. On the one hand, there has been a tendency to stress the practical skills of ministry to the detriment of the other theological disciplines. The practical field is regarded as a series of "how to" courses. On the other hand, it is possible to make them so theoretical that they fail to meet the concrete needs of the parish. In order to deal with the former tendency, Lutheran seminaries have been careful to ground practical theology courses in the knowledge and understandings imparted by the exegetical, systematic, and historical areas. As a way of insuring that the latter approach does not prevail—overemphasizing the theoretical—resident field education and vicarage components have become curricular requirements. The purpose of these programs is to assist the seminarian in relating the academic dimension of theological education to learning by experience in ministry through competent supervision.

In his *Summa Theologiae*, Thomas Aquinas argues that Christian theology is one science. He appeals to the scholastic principle that the unity of a potency or habit must be judged from the unity of its formal object. For instance, a person, a donkey, and a stone, though different things, agree in that which is the formal object of sight, that which is colored. The comparison applies to theology, he says, because it borrows its principles from the science of God made known by divine revelation. Theology deals with a variety of subjects (sin, grace, Christ, Sacraments, etc.) but there is one formal object involved. The *ratio formalis objecti* is the knowledge of God in Scripture.[5]

This comparison also applies, in a most significant way, to the classical curriculum of Lutheran seminaries. Although diverse in content and methodology, exegetical, systematic, historical, and practical theology have one formal object, one "common denominator"—the life-giving Word of God. This Word, in turn, is at the center of the pastoral vocation. Consequently, in order to provide for a competent ministry of the Word, the seminary must provide a training which is both theological and practical in scope. Its theology must be to set forth God, the Father of the Lord Jesus Christ, who has made Himself known. Such a theology is necessarily based in study of the Scriptures and the Lutheran Confessions.

However, the traditional curricular emphasis on content does not abrogate the practical aspect of pastoral training. The Lutheran pastor is, after all, "a man with a message, a message which must be communicated to people so that they may participate in their ministry of building up the body of Christ."[6] The classical curriculum has served Lutheran seminaries well in fulfillment of their obligation to attend to the message and equip the messenger.

Nevertheless, the traditional fourfold pattern of theological studies which has dictated curricular organization in seminaries down to the present day has not remained unchallenged. Since the innovative proposal of Friedrich Schleiermacher in his *Brief Outline on the Study of Theology* (1811), criticism of the classical approach has reached such levels that it dominates the contemporary conversation on theological education.[7] Acquaintance with such criticism and the willingness to attend to its valid points is crucial for a theological institution celebrating its past as well as reflecting on its future.

Proposals for Reform

A variety of reasons have been adduced for the radical reform of the theological curriculum.

Some have argued, for example, that the increasing vocational specialization in the pastoral ministry has antiquated traditional systems of theological training. In a report on the state of theological education for the World's Student Christian Federation, Keith Bridston observes that Protestant seminary training "has been limited rather strictly to the ordained ministry for local churches and has been especially directed toward preaching, the ministry of the pulpit." Today, Bridston contends, the local pastor has a much wider range of responsibilities than ever before, and they are much more specialized.[8]

Others have pointed to changing conceptions of church leadership. Recent years have seen more and more stress on the pastor as group facilitator and conflict manager. Therefore, it has been suggested that a thorough transformation of the entire structure of theological education is in order. And, in point of fact, some of the more influential proposals for reform in the last decade have followed this course. They have essentially begun with an empirically based description of current functions of the ministry in American Protestantism and then asked how ministerial education should be conceived as practical preparation for that actual ministry. The answer has typically been to substitute new curricular ingredients in place of some of the traditional ones (e.g., increase the curricular time given to training in group dynamics and conflict resolution while decreasing the courses in historical theology).[9]

Of course, calls for reform based on the phenomenon of special-ization in the practice of ministry or the needs of church leadership do not necessarily entail the dismantling of the traditional fourfold pattern. But two proposals which have been widely discussed by theological educators today do envision an abandonment of the clas-sical curricular approach. For that reason—and because they at-tempt to analyze theological education from the nature of theology—they are especially illustrative of contemporary thinking about sem-inary curriculum.

I. The first approach is represented by Edward Farley whose work, *Theologia*, "has sharpened the critical level of reflection on the na-ture of theological education as a theological problem" more than any other recent publication.[10]

Farley's thesis is that theological education needs a recovery of what prior to the nineteenth century was called "Divinity," and in his book is called "Theologia": the panoply of intellectual tasks con-nected with a cognitive disposition toward divine things. According to Farley, "Theologia" has two basic aspects: first, the cognition of the soul which attends faith and has eternal happiness as its goal; and second, the comprehensive intellectual enterprise of under-standing which enlarges this cognition, thus generating the histor-ical development of Christian thought. The problem is that with the advent of the Enlightenment, "Theologia" became fragmented into separate self-sufficient academic disciplines. In other words, the problem of theological education is the pluralism of theology—the splintering of theology, traditionally seen as the virtue of wisdom, into atomistic disciplines.

Farley's critique of the so-called "theological encyclopedia" sug-gests that their organization of the disciplines into a fourfold pattern has in fact contributed to the fragmentation of theology. Conse-quently, in order to restore the unity of theology one must go beyond "the functional unity" of service to the church and to ground the unity of theology in the very nature of the theological task itself."[11] Farley writes:

> the main thesis of this essay is that a significant reform of
> theological education, which addresses its deepest problems
> must find a way to recover *theologia*. Without that recovery,
> theological education will continue to perpetuate its enslave-
> ment to specialties, its lack of subject matter and criteria, its
> functionalist and technological orientation.[12]

What has been lost in the splintering of theology is any concern for or reflection on the substantial meaning of faith; the essence of Christianity, as an ecclesial, redemptive existence. In a sense, then, there is no theological justification for theological education itself today.

In order to effect the rescue of theological education Farley's proposal calls for the recovery of theology as *habitus* and the essence of Christianity as the substantial principle of theological education. The rejuvenation of theology as *habitus* formulates theological education as wisdom and not merely occupational training (which, Farley believes, is promoted through the fourfold pattern of theological encyclopedia). The essence of Christianity as principle of theological education thematizes it in terms of faith itself as a redemptive process. Such faith exists in the social matrices of believer, church leadership, and scholarly inquiry. The traditional approach fails to deal with what Farley terms the "pre-reflective habit of faith."

It was clearly not the intention of Farley's first book, *Theologia*, to give anything so routine as a "new curriculum" for seminaries. However, he does describe the structure of theological study in his sequel, *The Fragility of Knowledge*, and draws some curricular implications.[13]

"Insofar as schools or programs of study teach theology," Farley observes, "they are teaching modes of interpretation. In short, theological study is, in the broad sense of the word, hermeneutic study. It is learning what is involved in the interpretation of tradition, action, truth, and work as they come together in situations."[14]

Tradition, action, truth, and work are the primary hermeneutic modes of theology. The interpretation of tradition recognizes that the Christian faith, as an historical reality, embraces temporal, institutional, moral, and linguistic dimensions. According to Farley, such an interpretation "will not necessarily be advanced by shopping from a school's list of electives in the field of church history." Rather, it requires grasping "the dimensional complexity of the historical phenomenon." Christianity is not a collection of isolated figures and epochs but a movement "that is rooted in ancient Israel, has originating events, periods of classical formation and reformation, and periods of breakup and of challenge to its classical historical forms."[15]

The interpretation of action centers on the question of how to exist responsibly in a situation with specific outcomes in view. Farley cautions against reducing action to activity. Instead, the "formal pedagogy of action attends to the constitutive features of the situation of action and of its interpretation. The subject of this pedagogy is future, possible, preferred action, corporate and individual."[16] In Farley's scheme, subjects included under this rubric would be the action of social entities (communities and institutions) and such current issues as the nuclear threat, ecology, and social reform.

The third mode of interpretation which comprises theological study is that of truth. Ironically, Farley sees "the question about the truth of the faith as marginal for most programs of study in current clergy education."[17] This is the case because the settling of the truth question is based on the interpretation of Scripture. For Farley, theological education should reject the "precritical" equation of truth with content of the Biblical text. The Christian truth-claims are not propositions but attested mysteries, and there are many interpretations of the mystery which must be assessed for their truth. Nothing is "true which is not mediated in some way through the historic process and its paradigms."[18]

The final mode of interpretation is that of work or vocation. The fundamental point is "that the believer need not live in a dichotomy that severs work from the spiritual and churchly life."[19] In other words work involves issues that are not outside the realm of theological interpretation and reflection (e.g., survival, power, human accomplishment). In addition to this general understanding of work there is, of course, the Christian's "occupation" in the ecclesiastical community. Ministerial education demands that the student consider church leadership as "work" which calls for interpretation and not just occupational training.

For Edward Farley, then, theological education has to do with aims, not just subject matter. The following statement summarizes well his proposal for curricular reform:

> The aims of an educative effort answer the question, What will the course of study do to fulfill the needs or agendas projected for or by those who take it? . . . Aims are expressed in the grammar of infinitives and the language of purpose: to communicate information about, to facilitate skill in. Theological study can aim to form the student spiritually, to create scholars, to train or sharpen church-leadership (ministry) skills, to inform the student about the gospel and the church's tradition. . . . A major argument of this book is that the aim of theological study, as *theological*, is not to teach clergy skills, provide spiritual formation, or mold scholars but to communicate and discipline basic modes of interpretation already at work in the believer's situation.[20]

II. A second popular proposal for the reform of the theologial curriculum is based on the task of theological inquiry personal formation. The most influential advocate of this proposal today is Charles M. Wood.

In his book, *Vision and Discernment*, Wood contends that theology is not merely the imparting of doctrines or skills. It is "a critical inquiry into the validity of Christian witness."[21] As such, theology involves three main sorts of questions, each of which is the leading question of a particular dimension of theology.

> Since the aim of theology is to examine the validity of Christian witness as Christian witness, i.e., according to its own intrinsic criteria, each of these leading questions may be seen to derive from a particular formal, constitutive feature of that witness. Together, they constitute a comprehensive inquiry into the validity of Christian witness as such.[22]

The first of these questions is that of the "Christianness" of any alleged Christian witness. That is to say, one of the features of the concept of Christian witness is that such witness is not to one's own convictions but to Christ. The second question has to do with truth. To bear witness is to posit something as true. It is natural enough, then, to ask, is this witness really true? What claims to truth does it make and how are they to be judged? The third principal question relates to Christian witness as an attempt to convey a message. The critical question theology must raise is: Is this witness appropriately enacted? Is it related to its context?[23]

Inquiry into the first question is developed within historical theology; inquiry into the second question is developed within systematic theology; and inquiry into the third question is developed within practical theology. These three dimensions are distinct, but they are closely related. Historical theology, as Wood perceives it, is more than the study of the history of Christianity. "It is a study of the Christian tradition which seeks to discern what makes Christian witness Christian. It asks by what criteria the 'Christianness' of something might be judged, and it asks how such criteria might be applied in various sorts of cases; and it proceeds then to make appropriate judgments and proposals."[24] Similarly, systematic theology entails more than the study of "theo-logic." It "aims to discover and display the sorts of meaning the discourse and activity of Christian witness involve, including the sorts of claims to truth which that witness may make."[25] Finally, practical theology is much more than the study of practice. Practical theology examines Christian witness

in terms of its enactment. "It asks by what standards this practice
is to be judged, and it proceeds to make the relevant judgments
concerning past, present, or prospective instances of it. . . . Christian
witness is borne by the actions of Christians and Christian communities, and by their very being as Christians and communities."[26]

The exercise of these three dimensions of theology involves theological formation or, and Wood uses the same term as Farley, the
theological *habitus*. This means that theological education is something quite different from indoctrination. Being critical, in the sense
that Wood has in mind, is more of a "character-trait" than a skill.
Indeed, the development of the theological *habitus* is not dependent
on the acquisition of ministerial skills, but judgments regarding the
content of Christian witness and its appropriateness to its context.
This means, says Wood, "understanding the entire curriculum as
really and truly a theological curriculum, that is, as a body of resources ordered to the cultivation in students of an aptitude for
theological inquiry."[27] Accordingly, courses in sociology of religion,
psychology, or African history may have a significant role in a theological curriculum if such courses provide the concepts and skills
needed for the development of theological judgment. Conversely,
courses in church history or Biblical languages may be non-theolog-
ical in terms of the purposes they really serve.

Reformation or Revolution?

The two proposals for the reform of theological education sketched
above are by no means the only ones discussed in professional circles
today.[28] However, they do indicate that more than a reformation of
the theological curriculum is being suggested. For both Farley and
Wood the absorption of more theological knowledge is not enough;
it is a habit or mind, an attitude, a sense of awareness that is needed.
From their perspective a revolution in pastoral preparation is needed.

As Concordia Seminary marks its 150th anniversary the admonition behind these contemporary proposals must be heeded even
though the content of the proposals are seriously flawed. The admonition is that theological education must develop in seminary
students the actual "doing" of theology. The notion of *habitus* which
both Farley and Wood stress is essential—pastors must think theologically and not just technically. The training of the "theological
mind" is central to theological education.

Yet, the revolution in seminary education which Farley and Wood
seem to call for in displacing the traditional fourfold curricular approach is unwarranted. For that for which they yearn—a unifying

thread—is clearly there in the Lutheran application of the traditional approach. As noted earlier in this discussion, the Word of God is the focal and unifying point of Lutheran theological education. While Farley's proposal makes the pre-reflective faith experience in all its contemporary matrices the source of the unity of theological education and Wood places the activity of critical inquiry in the same central position, theological education at Concordia makes the Holy Scriptures the unifying principle of theological education. God's revealing activity in the Scriptures and the Savior provides the unity in the face of the pluralism of the four theological disciplines. Theology is indeed a genuine wisdom. Its unity is established on the Word of God who is one and on the Gospel of Jesus Christ which is one. The curriculum of Concordia Seminary must be continuously studied and adapted so that it can more adequately prepare men to serve the church in today's world. But such reformation dare never lead to revolution in terms of the role of *sola scriptura* in pastoral preparation.

Notes

[1] Quoted by Arthur C. Repp, "Pastoral Training of The Lutheran Church-Missouri Synod," in *Toward a More Excellent Ministry*, edited by Richard R. Caemmerer and Alfred O. Fuerbringer (St. Louis: Concordia, 1964), pp. 64-65.

[2] The first religious denomination to make provision for the training of pastors by special professors appointed and supervised by the denomination was the Dutch Reformed Church in 1784. Action by other church bodies followed soon thereafter. See William Adams Brown, *The Education of American Ministers* (New York: Institute of Social and Religious Research, 1934), pp. 74-79.

[3] *Ibid.*, p. 119.

[4] Conrad Bergendoff, *The Lutheran Church in America and Theological Education* (New York: Lutheran Church in America Board of Theological Education, 1963), p. 5.

[5] *Summa theologiae*, I-I q. 1, a. 3, ad. 2.

[6] Repp, p. 70.

[7] Schleiermacher identified the theological character and unity of the separate disciplines with their orientation to a particular purpose that of "church leadership." Equipping individuals for church leadership can not be accomplished through the mere mastery of techniques. According to his *Outline*, church leadership requires "scientific knowledge" as well as "practical instruction."

[8] Keith R. Bridston, *Theological Training in the Modern World* (Geneva: World's Student Christian Federation, 1954), p. 16.

[9] Charles M. Wood, *Vision and Discernment* (Atlanta: Scholars Press, 1985), pp. 3-4.

[10] Francis Schussler Fiorenza, "Thinking Theologically About Theological Education," *Theological Education*, Volume XXIV, Supplement II 1988, p. 90.

[11] *Ibid.*

[12] Edward Farley, *Theologia: The Fragmentation and Unity of Theologial Education* (Philadelphia: Fortress, 1983), p. 156.

[13] The essays in this volume explore theological education in the contexts of university education, clergy education, and church education on the basis of the hermeneutic approach outlined in *Theologia*.

[14] Edward Farley, *The Fragility of Knowledge* (Philadelphia: Fortress, 1988), p. 173.

[15] *Ibid.*, p. 149.

[16] *Ibid.*, p. 154.

[17] *Ibid.*, p. 150.

[18] *Ibid.*, p. 152.

[19] *Ibid.*, p. 160.

[20] *Ibid.*, pp. 142-43.

[21] Wood, p. 21.

[22] *Ibid.*, p. 37.

[23] *Ibid.*, p. 39.

[24] *Ibid.*, p. 42.

[25] *Ibid.*, p. 46.

[26] *Ibid.*, p. 47.

[27] *Ibid.*, p. 94.

[28] See, for example James M. Gustafson, "Reflections on the Literature on Theological Education Published Between 1955-1985," *Theological Education*, Volume XXIV, Supplement II, 1988, pp. 9-86.

The Importance of
Old Testament Studies
for Lutheran Theology

HORACE D. HUMMEL

The formulation of the topic cries out for more precise definition. Not only does "Old Testament" cover a wide variety of literature written over something like a millennium, but "Lutheran theology" of one sort or another has been around roughly half as long itself.

It would be tempting to offer simply a sort of historical sketch. But that would hardly address the aspect of "importance" in the title in any definitive way. Many other works have done a creditable job of that. Perhaps the best of those readily available is: *Old Testament Theology: Its History and Development,* by John H. Hayes and Frederick Prussner (John Knox, 1985). We cannot ignore aspects of that history; like it or not, all of our horizons have been shaped somewhat by it, whether positively or negatively. Nevertheless, our concentration will not be there.

An obvious pitfall is the hiatus that has always been present to one degree or another between what is taught in seminaries and universities, and the actual life, piety, and worship of local parishes and parishioners. Obviously, the latter is far more difficult to assess than the former. Not only is it the professors who tend to write the bulk of the literature, but also the variation from location to location is probably greater on the parish level.

In any case, this hiatus really became acute only about the middle of the post-Reformation period with the rise of the historical-critical method and its professed claim to be "scientific." The flip side of that desire to be "scientific" became a desire to be "free" of dogmatic and ecclesiastical controls and strive for "objectivity." It is nearly a truism to remind ourselves that almost synonymous with the rise of the historical-critical method was a shift in major context from church to secular university. Only in recent years, more or less concurrent

HORACE D. HUMMEL is Chairman of the Department of Exegetical Theology at Concordia Seminary, St. Louis.

with the rise of the so-called "new hermeneutic," has it become widely acknowledged that such "objectivity" is impossible. The only impossible presupposition is that one has no presuppositions.

As a result, "hermeneutics" has come much to the fore in recent years. In some respects, the results have been salutary: there is no reason why a confessional-traditional hermeneutics, such as has always officially been championed by the Missouri Synod, and as briefly attempted here, should not hold its head high as, at very least, as honorable and defensible an approach as any other. It also behooves the pastor/preacher to clarify in his thinking *why* he does what he does with a Scriptural text, even though those theoretical underpinnings may often remain unenunciated in a parish context.

In practice, however, a confessional-traditional approach is rarely honored in academic circles. Since "science" is still taken to imply "openness" to virtually any option, any person or group making ultimate *truth* claims is automatically suspect, at best. An implicit relativism still reigns supreme, as evidenced by the frequent preference of "religion" over "theology," and, even more obviously, of "Hebrew Scriptures" over "Old Testament."

No one would deny the appropriateness of such a stance in an avowedly secular context such as most universities in a society where church and state are properly distinguished. The problem assumes far greater dimensions, however, when the difference between *church* colleges and seminaries, on the one hand, and secular institutions becomes blurred. All too often teachers in the former have simply modelled their own instruction after that which they themselves received in earning their advanced degrees, more often than not in some other context. Any real ecclesiastical supervision or discipline is renounced as inimical to some "scientific *search* for truth." To no little extent, one could divide liberal (mainline) seminary faculties from "conservative" or confessional ones by the extent to which such an attitude has been able to establish itself.

As a result, the fragmentation of seminary curricula, a lack of interaction between departments, has emerged as a major problem today. If the exegetes no longer provide "raw material," as it were, for dogmatic, homiletic and other applications, those disciplines will inevitably look elsewhere for usable material. Perhaps nowhere have the end-results been more deleterious to all concerned than in the case of the Old Testament.

Even avowedly confessional seminaries have been affected by the situation. Not only is a general *Kulturkampf* (cultural battle) involved, from which seminaries could not totally isolate themselves, even if they wanted to, but a very real problem arises already in the question of how Biblical specialists shall be trained for service in a confessional/conservative church. Seminaries, such as ours, commonly have graduate programs, offering at least a master's (S.T.M.) and perhaps a doctor's (Th.D.) degree upon successful completion. Hopefully, these do a creditable job of training some in the skills and art of integrating and applying confessional principles of Biblical interpretation. However, resources are usually limited for much advanced work in the important philological component of in-depth Biblical exegesis (cognate languages, history, archaeology, etc.). In addition, the simple danger of "inbreeding" cannot be dismissed.

So where shall prospective professors of exegesis be advised to study? Many "mainline" seminaries also offer graduate programs, but their philological facilities are rarely any better than in conservative institutions. Furthermore, it proves very difficult, if not impossible, even to participate in most courses without subscribing to some version of historical-critical methodology.

An attractive (though usually expensive!) alternative is to earn a *Ph.D.* (not a Th.D.) at some university by majoring in *philology,* usually classics in the case of the New Testament and "Ancient Near Eastern Studies" in the case of the Old. This approach runs the risk of producing graduates who will be skilled in some aspect of philology but never be able to integrate it with theology (hermeneutics) in the classroom.

On the whole, however, experience seems to demonstrate that, all other things being equal, this approach is, at least for many, the most useful in the long run. If the individual himself had solid theological training before matriculating at the university, virtually all the pressures at a seminary will propel him to do the necessary synthesis with confessional theology on his own. The obverse is far more difficult, almost approaching impossibility: that one with an advanced *theological* degree master the philology on his own.

If this thesis be granted, it remains for most churches, including our own, to "put their money where their mouth is" by providing sufficient scholarship money for such training.

(Of course, similar problems confront us in many students, although that is only marginally relevant here. However, it must be noted that creeping secularism impacts also Christian families' inability to impart early Biblical formation, and the general neglect of language skills at more elementary levels is certainly not least evident when it comes to mastering Hebrew!)

An opposite extreme to the picture just sketched must also be

granted, although it is also an instance where the axiom applies
that "abuse does not nullify the use." Confessional exegesis, by definition, claims to possess and help enunciate THE truth of the Gospel. But there seem always to be some who would invoke such claims
prematurely, by limiting it too severely to certain formulae or modes
of expression. Although it is often said that, within limits, we have
no "official exegesis," some would seem to deny that at times in
practice. Nevertheless, even though it may sometimes seem that
"with friends like that, who needs enemies?", it should not provoke
us into losing sight of the fact that our *major* enemies today do not
lie in that direction.

   Although the need and power to exercise oversight and discipline,
if necessary, should be used cautiously and judiciously, a confessional church cannot subscribe to secular principles of academic
freedom and absolve itself of the responsibility to see to it that its
magisterium as well as its ministerium remains answerable and
responsible. "Councils may err" and often have, as the Reformation
insisted, but at times that risk must be taken.

   If one tries to develop our main topic somewhat inductively, it
will be noted at once that neither in Scripture itself nor in our
Symbols is there any explicit section on "Old Testament hermeneutics" or the like. In both, however, there is ample material for developing such a locus, as began to be done already in the later stages
of the Reformation. All conservative, traditional principles of interpretation must build upon the foundation laid in the New Testament,
and, according to its own testimony, to a large extent by our Lord
Himself. Obviously, with the exception of 2 Peter, the "Scriptures"
appealed to there are always what we have come to know as the
"Old Testament."

   Those Old Testament Scriptures, in general, as well as in spe-
cifics, are the promise, the type (and/or contain the prophecies) of
which Christ is the fulfillment, antitype, or answer. In Him they
ultimately find their unity, infallibility, and other aspects of their
authority. This must be stressed, because it is by no means self-
evident to unaided reason. Even the label we prefer for our hermeneutics, "historical-grammatical" rather than "historical-critical," may yield only a "historical faith," without Christological or
explicitly evangelical reference and application. After all, what we
know as "Old Testament" was, and still is, claimed also by Judaism,
which by definition does not confess Jesus as the Christ. Sometimes
it is said that the church receives the Old Testament anew from her
Lord, or else the "veil," of one sort or another, "remains unlifted" (2

Cor. 3:14). Nor should we forget what "slow learners" the disciples were; even after the post-resurrection appearances at Emmaus (Luke 24:44-49), in fact, on the very verge of the ascension, they were still unable to pose the right question (Acts 1:6-8).

We cannot retrace here the tortuous route by which the Spiritual — that of the Holy Spirit — enlightenment granted at Pentecost was maintained and developed. The first and perhaps the archetypical challenge down to the present day came already in the second century from Marcion, who would expunge the Old Testament from the canon completely as the witness to an entirely different deity and religion. Although promptly condemned, his ghost endures. One must even ask if the thousands for whom the Old Testament remains a closed book are not *de facto* Marcionites. And the label is surely applicable to much "scientific" study of the Bible; even if nothing is *per se* objectionable, the results remain "Marcionite" if the results are in no way related to the Gospel and the mission of the church.

Nor should it be forgotten that Marcion was forced by consistency to promulgate also an "edited" version of the New Testament. The adjective "New" remains essentially meaningless if the major referent is not the Old Testament. If the "New" Testament and Christ are not the fulfillment — and embodiment, if you will — of the Old Testament, it will inevitably find its "fulfillment" or ultimate meaning, if any, somewhere else, probably in the hopes and "spirituality" of the natural man. Again, one may formally be very "Biblical," but substantially not so at all.

To a certain extent, we may find a certain overcorrection of Marcionitism in the so-called "allegory" of the early and medieval church, especially in the influential Alexandrian school of exegesis. Also Luther, like other Reformers, is well-known for his ridicule of that method's excesses, and insistence upon "one, literal, grammatical" sense, or the like.

Yet we do well not to cry "allegory" too glibly. Ironically, to most modern, "historical" exegesis, not only the New Testament's use of the Old, but also Luther's and virtually all traditional use of the Old Testament will be dismissed as "allegorical," or at least as some species of "reading into" the Old some meaning, which does not appear grammatically and "historically" to be evident. At some point, one must either *confess* that Jesus Christ is LORD (Yahweh), also of the Old Testament, or one has some other confession of faith. (We recall that real neutrality or presuppositionlessness is impossible.)

Of course, there are valid and invalid ways of reading and confessing the Old Testament as also *Christian* Scripture. We need to recall that "allegory" was popular for so long precisely because it seemed to render meaningful and useful even the most difficult parts of Scripture. Even today, many who find some "spiritual" meaning in the Old Testament and even preach on its texts, but in no way anchor that meaning in any grasp to original, historical situation or context, may rightly be called "allegorists." Yet the solution is assuredly not to abandon the Old Testament to the "historical-critical" wolves, who, often as not, are unable, or even uninterested, to provide foundation for Christian use.

And herewith we come to what is probably the heart of the modern dilemma, one which threatened already in Reformation times and which has, on the whole, seemed to grow exponentially ever since. If there is anything which is likely to be emphasized in Biblical studies today, it is the necessity of attention to original, historical context. Yet all too often, what seems to result is a sort of paralysis, such a fear of "allegorical" "reading into" the text some alien meaning, that no meaning at all will be ventured! Many versions of the so-called "new hermeneutic" propose to overcome the aridity of historic*ism* by trying to put accent on "what the Bible means to *me,*" that is, upon the subjectivity of the individual reader on a par with the objective text, on "what it means" as somehow an entity divorceable from "what it meant." However well-intentioned, it is difficult to see what kind of controls or discipline there can be to such a method. Bugenhagen's old axiom, which once appeared at the beginning of Nestle editions of the Greek New Testament, works much better for all of Scripture!" *Te totum applica ad textum; rem totam applica ad te"* ("Apply yourself totally to the text; apply it totally to yourself"). I have often punned on the commonality, but also ultimately the vast difference between a purely "*h*istorical" exegesis in contrast to a "*H*istorical" one (= His story, the Gospel), or between a "spiritual" (purely personal and subjective) vs. a "Spiritual" one, that is, led and controlled by the Holy Spirit, as He witnesses to ultimate intent in the initially external "means of grace" (Word and Sacrament).

Some of the modern dilemma is presaged already in the Reformation, especially in the differences between Luther and Calvin and their heirs. Ironically, even though Luther was academically an Old Testament specialist and wrote and preached voluminously on the Old Testament, also Lutherans must admit that they usually find much more immediately in Calvin's commentaries what they expect to find in a commentary than they do in Luther's. The difference should not be overstated, or course, but generally Calvin gives much more attention to grammar and historical context than does Luther. Ultimately, perhaps Calvin does so too much; while New Testament or Christological application is by no means ignored, it scarcely dominates as it does in Luther.

Hence, externally at least, it is surely no accident that Calvinism has down to the present day "majored" in Old Testament far more than has Lutheranism. After the Enlightenment, I do not believe it is too much of an oversimplification to see the one-sided "historicism" of critical research as heavily indebted to Reformed covenantal accents all along. When Lutheranism did attempt to pick up Luther's "Christological" emphasis in a historico-critical context, some disjunction of history and revelation, of fact and faith, always seemed to be close at hand (e.g., Eissfeldt in a classical exchange with Eichrodt).

The orthodox appeal to Old Testament proof-texts almost as freely as to New Testament gave credence to their claim that both testaments were equally Word of God (the prophets *and* apostles *"ut limpidissimos purissimosque Israelis fontes"*). While formally that confession has never been retracted, I would judge it as functionally rather moribund. Ironically, much present-day orthodoxy fastens one-sidedly on two themes. Each is valid, indeed indispensable, yet only as part of a totality.

One theme often so misused is that of "Messianic prophecy," where all too often isolated verses are quoted atomistically, while the surrounding context is either ignored, or treated as though an evangelist or apostle had written it (so especially parts of Isaiah). Properly deployed, these passages are simply foci (especially visible mountain peaks) of the Messianic (Christological) content of the entire Old Testament. Not only are they—and is it—all fulfilled in Christ, but they continue to be "fulfilled" in the faithful in Word and Sacrament, and all of it will be consummated at our Lord's Second Coming.

It is increasingly being recognized that explicit prediction must be accompanied by a sense of *"typology,"* the conviction that the salvific events, persons, rites, institutions of the Old Testament are "shadows"—predictions—of Christ, and must so ultimately be interpreted by one who faithfully echoes the New Testament's use of the Old Testament. These, too, are actualized in us by the Spirit and will likewise be consummated at the eschaton.

Typology, of course, is subject to abuse, and long Lutheran contact with Catholic (especially on priesthood and sacrifice) and Reformed misapplication (Cocceius, etc.) has probably contributed to neglect. But if we but look at much "evangelicalism" all about us, at least of the millennial variety, it is clear that "prophecy" also is subject to all sorts of caricatures.

The second major caricature has to do with "Law." Few, if any, would subscribe to the simplistic equation of the Old Testament with "Law" and the New Testament with "Gospel" (in direct contraction to the accent on "Messianic prophecy," of course), but at a more visceral level the misconception dies hard. There are, indeed, sections in St. Paul, as there are in Luther, that would appear to dismiss the Old Testament as simply "Law." But read on! The temptation to misunderstanding is perhaps especially strong to orthodox Lutheranism with the laudable centrality of its dogmatic "Law-Gospel" emphasis.

Much of the confusion is translational: St. Paul's νόμος as well as the Old Testament's *torah* both tend to be translated as "Law." Yet, however translated, the vocables in both testaments are multivalent, and by no means equivalent. I have long argued that *torah* might more accurately, as a "dynamic equivalent" translation, be rendered "Gospel" in its broad sense or at least "Word," rather than "Law." This preferable rendition is perhaps most urgent in the simple *reading* of Old Testament lessons, where little if any accompanying explanation is possible. Otherwise, at best, we run the risk of undermining all that we teach about the Old Testament—and perhaps subliminally subvert ourselves as well. Since virtually no common English translations do this, it is incumbent upon the pastor or other lector simply to *make the substitution*.

During the era of "Biblical theology" much academic excitement turned on the Old Testament and much of it also proved useful to orthodoxy. But that age is past, and, hence, perhaps, the task of proclaiming the Old Testament *evangelically* is today as difficult, but as urgent as ever, if we really mean what we say about *tota Scriptura*.

Holy Baptism and Pastor Walther

NORMAN E. NAGEL

In the Church of the Good Shepherd in Langenchursdorf, Saxony, on October 11, 1811, an infant was baptized Carl Ferdinand Wilhelm, a son of the pastor, Gottlob Heinrich Wilhelm Walther. The baby was five days old. To baptize a child so soon was long since the baptismal usage, a usage which matches the doctrine of holy Baptism.

This child came into the heritage of generations of pastors. His father, grandfather and great-grandfather were pastors of the church in Saxony since the Reformation. Although this heritage was his birthright, he became conscientiously a Lutheran only when he was a student at the University of Leipzig.

At his Baptism the agenda used was that of 1771, the last in the tradition of the Saxon agendas of 1539, 1540, 1555, 1580 and 1624. Its title ran: Agenda, that is, the Church Order for the ministers of the churches in the principality of Duke Henry of Saxony, our gracious lord, how parsons and pastors are to conduct their offices and services, presenting a newly improved version of the Church Order of Elector Augustus, enlarged with many collects of the Superintendents for all weekdays, Sundays and feast days. Leipzig: Johann Friedrich, Junius, 1771.[1] This represents the so-called Duke Henry's Agenda. F. Hort says of it:

> The order given the Saxon liturgy by Henry's Agenda characterizes its subsequent particular development. Here one can see most clearly what particularly developed in the services, their liturgical character, and what remained permanent and typical.[2]

For Walther to recall his Baptism was to recall the Agenda of 1771. He took it with him to Perry County and to St. Louis.

NORMAN E. NAGEL is Chairman of the Department of Systematic Theology at Concordia Seminary, St. Louis.

At his Baptism one godfather was the pastor of Bräunsdorf, where
Walther later succeeded him as pastor. Walther's examination (*examen pro candidatura*) was April 26, 1836. His call came by way of
the Count of Einsiedel, patron of the parish, and he was ordained
on the second Sunday after Epiphany in 1837, January 15.[3] Walther
was pastor in Bräunsdorf for only two years. In those two years
seventeen children were baptized by him. In Walther's own hand
there is a note written in the church register at the end of his time
as pastor in Bräunsdorf. "These entries were made with my own
hand as pastor of this church"—a sort of testament as he laid down
his pastorate there and turned toward emigration.

There was more than one ground prompting him toward emigration, but one of them was certainly the doctrine of holy Baptism,
its administration, and the responsibilities that go with these for a
Lutheran pastor. We are given a glimpse of the pastoral care involved by the fact that half of the children he baptized in Bräunsdorf
were born outside of wedlock. This fact was discovered by Professor
August Suelflow during his recent research in Bräunsdorf. He sees
this fact not so much as evidence of galloping fornication but of the
social and economic situation of that time. According to the social
usage of the time (responsibility to care for wife and family) they
were simply too poor to marry. This was the time after the Napoleonic wars and in a region devastated by them. We have only to
recall the Battle of the Nations near Leipzig. What all suffers loss
during a war and its aftermath!

It was also the time of the Awakening. These young people found
in the young Pastor Walther a pastor who was compassionately there
for them in their need. The names of those who were said to be the
fathers (*annehmendlich*) he wrote straight into the church book. He
led them the way of repentance and faith to the font, dealing with
them as God's deputies for their children. These poor, baptized, and
faithful mothers brought their illegitimate children to this pastor to
be baptized, and he showed himself to be there for them in baptizing
their children as our Lord's servant and deputy and their pastor.
Mark 10:13-16 is evidenced in the liturgy of holy Baptism at least
since the seventh century.

In contrast with the foregoing we may set the advice of the ra-
tionalizing liturgiologist G. F. Seiler. "In such cases something quite
different is to be said than of the baptism of a legitimate child."[4] He
provided a special order for the baptism of the child of poor parents.
What we have seen here of Pastor Walther in Bräunsdorf we shall
see again in Missouri.

There were other similar needs and pressures. Walther tells of them in his *Short Account of the Life of the Late Reverend Pastor Johannes Friedrich Buenger who showed such Faithfulness as Pastor of the Evangelical Lutheran Immanuel's Congregation in St. Louis, Missouri.* From Walther you know what you are getting. Proceeds from the sale of this book were for the Orphans' House of the Child Jesus. This had been founded by Buenger as was also a hospital. Walther was his confessor. They were brothers in the office of pastor (*Amtsbrüder*) until Buenger's death in 1882.

In this biography of his brother pastor, Walther recalls the pressure under which they had to work as pastors in Saxony. Walther himself was denounced for following the Absolution in the Agenda of 1771, and so for not obeying the directive that the Enlightenmentized Agenda of 1812 was to be used exclusively after January 1, 1813. He was summoned before the church court and ordered to obey this directive. His compassion went out to the people who also suffered under such pressure.

> Faithful Lutheran lay people were put in no lesser distress of conscience at that time in Saxony. They were expected to accept as their shepherds and pastors *(Seelsorger)* men who were quite clearly false prophets. By such men they were expected to have their children baptized and confirmed, from them in confession to be absolved and be given the holy Lord's Supper. . . . Their need was acute whenever a child was born to such faithful parents. In the agenda [1812] there were five orders for Holy Baptism, only one of which could possibly be called tolerable *(einigermaszen erträglich)*. The father would then hasten [with the child] to his unfaithful pastor, and there humbly have to beg that this one order might be the one used. Such a plea was only seldom granted. So it was often the case that the father returned home from the church with a deeply wounded conscience, his child having indeed been baptized in the name of the Father and of the Son and of the Holy Spirit, but with the addition of rationalistic verbiage.[5]

A footnote here adds to the picture. "Moreover, at that time there were pastors in Saxony who did not even baptize with the words of the Triune Name." This fact is also attested by Seiler. He at least respects the name of God as a Biblical expression. His advice:

> In the place of the words Father, Son and Spirit one cannot put the faith in the almighty, all-wise and all-kind God. . . .

We may not prescribe to those who hear us what they are to believe; they are so diversely disposed. On the other hand, we are not bound to leave out the biblical expressions for the sake of love, and be too clever in keeping people contented.[6]

Similar circumstances in Prussia are reported by Martin Kiunke in his book on Scheibel.[7]

Walther reports an account given him in 1836 by a candidate of theology who was there as a godfather.

A couple of days after his wife had given birth to their child, Mr. H., a faithful Lutheran layman, went to Pastor S. He requested that at the forthcoming baptism that formula of the five in the agenda would be used, which was the only one which accorded with Scripture. Pastor S. received him with more than exemplary humanity and most willingly accepted his request. In view of this Mr. N. N. with his wife and myself and those who had been chosen to be godparents went without misgivings to the church. The baptism began. He read the desired formula up to the part where the Our Father should follow. There he inserted a prayer he had made up himself, proceeded forthwith to the name giving and then spoke the Apostles' Creed himself as "We believe . . ." instead of putting it as questions to the sponsors. He left out the question "Do you renounce the devil . . ." and then simply did the baptism. We were astonished and, without exaggeration I can say crushed by the way we had been dealt with. There we stood as those who had been deceived. Thereupon we hurried to see Pastor S. in his panelled chamber in the sacristy. We confronted him with his having broken his undertaking. At first he denied it. From the agenda it was pointed out how he had not followed the first formula. This he could not deny. With scarcely containable anger he said he would make good what had been left out, although he supposed that all that was contained in what had been said. We then went and sat down in the church gaped at by the midwife and godparents of the next child to be baptized. Before Pastor S. proceeded to that baptism he came angrily to us and said, "You will write down your names for me." Then he did the other baptism, with great fluster swiftly taking their promises one after another. Then he turned to the sacristan and snorted, "Have those people step forward." We stepped up to the font. Mr. N. N. took the child in his arms after Pastor S. had loudly remarked,

"These people have taken in hand to make prescriptions for a teacher of religion. I make this concession to you because I have regard for your weakness." Then word for word from the agenda the question, "Do you renounce the devil?" This was greeted by bystanders with sniggers and exclamations of astonishment. Then the giving of the sign of the cross on breast and forehead. He then summoned me to him in the screened off place and said in the hearing of all: "But you, you want to be a scientific and educated man. Show me where 'Do you renounce the devil' is required." This was something contrary to his viewpoint. I answered. "I do not have to show you a place in the Bible. You are a servant of the church and bound by your ordination. You have broken what you promised. You should not have promised what is against your conviction."[8]

Walther observes how a candidate of theology might recall a pastor to his ordination vow, and then thinks of how it would be with the poor and uneducated, a weaver or a trousers tailor. This eye-witness account and Walther's telling of it show how vividly it stayed with him. Here was not the faithful way with holy Baptism. Was this tolerable? Was there no way out? Walther recounts the situation:

How gladly the faithful Lutheran preachers and people would then have spared nothing for permission to join together in a separate Lutheran free church—so far had things gone, so deep the deterioration in the territorial church. At that time it was quite unthinkable that they would be granted the freedom to do this. Emigration appeared to them as the only way out, emigration to a land where religious freedom reigned, emigration from a land where oppression of conscience grew ever more intolerable threatening to choke the life of faith. In addition there was the warning example which the Saxon Lutherans saw happening to the separate Prussian Lutherans. Many of them had struggled faithfully and hard against the Union but in vain. They had suffered heavy persecution. When they applied for permission to emigrate, their plea was flatly rejected at the instance of Altenstein, the Minister for Culture, and this in spite of a Prussian law of 1818 which expressly permitted emigration. It was therefore no groundless fear when the Saxon Lutherans saw a similar fate ahead for them as for the brave Prussians, if they did not attempt to be let go peacefully. Their resolve toward such an attempt was strengthened by further events in Prussia. Toward the end of the year 1837 the tyrannical prohibition of emigration was abrogated by royal decree. Pastor Grabau with a large flock of Prussian Lutherans then emigrated to America, and Pastor Kavel with a small group of them to Australia. In Saxony the territorial church had not formally established a Union of Lutherans and Reformed with a specific law, but for some considerable time that was already *de facto* the case.[9]

Walther writes of Buenger:

So then he also joined the quietly organized association of those who planned to emigrate. He did not come to this with any joy, but with deep ache and pain in his heart at having to leave his fatherland so dear to him. He did not do it in the hope of finding good days in America. On the contrary he saw clearly the many and great privations. That which alone moved him to go to America was release from burdens of conscience, and the precious boon of freedom to serve God according to His word.[10]

What that meant for the doctrine and practice of holy Baptism we may read in a comparison between the agenda of 1812 and the Missouri Synod agenda of 1856.

In the 1812 agenda the intrusion of Rationalism and also Pietism are clearly evident. It had the title, *Church Book for the Evangelical Divine Service of the Royal Saxon Land, issued by All-highest Decree, Dresden in the Royal Court Printery, 1812*. In the Foreword to the second part we read:

This second part of the Church Book shall take the place of that agenda which until now has been in use, the agenda which was first issued in the year 1539 and subsequently improved and enlarged. [This second part of the Church Book] shall be used exclusively by all pastors of the Royal Saxon Land in all that is done in the Divine Services beginning January 1.[11]

We have already observed the omission of the old Absolution. By then this may not have upset too many. Holy Baptism, on the other hand, went deep into the Christian life of the people. Here changes had to be made more cautiously and transitionally.[12] The old order for holy Baptism could not simply be put out. It was weakened and relativized. Four further orders were provided, all legally prescribed. The first order, an "improved" version of the traditional order, was regarded by Walther as barely tolerable (enigermaszen erträglich). It has a number of expressions which put man at the center, along with such phrases as "with touched hearts." While the almighty and all-kind God is praised for having created the child with reason and immortality, there is only passing mention of sin. Of the further four orders one can only say, the more, the worse.

Walther described the Church Book of 1812 as "in part clearly denying the divine truth, in part containing formulas which miserably watered down the Christian doctrine." He wrote further:

> In addition there was also this that no one enquired of the rationalistic unfaithful preachers whether they did things according to the agenda. To them it still rang too Christian. On the other hand a faithful Lutheran preacher was not permitted to depart one jot from the agenda. If he did and it was reported to the authorities, he was rigorously called before them to answer for it.[13]

Clearly the Saxon agenda of 1812 would not be the one used by the emigrated pastors, but rather that of 1771. Concordia Historical Institute has a copy of this from Immanuel Church, whose pastor was Johannes Buenger.

The first event in the history of liturgy in the Missouri Synod was the publication of an agenda in 1856. Its announcement appeared in *Der Lutheraner* of November 4, 1856: Church-Agenda for Evangelical Lutheran Congregations of the Unaltered Augsburg Confession, put together from the old orthodox Saxon Church-Agendas and published by the General German Evangelical Lutheran Synod of Missouri, Ohio and other States.

> Finally we have the pleasure of being able to announce to our dear readers that this work, so long awaited and desired, is completed and lies ready to be sent to all who want it. The work falls into four parts. The first part contains the formulas for the following official acts (Amtshandlungen): 1. the baptism of children, 2. the confirmation of emergency baptism, 3. adult baptism. . . .

At the end comes the following notice. "A copy (one volume fully bound in leather, gold embossed and with cover ornamentation) $2.00. The work can be obtained through Mr. Ed. Roschke, care of Prof. C. F. W. Walther, St. Louis, Missouri."

Thus this agenda was in continuity with the old Saxon agendas. It was characteristic of the Confessional Awakening to recognize the Enlightenment as a wrong turning, just as the Reformation had so recognized Scholasticism. The Lutheran liturgical heritage lived on again in Missouri, just as was later also the case in doctrine with Walther's edited and enlarged publication of Baier's *Compendium* in 1879. Similar continuity (*Kernlieder*) was evidenced in the *Church Hymnbook for Evangelical Lutheran Congregations of the Unaltered Augsburg Confession* of 1847, and also in the publication of Luther's Writings 1880-1910.[14]

In liturgical matters Walther was no theoretician but rather a churchly theologian and pastor. The agenda of 1856 did not flow out of his pen. It was the result of the careful ("finally" and "long awaited") work of the surrounding pastors under his leadership.

What of Holy Baptism? The same "old" thing.

Without any Foreword the orders are simply presented very much as in 1771. Luther's Foreword of 1526, which is still in 1771, is omitted. Holy Baptism begins with the old admonition, "Dear friends in Christ. We hear every day from God's word . . . He himself has *commanded* to bring little children to him, and has *promised* to receive them into His Kingdom" just as in the Saxon agenda of Duke Henry in 1539 whose Foreword was signed by Justus Jonas, Georgius Spalatinus, Caspar Creutzinger, Fridericus Myconius, Justus Menius and Johannes Weber. In Missouri 1856 the language is somewhat updated and smoothed out, just as had earlier been done in Pomerania in 1542, Prussia in 1568, Mecklenburg in 1552, Wolfenbüttel in 1569, Mansfield in 1580 and Lauenburg in 1585. The 1856 Missouri agenda was in principle the heir of Saxon antecedents. The influence of Loehe should be noted—not so much theoretically as in supplying particular liturgical pieces which filled out a gap. The agenda of 1771 lacked ordination. This omission was supplied by Loehe's second order (his first was the old Saxon one).[15]

The first part of Loehe's *Agenda for Christian Congregations of the Lutheran Confession* was published in 1844. It was dedicated to Wyneken. The second edition with the second part, which contained holy Baptism, came out only in 1859. This time the dedication was to Wyneken and Huschke. In the Foreword to the second part Loehe expressed a desire for "ascetic associations (*asketische Vereine*) . . . who would . . . of necessity often go beyond the sixteenth century."[16] Walther had little such desire. In part they travelled a common way; in part they went different ways. We may observe something of this here.

The greatest thing lacking in the traditional Saxon order for holy Baptism was our Lord's mandate of Baptism. Luther had set aside the consecration of the water for which the mandate was used. In his setting aside this misuse of the words of institution these words also disappeared, but not really; they are centered in "Baptism itself."[17]

The 1856 Missouri agenda begins with the introductory admonition of the 1539 Saxony agenda in the way of the 1771 Saxony agenda and then adds to this the introductory admonition from the 1626 Coburg agenda within which come the words of institution. Other orders of holy Baptism which included the words of institution and which were available in Missouri were those of the 1543 Schwäbisch Hall and 1614 Goltz agendas. These were to be found in Höfling's work *The Sacrament of Baptism* which was published in Erlangen in 1848. In the 1856 Missouri agenda is mostly the best, also the shortest, and the liturgically most cogent words of institution. We give the English translation of the 1856 Missouri agenda which was published in 1881.

And since in baptism there is Christ our Lord's, will and command which He has given to His beloved disciples, when He says in the last chapter of Matthew: Go ye and teach all nations, baptizing them in the name of the Father, and of the Son, and of the Holy Ghost; and also His comforting promise which He added thereto in the last chapter of Mark: He that believeth and is baptized shall be saved; but he that believeth not, shall be damned: therefore these two things, God's command and promise, ought to be the reason of your bringing this little child hither to this blessed baptism that it might be baptized in the name of God.

Do you, therefore, listen attentively and mind diligently both the prayers and the divine Word.

Receive the sign of the holy cross both on forehead (+) and breast (+).[18]

Loehe's agenda of 1859 has this admonition from the 1626 Coburg agenda as the fifth admonition, and the final one with the first exorcism.[19] The 1856 Missouri agenda stops short of this with the words "mind diligently both the prayers and the divine Word." Also omitted are Coburg's words "and in your sighing say inwardly, 'Depart, you unclean spirit. . . .' "

Following the admonition comes the signing with the cross and the naming of the child. Then two prayers from the *Little Book of*

Baptism in the wording of 1771: "Almighty eternal God . . . " and the Flood Prayer. At the end of the latter comes the footnote:

> Here in some places in the Evangelical Lutheran Church exorcism is used with following words, "I adjure thee, thou impure spirit, by the name of the Father (+), and of the Son (+), and of the Holy Ghost (+), that thou go out and depart from this servant of Jesus Christ. Amen."

Then comes "the holy Gospel of St. Mark" (10:13-15). *The Little Book of Baptism* included verse 16 followed immediately by the baptizer's laying his hands upon the child's head with the Lord's Prayer kneeling. (1856 has verse 16.) Next an admonition to the sponsors which takes more than seriously the "teaching them to observe all things whatsoever" of the mandate.

> Furthermore I remind you who are acting here in the place of the child . . . to faithfully and diligently instruct it: In the first place, in the Holy Ten Commandments, that it may well learn to know from them both its sin and will of God;
>
> In the second place, in the Christian Creed, that it may know where it shall seek help and grace in order to live according to its faith and God's will;
>
> In the third place, in the Lord's Prayer, that it may call upon and ask God for grace to lead a Christian life and resist Satan;
>
> In the fourth place, do also remind it of its Holy Baptism, that is, of the covenant it is now here making with God Father, Son, and Holy Ghost, that it may receive comfort therefrom in every temptation, anguish, and trouble against that vexatious spirit, the devil (*wider den leidigen Teufel*), against the world and its own flesh;
>
> In the fifth place, of the most venerable Sacrament of the Altar, that is, of the true body and blood of Jesus Christ, what it is and for what purpose it has been instituted [cf. LC V, 2].
>
> In the sixth place, of Confession and Absolution, that it may know, when by reason of the weakness of its corrupted flesh and blood it again after baptism falls in sin, to get rid of it, comfort itself, and strengthen its faith, until God fulfills in it what He now begins in the baptismal covenant, and it be saved therein.
>
> This, then, you intend to do freely and willing? Answer: "We do" (*Ja*).
>
> May God, our dear Lord, grant us this, and with His grace fulfill what we cannot do.

Now, in order that our dear Lord and Savior Jesus Christ who is come into the world to seek and save poor sinners, may receive into His grace this present child also, may embrace it, bless it, lay His divine hand upon it, graciously grant it the Holy Ghost, true faith and everlasting life: we will futhermore offer it to Him, by saying the Lord's Prayer with faith and devotion; we shall, therefore, kneel down together and pray: (Here the minister shall lay his hand upon the child.) Our Father . . . .

With this rubric the wording comes again in step with the Saxony agendas of 1540 and 1555. The movement to the font has been lost in the 1856 Missouri agenda; they are already there. Nevertheless it still has the blessing which goes with this movement and marks the conclusion of this part of the liturgy. "The Lord preserve thy going out and thy coming in from this time forth and even (+) forevermore. Amen."

This with the signing is as in the Saxony agenda of 1771.

Then the minister shall make (lasze) the child renounce the devil through his sponsors, saying:
N: Dost thou renounce the devil?
  Answer: "I do."
And all his works?
  Answer: "I do."
And all his pomp (Wesen)?
  Answer: "I do."

The interrogationes de fide follow as in Saxony 1771, and as evidenced since the beginning of the third century.[20] The English translation declines "Wesen" as in the German of the Little Book of Baptism, and chooses "pomp" from its Latin translation and the Agenda Communis of 1512.[21]

Then comes "baptism itself with the word of God."

Hereupon the chrism-cloth (Westerhemd) is spread over the child, and the minister, with laying of hands, says: The Almighty God and Father of our Lord Jesus Christ who has regenerated thee by the water and the Holy Ghost and has forgiven thee all thy sins, strengthen thee with His grace unto everlasting life. Amen.
Peace be with thee. (+) Amen.

The lineage of what we have here is clearly traceable back through the Saxon liturgies to the *Little Book of Baptism* of 1526 and 1523 and what flows into them via the *Agenda Communis* of 1512 from the earliest baptismal liturgies. Noteworthy additions are the mandate in the way of the 1626 Coburg agenda and the weighty admonition to the sponsors. Antecedents for the latter may be found in the 1533 Brandenburg-Nuremberg agenda and the 1540 Brandenburg agenda.[22] We may recall what Graff found as characteristic of the Church Orders of the sixteenth century: "the need always and again to set down the true Lutheran understanding of baptism."[23] In contrast with this the admonitions of the nineteenth century were expressed in only quite general terms.[24]

In his collection of baptismal formulas Loehe mentions Coburg's following Mark 10 with the obligation of sponsors.[25] What Loehe called the obligation is in the 1856 Missouri agenda the admonition to the sponsors. It is taken almost word for word from the 1626 Coburg agenda.[26] Some words are left out for the sake of brevity and the language is updated. There is a change which is liturgically more potent and emphasizing of grace. In the 1626 Coburg agenda after the sponsors have answered "Yes," we have, "God help us do what we are unable to do." The 1856 Missouri agenda has: "This grant us our dear Lord God, and fulfill with His grace what we are unable to do." (This is as in 1540.)

We may observe how the liturgical work for the 1856 Missouri agenda was well informed in its tradition and not mechanically done. All the more striking then is the taking over of such a dubious expression of the idea of covenant: "which it (the child) now makes with God Father, Son and Holy Ghost." Loehe's 1859 agenda has incidental mention of covenant. It is not there in the *Little Book of Baptism* nor in the Saxon agendas. One can only ask whether here we have a lack of care or of theological insight or an unreflected taking over of an alien line of thought.[27]

This confronts us with the question of influences. In 1804 Seiler commended his collection as work done "with regard for the spirit of our time" (*mit Rücksicht auf unsern Zeitgeist*).[28] The work in which Walther was involved might be characterized as "without regard for the spirit of his time." What he had regard for comes to clear expression in his *Pastoral Theology* of 1872.

Primary, when he speaks of Baptism, is the name of God, and so Baptism is done by the Lord. Luther, as usual, is adduced as witness.

"In the name of" refers to the person of the doer, so that the

name of the Lord is not only to be uttered and invoked while
the work is being done; but the work itself is to be done as
something not one's own—in the name and stead of another.
Matthew 24:5, Romans 1:5 . . . there is great comfort and a
mighty aid to faith in the knowledge that one has been baptized, not by man, but by the Triune God Himself, through a
man acting among us in His name . . . in this way without
doubt it saves (so macht sie gewiszg selig).[29]

Further witnesses are Brenz, Deyling, Fecht, Scherzer and Gerhard.
Clearly Walther does not strive for originality or any novelty but
rather for faithfulness to what our Lord has said and given us as it
has been faithfully confessed and handed on to us.

In the Smalcald Articles we Lutherans therefore confess: "Therefore we do not agree with Thomas and the Dominicans who forget
the word (God's institution) and say that God has joined to the water
a spiritual power which, through the water, washes away sin."[30]

In Walther's *Pastoral Theology* the theology is of the words of
God in the way of Scripture and the Confessions, and the theology
is pastoral. So great are the gifts of Baptism that no one may be left
in doubt that he has in fact been baptized. "If there is here no
absolute certainty to be had, those who stand in doubt are to be
baptized as unbaptized persons."[31] Walther quotes Augustine, Bald-
win, John of Damascus, Canon 19 of Nicaea, Canon 8 of Arles, Tar-
nov, Basil's Epistle 78, Dedekennus, Fecht, Gerhard, Hornbeck, Tre-
senius, Leo the Great, with Luther having the last word. The same
pastoral care may be heard in in the discussion of emergency Baptism, as perhaps also echoes his days as pastor in Bräunsdorf. Those
who bring a child to Baptism may not be members of another parish
(1 Pet. 4:15).

Parental responsibility, on the basis of which those brought
for baptism are to be baptized, the mother has by herself,
even when the father is unwilling for the child to be baptized
(1 Cor. 7:14).[32]

And there is perhaps a further echo from Bräunsdorf.

As soon as there has been announcement of a baptism to be
done a preacher is to write the entry in the church book,
clearly and in proper order, giving the relevant data: day and
hour of the birth of the child to be baptized, its name or names,
as also the names, status and present address of the father
and of the mother, and finally the names of those selected to

be sponsors. Not yet to be entered is the time of the actual
baptism. That is to be done only after it has in fact taken
place. A preacher who is not conscientious in this matter takes
upon himself a heavy burden that he has to answer for, because after some time the church book is the only sure record
there is that the child to be baptized has in fact been baptized.[33]

Stronger than any Bräunsdorf echo is the pastoral care that no one
be allowed to be left with any grounds of uncertainty whether he
was indeed baptized, whether that be any question of confession of
the Holy Trinity, or the entry in the church book.

In his *Pastoral Theology* the theology is profound and pastoral;
it is also practical. He discusses what there is for a pastor to do in
the care of living unnatural births *(Miszgeburten)* and also how old
a child may be for the baptizing still to come before the teaching.
In casuistry Walther provides no canon law rules. The pastor is to
take account of the specific facts in each case and do what is his
office to do. He makes no necessity or law out of what he lists as
the baptismal usages.

To the baptismal usages which are observed in our church
belong: 1. a recall of original sin; 2. the name giving; 3. the
so-called lesser exorcism; 4. the signing with the cross; 5.
prayers and votum; 6. the greater exorcism; 7. the reading of
Mark 10:13-16; 8. the laying on of hands; 9. the Lord's Prayer;
10. the renunciation with the Apostles' Creed; 11. the usage
of sponsors; 12. the putting on of the baptismal garment *(Wes-
terhemdchen)*; 13. the blessing.[34]

These usages are then differentiated in the way of the Gospel. Walther
follows Gerhard's threefold division.

1. What has been mandated by God; 2. Some things freely
observed by the apostles; 3. Some things added by churchmen.

This is in contrast with the *Little Book of Baptism* which has
only two classes: Baptism itself, and what men have added.[35] What
is the worth of putting between these two that of apostolic usage?
It has the worth of making some ponderable distinctions. Of particular weight for Walther are the *signum crucis* and the *abrenuntiatio*,
while the exorcisms clearly belong to the third class. Of exorcism
he says:

Since this clearly belongs to those ceremonies which first need an explanation so that they be done without misunderstanding, it is best, where there is the usage, not to set it aside hastily, and still less to work toward its reintroduction.[36]

On the other hand, the *signum crucis* is not merely, as it says in the Saxony agenda of 1812, "given as a reminder."[37]

Concerning the renunciation and the confession of the creed in baptism, Rudelbach writes, among other things, the following: "For a baptism to be recognized in the church as a baptism the church has, for as long as we know, had regard for two things, namely the renunciation of the devil and the confession of the Christian creed. That these two parts are organically bound up with the words of baptism we shall undertake to show."

Rudelbach adduces the words of the apostle Peter (Acts 2:38), and also Hebrews 6:1 and 9:14 and 1 John 3:8.

After he [Peter] has shown the only way of redemption, and before the incorportion into the kingdom of Christ through Baptism, he puts the μετάνοια, the "repentance from dead works" (*Umkehr von den todten Werken. Umkehr* goes nicely with what Jerome tells of turning from west to east before baptism. Also Ambrose *De initatis* 2.) as it is also called in the apostolic Scripture. Only by way of this do they come to Baptism. . . . It was indeed the purpose of the coming of Christ into the world "to destroy the works of the devil," and when we, as those who have been redeemed, have lively grasp of this, it is quite clear how the creed is implicit in the words of Baptism and its confession precedes Baptism, and so also preceding this, as the indispensable prior step, the renunciation of the whole kingdom of darkness and its prince.[38]

So the "what" of creed and renunciation are given; formulation may vary. Such formulation we have from Tertullian. He speaks of the renunciation as simply there in the liturgy as everyone knows, and so it provides an indispensable ground from which consequences may be drawn (*De Corona* 3).

Something that was generally recognized in the church toward the end of the second century must already have been known without question as apostolic in the first century. We stand here at the border of the age of the apostles. Who could ever imagine that the renunciation was invented by any

teacher of the church of the first or second apostolic διαδοχή
(Folge, succession). It was a time when direct pupils of the
apostles were still living, such as Polycarp, the disciple of
John. They, and indeed the whole church, would have shown
loud and formal rejection to anything that appeared as such
an invention or novel private opinion strange to the church. . . .
(Justin Martyr is quoted. Ap, I, 61) The matter itself does not
depend on such witnesses, since the witness of the apostles
themselves has put it clearly. Not the "what" but only the
formulation is clearly then all that remains to discuss. . . .
What cannot be left out of this is the renunciation not only
of all sin and works of darkness, but also of their author, the
devil, by name. The form which does this we may never surrender; that would be surrender of our communion with the
catholic *(allgemein),* holy church.[39]

Here Walther has been running with Rudelbach, a Dane who resigned his pastorate in Saxony in 1845 because of unionism.[40] Here
and elsewhere we recognize in Walther his pastoral recognition of
the dread earnestness of salvation's either/or in Baptism: either the
name of the devil or the name of God; either the kingdom of darkness
or the kingdom of light. Hence is the general practice of Baptism no
later than the second Sunday after the birth.[41] We observe also the
catholic and apostolic theology. As a theologian Walther had no
desire to invent something novel and separatistic. What has been
given us from the Lord he would give on, as Paul speaks of *paradosis*
in 1 Corinthians 11:23 and 15:3. He is at his best when he rejoices
that what he confesses rings with that which is apostolically and
catholicly confessed, with the ancient liturgies, the church fathers,
and the confessors of the Confessions.

This *paradosis*, this heritage, this confession, was threatened in
Saxony. But in America there were dangers also. The full title of
his *Pastoral Theology* was *American Lutheran Pastoral Theology.*
Lutheran and pastoral it was without any doubt, but how American?

Walther rejoiced to see a door opening wide to those who spoke
English, and wrote in encouragement toward this to Pastor August
Crull:

God has indeed clearly now opened to us a wide door to the
people who speak English. This sets before us a great work
now plain to see, just as much in the south as in the north.
Less and less do we confront the misgivings which see in what

original Lutheranism stands for (*Altluthertum*) something "formalistic" or "semi-Roman."[42]

Where there is the need and opportunity one should preach, comfort and teach in English, and that for the Gospel's sake. Thus Walther urged Crull whom he saw as well able to do this. Competence in English was not to be found in everyone in that generation. We have seen some labored and not always felicitous English in the 1881 translation of the 1856 agenda. This next generation, wanting more English resources, drew in some English things from other traditions. This development was responded to in the Agenda of 1917. German, shaped by Luther, did not always go easily or fully into English shaped by a different tradition.

To be American, to speak in English, might not result in a de-lutheranization. Walther's liturgical work and his *Pastoral Theology* were not American in the way of Schmucker. Walther saw the greatest threat in a Methodistic Americanization. As a result of his work, the Missouri Synod was not in need of rescue from such impoverishment. So far from falling into the ways of Methodism (little liturgy and lay preachers) we find Walther being not altogether displeased when the Missouri Synod was called Puseyite.[43] So the history of the liturgy which Reed recounts is not that of the Missouri Synod. In Reed the *Kirchenagende* of 1856 receives barely a mention and its English translation of 1881 none at all. Walther also receives no mention.[44]

In liturgy, doctrine, pastoral theology, and so in Baptism also, Walther served the continuity of the Saxon tradition. To become American did not mean less Lutheran, but rather the way of the door opening wide for the Gospel (1 Cor. 16:9). This could not be turned away from, any more than Pastor Walther could turn away from those who brought their children to be baptized in Bräunsdorf. Baptism holds through.

As encomium Luther's words may serve:

Blessed be God the Father of our Lord Jesus Christ, who according to the riches of his mercy has singularly preserved in His church this sacrament, unbesmirched and unpoisoned by statutes laid on it by man, and has kept it free for all nations and conditions of men.[45]

The Lutheran way of liturgical *paradosis*—apostolic, catholic and confessional—as evidenced by Walther is expressed by Luther in a letter to two parsons:

Since Baptism among us is the same as was and has continued from the beginning of Christianity . . . if some one would change or do away with anything that has so long been done, he ought and must prove conclusively that it is against God's word, and if he cannot, then "what is not against us is for us" [says Christ].[46]

In conclusion, all that Walther confessed of holy Baptism may be put under the touchstone of how this was preached and prayed. The sermon which Walther preached on the Gospel of Trinity Sunday in 1844, begins with this prayer.

Triune God, Father, Son and Holy Spirit. Unto You we all were baptized. There Your most holy Name was put upon us, and there You become again our dear Father and we Your dear children. There You have forgiven us all our sins, washed clean our souls, made us Your temple, regenerated us to eternal life and received us into a new kingdom of grace and salvation. Please look upon us all therefore, You who are our faithful convenant God, in grace this day also. Show to all those among us who have lightly regarded their Holy Baptism what incomparable good they have scorned, a good greater than which cannot be imagined. Guide them with repentance and contrition to the spring of that salvation, which You have opened up for them, that they may return to it. Awaken in us all, we pray You, soul's thirst and faith's courage by the words of Your sacrament of overflowing grace. From now on draw us daily to that fountain which flows free and open against sin and uncleanness, which You have promised and given to all citizens of the New Testament Jerusalem, and so also to us. Hear us, O Triune God. Amen.

The sermon concluded as follows:

Ponder this: When everything comes against you as a challenge and an uncertainty, your Baptism nevertheless stands sure. It is a fact which surely happened on a specific day, and God does not now take His Word back. With His Word God has, so to speak, made Himself your captive. Only do not let Him go. Do not let faith's hand come loose from this the covenant of grace. He cannot let you go.[47]

Notes

[1] Dr. Luther did not write up a new Order of Holy Baptism. Others were producing orders,

and he was being pestered to do something. He translated the current *Agenda Communis* with remarkably little change. No one should suppose he was putting out a new Baptism, nor should anyone be prompted to doubt whether he was indeed baptized. This was the *Little Book of Baptism* of 1523 which was refined in 1526. From 1529 this was included with the *Small Catechism*. It settled into usage in the form of the Saxon agenda in 1539.

1539's *Kirchenordnunge zum anfang* was prompted by a visitation earlier that year (Albertine Saxony). It overcame the abrupt beginning of the *Little Book of Baptism* (1526) by putting first an admonition: "Dearly beloved in Christ. We hear every day from the Word of God, perceive it, also, by our own experience in life and death, that we from Adam's fall are all conceived and born in sins ... our Lord Jesus Christ has borne the sins of the whole world, and has redeemed and saved from sin, death, and damnation poor little children no less than grown persons. . . . He himself has commanded to bring little children to Him, and has promised to receive them into His kingdom." Thereafter the order went according to the *Little Book of Baptism*. Before going to the *Little Book of Baptism* 1540 and 1555 have the name-giving, exorcism, sign of the cross, then the *Little Book of Baptism* to Mark 10:13-16. Inserted here is a lengthy admonition expounding this Gospel; this then loses the immediate connection between Christ's hand and the pastor's. After the admonition comes the laying on of hands with the Lord's Prayer. Then the movement to the font with votum (The Lord preserve thy coming in ... "), and thereafter an admonition to the godparents with the Gospel its starting point. What our Lord Christ so heartily wishes to do and has promised, He surely does, though it be done through a man's voice, who is here His instrument (*mittel*). Christ's saving work is extolled and the godparents accept their part in the Christian nurture of the child: " ... that it be taught the Ten Commandments, the Christian Creed and the Lord's Prayer and whatever else is necessary for salvation to know and to believe." "This then you are willing, as God gives you grace, gladly to do? The godparents answer 'Yes.' The baptizer: This grant us our dear Lord God, and fulfill with His grace what we are unable to do." If this is too long or the child is weak the short form in the catechism may be used. What follows is as in the *Little Book of Baptism* to the end.

1539, 1540 and 1555 represent the so-called Duke Henry's Agenda. This was augmented in 1580. This was called after the Elector Augustus and was presented to the synod of 1580 by Jacob Andreae. Andreae had a considerable hand in the Württemberg *Kirchenordnung* of 1559, parts of which appear verbatim in this *Kirchenordnung* of Elector Augustus of 1580. It was also adopted in Coburg where it became the basis of the *Casimiriana* (1626). The editor of this *Kirchenordnung* was John Gerhard. 1580 "became the model for the whole of Ernestine Saxony," and continued its sway despite the political and confessional vagaries of various Saxon princes." Berbig, "Zur Composition der Casimirianischen Kirchenordnung v. J. 1626," *Deutsche Zeitschrift für Kirchenrecht*, XXVIII (1897), p. 177. After 1547 (Mühlberg) care for the heritage of the Reformation passed increasingly from Albertine to Ernestine Saxony, as did the electorship, which in 1806 became kingship (cf. 1812). As regent for them as minors the Elector Augustus signed the Formula of Concord for his nephews John Casimir (Saxe-Coburg) and John Ernst (Saxe-Eisenach) (BKS, p. 763, n. 2). There is something of a parallel here with the ancient councils which confessed the creed and then added canons regarding how things were to be done in the church—doctrine and practice. Similarly the Book of Concord and the Kirchenordnungen, with the former overlapping and informing the latter. Berbig gives the sequence of 1580 as follows:

a) Reine Lehre—Glaubensbekenntnis (Wort). b) Mittel, sie rein und unverfälscht zuerhalten (Sakrament). c) Agende (Gottesdienstordnung). d) Verwaltung und Dienst am Wort (der Pfarrer). e) Ehesachen. f) Lehranstalten, Schulen, und Universitäten (weil hier die Diener am Wort ausgebildet werden). g) Kirchenvisitationen—Superintendenten—geistliche Gerichte. h) Die General-Artikel. (p. 179)

The way of this sequence lives on in Walther.

In the recent doctoral work of Eshetu Abate, "The Apostolic Tradition: A Study of the Texts and Origins, and its Eucharistic Teachings with a Special Exploration of the Ethiopic Version," one may observe that however early was the *Apostolic Tradition* it was never canonical. There is that which is first, and that which follows from it as second, however much they may have in common, and the more the better. This is no individual enterprise. The very notion of writing up or improvising liturgies is utterly alien to Walther and the tradition of which he was a grateful heir. Holy Baptism was done as in the agenda. When an alien agenda was imposed, it was better to leave for America, and there follow "the old orthodox Saxon church agendas." "Baptism belongs to the church, not to the minister." *Amerikanisch-Lutherische Pastoraltheologie* [St. Louis: Printery of the Synod of Missouri, Ohio and other States, 1872], p.123, see n. 28) (Cited hereafter as PT).

The text of 1539, 1540 and 1555 is in E. Sehling, *Die Evangelischen Kirchenordnungen des XVI. Jahrhunderts* (Leipzig: Reisland, 1902), p. 266f., and of 1580, p. 359ff.

The text of the *Little Book of Baptism* (1526) is in *Die Bekenntnisschriften der evangelish-lutherischen Kirche* (Göttingen: Vandenhoeck & Ruprecht, 1986 [10th printing]) pp. 535-541. Since 1529 this was included with the Small Catechism. *Luther's Works* (Philadelphia: Fortress, 1965), p. 51, pp. 107-109. For *Agenda Communis* see F. Schmidt-Clausing, *Zwingli als Liturgiker* (Göttingen: Vandenhoeck & Ruprecht, 1952), pp. 146-164.

1624 has *jetzo aufs neue*, and so to 1771. This agenda was included in the *Kirchenbuch* of the same year and printer. The Concordia Historical Institute has a copy of this from Immanuel Church in St. Louis which was served by Pastor Buenger. Its title speaks true. Vollständiges Kirchenbuch darinnen die Evangelica und Episteln auf alle Fesh- Sonn- und Apostel-Tage durchs ganze Jahr die Historien von dem schmerzlichen Leiden und der fröhlichen Auferstehung des Herrn Christi, sammt der erbärmlichen Zerstörung der Stadt Jerusalem die drey Haupt-Symbola und Augsburgische Confession und viel Collecten auf die Sonn- und Fest-Tage und unterschiedliche Fälle wie auch der kleine Catechismus Lutheri, die Kirchen-Agenda, Ehe-Ordnung und allgemeinen Gebete, die in den Chursächsischen Ländern gebraucht werden, enthalten Anietzo von neuem mit Fleisz übersehen, und mit einer besonderen Vorrede herausgegehen. See also *Leiturgia* V, ed. K. L. Müller & W. Blankenburg (Kassel: Stauda, 1970), B. Jordan, "Der Taufgottesdienst in Mittelalter bis zur Gegenwart," pp. 426-472.

[2] "Zur Komposition und Geschichte der Agende Herzog Heinrich's," *Zeitschrift für kirchliche Wissenschaft und kirchliches Leben*, vii (1886), p. 483.

[3] Martin Günther, *Dr. C. F. W. Walther. Lebensbild* (St. Louis: Lutherischer Concordia-Verlag, 1890), p. 19.

[4] G. F. Seiler, *Allgemeine Sammlung liturgischer Formulare der evangelischen Kirchen* (Erlangen: Palm, 1804), III², xiv. P. Graff, *Geschichte der Auflösung der alten gottesdienstlichen Formen in der evangelischen Kirche Deutschlands* (Göttingen: Vandenhoeck & Ruprecht, 1937) I, 308: "In Schleswig-Holstein 1665 sollen eheliche und uneheliche Kinder nicht zusammen getauft werden, die einen vor, die anderen nach der Predigt!" Cf. J. W. F. Höfling, *Das Sakrament der Taufe* (Erlangen: Palm, 1848) II, 261 (Hereafter cited as Höfling).

[5] *Kurzer Lebenslauf des weiland ehrwürdingen Pastor Joh. Friedr. Bünger, treuverdienten Pastors der evangel.-Lutherischen Immanuels-Gemeinde zu St. Louis, Mo.* (St. Louis: Verlag von F. Dette, 1882), p. 36. Of the weight of pastoral care involved here, and of Walther's practice of Holy Absolution one gets no inkling in W. O. Forster's *Zion on the Mississippi* (St. Louis: Concordia, 1953).

[6] Seiler, p. v.

[7] *Johann Gottfried Scheibel und sein Ringen um die Kirche der lutherischen Reformation* (Göttingen: Vandenhoeck & Ruprecht, 1985), p. 329f.

[8] *Kurzer Lebenslauf*, p. 36f.

[9] *Ibid.*, p. 39f. For a documented account of the situation in Saxony see G. Herrmann, *Lutherische Freikirche in Sacksen* (Berlin: Evangelische Verlagsanstalt, 1985), pp. 20-38.

[10] *Ibid.*, p. 41.

[11] *Kirchenbuch für den evangelischen Gottesdienst der Könglich Sächsischen Lande* (Dresden: Royal Court Printery, 1812), p. iii.

[12] Graff, II, 51f.

[13] M. Günther, *Dr. C. F. W. Walther. Lebensbild* (St. Louis: Lutherischer Concordia-Verlag, 1890), p. 28f. Cf. Rudelbach's "Amtliches Gutachten über die Sächsische Kirchen-Agende vom Jahre 1812" in *Die Sacrament-Worte* (Leipzig: Tauchnitz, 1837) , pp. 92-97. He is shocked at the Creed's being paraphrased in the fourth formula. He points to the dangers that come with "Rücksicht auf die gegebene Zist." "What has been striven for in the new and recent time has been quite evidently to obliterate as much as possible what is uniquely Christian with the use of expressions of a universal sort which promote a deistic view.... Sin, grace, virtue, repentance, blessedness are in part so deformed by the influence of a philosophy that is from no Christian source, in part so robbed of all Christian content, that the proclamation of the Word in our time has always to contend against misunderstandings from that direction, and can never be diligent enough in pushing them aside and getting rid of them by the clarity of the Holy Scripture and the penetration of the lively Word" p. 94. For universal expressions see Lessing's *Nathan the Wise*, which is also useful as a preparation for reading the Church Book of 1812. For Rudelbach's Enlightenmentized use of "new" compare C. S. Lewis, "De Descriptione Temporum," in *They Asked for a Paper* (London: Bles, 1962), p. 15. Also some brewer's current top brands of beer. We

may similarly observe Walther using words in a Romantic way, but scarcely in the Agenda of 1856.

[14] *Kirchengesangbuch für evangelisch-lutherische Gemeinden ungeänderter Augsburgischer Confession* (New York: G. Ludwig, 1847). Walther enunciated as a criterion of selection, "that they express not so much the changing circumstances of individual persons, but rather contain the language of the whole church." C. S. Meyer, ed., *Moving Frontiers* (St. Louis: Concordia, 1964), p. 182. In this *Gesangbuch* we may observe the giving of the name in 190 stanza 7; the covenant made by God in 191 stanza 2 and 284 stanza 1; the renunciation in 191 stanza 5.

[15] K. Ganzert, ed., *Wilhelm Loehe Gesammelte Werke* (Neuendettelsau: Freimund, 1953) VII, 1, 353-362.

[16] *Ibid.*, p. 350.

[17] Luther's Works, Am. ed., vol. 53, p. 103 (Cited hereafter as LW); BKS, p. 538, 14. Paul Althaus the Elder, *Die historischen und dogmatischen Grundlagen der Lutherischen Taufliturgie* (Hannover: Teesche, 1893), p. 8ff. "Weshalb er [Luther] so nachdrücklich gerade die Recitation der Stiftungsworte vor dem Vollzugsakte 'um des Aberglaubens willen' verwirft." p. 15, n. 1.

[18] *Church Liturgy for Evangelical Lutheran Congregations of the Unaltered Augsburg Confession,* published by the German Evangelical Lutheran Synod of Missouri, Ohio and other States. Translated from the German (St. Louis: Concordia, 1881), p. 4.

[19] Loehe, *Ibid.*, p. 377. Although Loehe was then aware of it, he did not include it in his *Sammlung liturgischer Formulare der evangelisch-lutherischen Kirche, Erstes Heft* (Nördlingen: Beck, 1839). He was inclined to the view that short is beautiful. p. 20, n. 8.

[20] A. Hahn, ed., *Bibliothek der Symbole und Glaubensregeln der alten Kirche,* 3rd edition of 1897 (Hildesheim: Olms, 1962), p. 34. Acts 8:37. *Leiturgia* V, 50.

[21] BKS, p. 540, 21, F. Schmidt-Clausing, *Zwingli als Liturgiker*, p. 160. In both places the plural: *Et omnibus pompis eius.*

[22] Sehling XI¹, 180 III, 57.

[23] Graff I, 293.

[24] *Leiturgia* V, 614.

[25] *Sammlung*, p. 20.

[26] Höfling, p. 79f. The text as in Höfling is to be found in the *Vollständiges Kirchenbuch* of 1771 of Immanuel Church. It is written out on pages securely stuck in, and in a script so beautiful that it cannot be that of Buenger or of Walther. Was a calligrapher hired to do this (*christlich* is given a big C), or perhaps a thus gifted student (one *Umlaut* is not copied)? Was this done for other copies in use of Saxony 1771? What was thus written into Saxony 1771 was printed in 1856: both this Admonition to the Sponsors (right up to the Lord's Prayer), and the conclusion added to the first admonition ("And since in baptism" [n. 18] which has in it our Lord's mandate, similarly scripted and stuck in). From script to print there is a little updating and smoothing and shortening. The script is inserted to displace the lengthy exposition of Mark 10:13-16 as well as the admonition at the font (pp. 12-17, as in 1540). Thus also then in 1856 the verbs with duty and covenant are changed from the perfect to the present tense, thus connecting more clearly with "Baptism itself."

[27] That these words, which speak of an infant making a covenant with God, carry nevertheless no thought of synergism is clear from Walther's confirmation sermon on Palm Sunday, 1846. His text, 1 Peter 3:21, has *Bund* in it. Only faith that receives every good thing from God can speak this way. So also the prolepsis of the question addressed to an infant, "Wilt thou be baptized?" and the answer, "I will." "so ist nun die Taufe die Hand Gottes" "allein um Christi willen" "Denn auf den Galuben kommt es ehen an" "Wir sind getauft!" *Amerikanisch-Lutherische Epistel Postille* (St. Louis: Lutherischer Concordia-Verlag, 1882), p. 165f.

[28] In the preface of his *Sammlung*.

[29] PT, p. 110f. LW, vol. 36, p. 63; (also Luther's Works, Weimar edition, [hereafter cited as WA], vol. 6, p. 531, par. 18).

[30] PT, p. 115. SA III, 5.

[31] PT, p. 124.

[32] PT, p. 125. Cf. *Lehre und Wehre*, Nov. 1857, III, 327.

[33] PT, p. 129f.

[34] PT, p. 130.

[35] BKS, p. 538, 12; 537, 2: das von Menschen, die Taufe zu zieren, hinzugetan ist; denn auch wohl ahn solchs alles die Taufe geschehen mag. LW, vol. 53, p. 102f.

[36] PT, p. 136.

[37] PT, p. 133.

[38] PT, p. 139.

[39] PT, p. 140. "Diese Korrelation von Absage und Bekenntnis wird bei Tertullian und nach ihm inübrigen lateinischen Kirchengebiet geradezu zum Kernstück der Taufe." *Leiturgia* V, 99.

[40] Herrmann, *Lutherische Freikirche*, pp. 30-33.

[41] PT, p. 141, n. 2.

[42] L. Füerbringer, ed., *Briefe von C. F. W. Walther* (St Louis: Concordia, 1916), II, 80f.

[43] "Sie war so weit von Methodismus entfernt, dasz man sie als 'Puseyiten' betrachtet." *Der Lutheraner* of September 5, 1846, p. 2. Also *ibid.* April 4, 1846, p. 62.

[44] L. D. Reed, *The Lutheran Liturgy* (Philadelphia: Fortress, 1960), p. 176.

[45] *Babylonian Captivity*, 1520. WA, vol. 6, p. 526, par. 35; LW, vol. 36, p. 57.

[46] WA, vol. 26, p. 155, par. 29, in 1528.

[47] *Gnadenjahr. Predigten über die Evangelien des Kirchenjahrs von Dr. C. F. W. Walther. Aus seinem schriftlichen Nachlasz gesammelt* (St. Louis: Lutherischer Concordia Verlag, 1891), pp. 312, 322. At the end this stanza:

Was er theuer euch versprochen,
Wird von ihm niemals gebrochen,
   Sein Bund stehet ewig fest.
Lasset euch nur ewien Glauben
Nicht von Fleisch und Satan rauben.
   Gottes Hand euch nimmer läszt.
     Amen.

What He has, at great cost, promised you, will never be broken by Him; his convenant stands everlastingly sure. Let not your faith be robbed from you by flesh and Satan; God never withdraws His hand from you.

What He has so dearly spoken
Never shall by Him be broken;
   Firmly stands His covenant.
So let not your faith be stifled
Or by flesh and devil rifled;
   God's hand holds you confident.

Tune: *Alles ist an Gottes Segen*

    This stanza is the translation of Jon Vieker who is investigating the doctrine of Holy Baptism in the 1847 hymnal. Thanks are also due Scott Bruzek for his expert help in the research. H. J. Eggold, trans., *Selected Sermons* (St. Louis: Concordia, 1981), pp. 99-107.

    For his son Ferdinand, who was a big worry, Walther drew strength from his Baptism. To his nephew Johannes he wrote of his wife's churching as the usual practice. R. A. Suelflow, trans., *Selected Letters* (St. Louis: Concordia, 1981), pp. 39, 43. Also *Lebensbild*, pp. 214, 254.

Repristination Theology and the Doctrinal Position of The Lutheran Church— Missouri Synod

QUENTIN F. WESSELSCHMIDT

The question this paper addresses is whether the doctrinal position of The Lutheran Church—Missouri Synod is that of repristination theology. The epithet "repristination," when applied to a church's or an individual's theological stance, can be accepted as a badge of honor identifying one as a faithful steward of the Holy Scriptures as eternally true, of the Confessions in their doctrinal content, and of the writings of the Fathers of the church insofar as they are correct expositions of God's Holy Word. Or, the term can be used as a charge against the church or an individual of lack of scholarship, of close-mindedness, and of being an ostrich with its head in the sands of theological antiquity. Historically the Missouri Synod has accepted this characterization of its theology in the first sense of the term in the face of repeated charges that it was guilty of being repristinationistic in the second sense.

Theological repristination is the position of conservative, confessional theologians or churches over against modern liberal theology's opinion that doctrines are subject to change and development as contemporary learning and research open up new vistas or lead to conclusions that an accepted dogma or theological position is no longer tenable. There are basically two views on the development of doctrine in the church. One, rooted in ecclesial antiquity, holds that doctrine does not undergo change or development. This view does allow for explication of what was always implicit in Sacred Scripture and the apostolic message as the sole source of all religious truth. The other view maintains that the doctrine of the church has undergone change and either may or must necessarily continue to do so.

QUENTIN F. WESSELSCHMIDT is Chairman of the Department of Historical Theology at Concordia Seminary, St. Louis.

Of course, there can be a certain latitude within a repristinationistic approach to theology so that it may be a responsible or an
irresponsible position toward the teachings of the church. It can be
irresponsible if it is absolutely close-minded and opposed to all Biblical scholarship as if the church has nothing more to learn from the
Scriptures themselves. It can be responsible if it is open to and
supportive of Biblical scholarship which is bound to the explication
of Biblical truths on the basic of the *sola Scriptura* principle, and a
firm confessional commitment.

The first approach may honor the past for the past's sake and
seek to establish doctrine only by quoting, in addition to Scripture
and creedal formulae, former theologians, whether from the first
five centuries, the Medieval period, or the Reformation and post-
Reformation eras. The second approach considers the church a dynamic and vital entity that expects no new doctrine but is committed
to the continued mining of the original depository of divine truth
for its meaning and for application to the life of the church in every
age.

It is on the basis of this second Scriptural-confessional model,
which is open to responsible scholarship, that Dr. Francis Pieper
could declare in the Preface to his multi-volume *Christian Dogmatics:* "I consider it necessary to refute the unwarranted charge and
to remove any misgivings concerning the 'repristination theology'
and have therefore set forth in some detail the religious life of a
church body which is definitely committed to the 'repristination theology.'"[1] As we shall see, this was the position of the church for
much of its history and has remained the position of the LC—MS
even though a majority of denominations have preferred to subject
the truth of Scripture to human reason and contemporary whims of
religious fashions.

The charge of repristination arose in the nineteenth century in
the aftermath of the Enlightenment, the rise of romanticism, and
the extension of rationalism and free inquiry to theology. The sharp
criticisms and rejection of many accepted beliefs by modern theology
were in sharp contrast to the earlier position of Christianity. Orthodox Christianity has always maintained that the teachings of the
church, when rooted in Scripture and the apostolic tradition, are
static and abiding in content; the only changes allowed are in terms
of more lucid explications and sharper definitions of Biblical teachings as necessitated chiefly by the challenges of heresy. This was
the position of the early church and was best encapsulated in the
famous statement of Vincent of Lerins, who said in his *Commoni-*

torium: "In ipsa item catholica ecclesia magnopere curandum est, ut id teneamus quod ubique, quod semper, quod ab omnibus creditum est. Hoc est etenim vere proprie que catholicum" (In these very things also the catholic church must especially take care that we hold on to that which has been believed always, everywhere, and by all. For this is truly and properly catholic.).[2]

The early church spoke of an apostolic tradition but not tradition in the later Roman Catholic sense of allowing for magisterial interpretation and addition by papal fiat, but in the sense that the teaching of the church was synonymous with the teaching of Christ and the early apostles. Ignatius of Antioch wrote in his letter to the Philippians: "Of some who say: 'Unless I find it in the originals in the Gospel, I do not believe,' and when I said to them, 'It is written,' they answered me, 'That settles it!' "[3] The early church had a clear commitment to a body of dogma as a κανών τῆς ἀληθείας or *regula fidei*. The understanding was that the *regula fidei* was fixed and was to endure for all time. This is certainly clear in the statements of Irenaeus and Tertullian. Tertullian, for instance, said: " The rule of faith, indeed, is altogether one, alone immoveable and irreformable."[4]

This view of the church's teaching remained firm until the Middle Ages. It was the Reformation of the fifteenth and sixteenth centuries that opened up the way for critical investigation of dogma not in the sense of seeking change but for the sake of rooting out fallacies that had crept in over the years. The first serious questionings of accepted positions of the church for non-heretical purposes occurred in the case of Lorenzo Valla who, in his investigation of the Donation of Constantine, declared it a forgery and with the critical studies of the Apostles' Creed by Lorenzo Valla and Reginald Pecock, the bishop of Chichester.

Later Martin Luther in defence of Biblical theology established the principle that dogmas have no authority as decrees of councils and popes unless they are in accord with Scripture. Luther in this regard is noted for criticizing the crucial Nicene term *homoousios;* of course, his criticism was a criticism *verbi non rei.* The church's long-standing belief, in this instance, in the full divinity and co-eternity of Christ was Scriptural and therefore a continuously valid doctrine.

This open-mindedness to examine the traditional beliefs of the church to determine whether they were harmonious with Scripture and not human additions or misinterpretations continued with some of Luther's contemporaries and associates. Philip Melanchthon observed that certain Platonic ideas had influenced early Christian doctrine and that there were definite adulterations in Christian teachings following Leo the Great (Bishop of Rome, 440-461). One of Melanchthon's pupils, Matthias Flacius, in his pioneering work on church history, *The Magdeburg Centuries,* concluded that the succeeding centuries of church history were a continuous process of obfuscating various evangelical doctrines with an occasional witness to the truth. The purpose of these investigations into the history of dogmas was not to make or encourage change but to maintain the historic validity of Scriptural truths.

Although various individuals in the Reformation period began to turn a critical eye toward dogma of the church and would no longer agree unreservedly with Vincent of Lerins, interest in examining critically the dogmas of the church was curtailed by the turmoil of the religious wars of the sixteenth century, which occupied the mind of the church, and the strong conservatism of the late sixteenth and early seventeenth centuries which did not encourage further investigation.

However, a new attitude toward the historic teachings of the church developed in the late seventeenth and early eighteenth centuries. Beginning with men like Gottfried Arnold (1666-1714) and Wilhelm Muenscher (1766-1814) there emerged a renewed interest in the study of dogma. Arnold, a pietist, took the position that orthodoxy is fallible and that heretics and sectarians were the purveyors of religious truth. Muenscher, who belonged to the rationalist camp, set out to prove that doctrine had and does undergo change. Such a position clearly called into question the authority of accepted doctrines which were now beginning to be considered by some as fluid in nature.

Men like Arnold and Muenscher opened the floodgates of intellectual inquiry into doctrine and no longer respected Scripture or the creedal teachings of earlier Christendom as binding upon the church. They were followed by other men like F. Christian Baur (1762-1860), who applied the Hegelian view of history to Christianity. The consequence of this approach was the view that "Christianity is not a finished product expressed in the person of Christ and in the New Testatment, but it is the expression of an idea in progressive development."[5] Christianity is in a continual process of unfolding. Thus traditional, historic beliefs are discredited and a "new religion" emerges in the synthesis as either clarified or compromised truth.[6]

Of course, a more monumental figure than Baur was Adolph von Harnack (1851-1930), who claimed to find a twofold Gospel within the New Testament, namely, the "Gospel *of* Jesus" and the "Gospel *about* Jesus." The apostolic proclamation, which constituted the second gospel, is a superimposition upon and possibly a redirection and amplification of the first gospel. Therefore the teachings of the New Testament were no longer reliable and could not be considered reliable unless they could be purified by the critical minds of modern theologians.

Modern scholarship, growing out of romanticism, rationalism, the Enlightenment, and liberalism began to replace the authority of Scriptures, the Ecumenical Creeds, and the received tradition embodied in the confessional stance of historic denominations with the flexible, changing, reactions of its own findings. Theological truth could no longer be established by appealing to the Scriptures in its literal sense or to the historic witness of the church. A concept of objective truth was definitely undercut by the subjective approach of Friedrich Schleiermacher (1768-1834) who tried to objectify Biblical truth on the basis of subjective religious experiences. Schleiermacher spearheaded the reaction of romanticism to the unbridled rationalism of the French Revolution in Protestant circles in Germany. He held that religion is a mother of experiences and Christianity is a matter of Christian experiences. Thus, man becomes the locus of religious truth and his feelings the measuring stick of its validity.

The final decades of the nineteenth century witnessed a new assault on Biblical theology and the time-honored teaching of the church by the application of historical-critical research to Biblical texts and the study of dogma. Metaphysical agnosticism and historical positivism dominated the intellectual climate of the time. The theology of Albrecht Ritschl was dominant in the theological faculties of Germany, such as Berlin, Marburg, Tübingen, Jena, and Leipzig. Ritschl accepted the Schleiermachian emphasis on experience but wanted a more objective basis for that experience. In the place of religious feeling Ritschl emphasized the will and what he called "judgments of value." The proper object of theology was the historical reality of the Gospel as found in the New Testament. However, traditional dogma was to be rejected as too metaphysical. Rather, theology was to concentrate on the moral teachings of Jesus. While Ritschl posited the historical Christ who can be reconstructed by a rigorous application of historical criticism as a religious starting point, the traditional formulae regarding the person and work of Christ were considered mere abstractions and not necessarily related to the historical Christ. Traditional soteriological views, such as the formal imputation of righteousness, were rejected in favor of a communal salvation of a loving humanity primarily limited to the present existence. What a far cry this was from Athanasius' view of God's reason for the incarnation of Christ as detailed in his writing, *De incarnatione verbi* and in Luther's explanation to the Second Article of the Apostles' Creed!

One of the most famous disciples of Ritschl was Adolf von Harnack. Harnack saw set dogma as an enslavement of Christianity which must be a dynamic reality in the modern world. In order to maintain its freedom for each age he believed that Christianity must free itself from the intellectual doctrine of the past. Granted, Harnack was somewhat of a primativist in holding that the Gospel of Jesus is the only permanent aspect of Christianity and remains normative for the Christian religion; nevertheless, Christianity still ends up in his system propagating primarily a social gospel of providing a better life in the present order.

Over against such onslaughts against the traditional beliefs of Christianity, the nineteenth century emerged as a time of reaction and revival. There were numerous reactions to the theological liberalism that had crept into Christianity. In England the desire to return to the traditions and beliefs of the past surfaced in the short-lived Oxford Movement. Many devout British Christians yearned for the certainty of orthodoxy over against the vagaries of critical rationalism and the push for reform in politics as well as in religion. The movement was characterized by a resurgence of nostalgia for a unified Western church after the pattern of the earlier Middle Ages.

The leaders of this movement felt a strong sense of devotion to Scripture, but more in a devotional or disciplinary than an intellectual or dogmatic sense. Their interest in the past did stimulate a renewed interest in ancient thought and the practices of the early church. The Oxford Movement awakened the Church of England and a good portion of Protestant Christianity to the wealth of its pre-Reformation heritage. Although men such as John Keble (1792-1866), Edward Pusey (1800-1882), and Cardinal Newman (1801-1890) stirred a fresh interest in liturgy and spiritual discipline, there was little contributed by way of theology itself. One of the movement's main influences was in the renewed interest in and veneration of the church's past.

Lutheranism also was affected by nineteenth century romanticism and revivals like pietism, by the resurgence of national sentiment which fostered a feeling of indifference toward doctrinal distinctions between the Lutheran and Reformed churches. In Germany attempts were made to bring these two sides together in the Prussian Union of 1817 and 1830, with which both sides were soon disaffected. Confessional Lutherans were especially concerned about the doctrinal indifference manifested in the Union. One consequence of the spiritual reawakening, reaction to liberalism, and unionistic tendency within Lutheranism was a resurgence of interest in the Confessions.

This confessional revival also coincided with the publication of the Erlangen edition of Luther's works (1826), the tercentennial anniversaries of the Ninety-five Theses and the Augsburg Confession (1817 and 1830) and the issuance of a new edition of the Augsburg Confession in 1819. According to E. Clifford Nelson these developments gave rise to three different and yet somewhat similar movements within German Lutheranism.[7] The first of these movements is known as the theology of repristination, the initial chief exponent of which was Ernst Wilhelm Hengstenberg (1802-1869). Hengstenberg, an Old Testament professor at the University of Berlin, held that Scriptures were not to be subjected to the purview of literary criticism and urged a return to the authority of seventeenth-century Lutheran orthodoxy.

Akin to repristination theology was the Neo-Lutheranism of Wilhelm Loehe (1808-1872) and August Vilmar (1800-1868). This movement had close affinity to the Oxford Movement of England and stressed the similarity of the Lutheran church in confessional definition with the church of the New Testament.

The third movement, the Erlangen School of theology, was identified chiefly with Adolf von Harless (1806-1879), but also with Gottfried Thomasius (1802-1875), Johann C. K. von Hofmann (1810-1877), and Franz H. R. von Frank (1827-1894). Advocates of the Erlangen School took a less rigid view of the Confessions, which they considered an expression of the church's reaction to conflicts and errors of the time. Instead of looking back to Scripture, the Confessions and the writings of orthodox teachers, they saw theology as the product of an ongoing organic process.

The reawakening of Lutheran Confessionalism was stimulated in the early 1800s by rationalism, by a resurgence of German pride over against the oppressive tyranny of Napoleonic armies, the liberalization and watering down of theology as a result of the Prussian Union of 1817 and 1830 (in which union Lutheranism would eventually have been eclipsed by Reformed theology) and in pursuit of religious liberty. Many of the first Lutherans who flocked to the shores of America left Europe in the wake of this confessional revival.

They believed that the best way to preserve the truth of Scripture
and the Confessions from the inroads of rationalism and the com-
promises of unionism was to emigrate to America. H. E. F. Guerike
observes " . . . all of these Lutheran pastors who emigrated in the
year 1838 and afterwards were decisive and orthodox Lutheran Saxon
pastors. . . ."[8]

The fact that these Saxon Lutherans were committed to the
Confessions as well as Scripture is evident in the words of J. K. W.
Loehe's constitution for Lutherans in the Saginaw Valley, "We pro-
fess our adherence to the confessional writings of the Lutheran
Church, the Augsburg Confession, its Apology, both Catechisms of
Luther, the Smalcald Articles and the Formula of Concord—in short,
the Book of Concord of 1580 as it first appeared in Dresden."[9] This
same concern existed among the Missouri Saxon Lutherans and is
articulated in Walther's August 21, 1845 letter to Pastor J. A. Ernst,
in which he states that one of the basic principles for organizing a
synod is "That the Synod organize itself, in addition to the Word of
God on the basis of all the Symbols of our church, and if possible (?)
[sic], include also the Saxon Visitation Articles. However, I shall not
unconditionally insist on the latter, glorious, concise confession."[10]
The same commitment to Scripture and the Confessions is made
clear in Chapter II of the 1854 Constitution of the German Evangelical Lutheran Synod of Missouri, Ohio, and other States. The first
two conditions of Chapter II under which union with the Synod may
take place and fellowship with it may continue are:

> 1. Acceptance of Holy Scripture of the Old and New Testa-
> ments as the written Word of God and the only rule and norm
> of faith and life.
> 2. Acceptance of all symbolical books of the Evangelical Lu-
> theran Church (to wit: the three Ecumenical Symbols, the
> Unaltered Augsburg Confession, its Apology, the Smalcald
> Articles, the Large and the Small Catechism of Luther, and
> the Formula of Concord) as the pure, unadulterated state-
> ment and exposition of the divine Word.[11]

Also in the first of his propositions on "The Proper Form of an Evangelical Lutheran Congregation Independent of the State" Walther
states:

> An Evangelical Lutheran local congregation is a gathering of
> believing Christians at a definite place, among whom the
> word of God is preached in its purity according to the confes-

sions of the Evangelical Lutheran Church and the holy Sacraments are administered according to Christ's institution recorded in the Gospel, in whose society, however, false Christians and hypocrites will always, and manifest sinners may sometimes, be found. [12]

The same holds true in the 1843 Constitution of Trinity Lutheran Church in St. Louis when it states:

Our congregation acknowledges all canonical books of the Old and the New Testament as God's revealed Word, and all the Symbolical Books of the Evangelical Lutheran Church as the form and norm derived from God's Word, according to which, since they are taken from God's Word, not only the doctrine in our congregation is to be taught and examined, but also all disputes which might occur, in doctrine and religion, shall be judged and regulated. These are the three chief Symbols, the Unaltered Augsburg Confession, the Apology of the same, the Smalcald Articles, Dr. Luther's Small and Large Catechism, the Formula of Concord, and the [Saxon] Visitation Articles.[13]

Over the years synodical leaders regularly appealed to the Confessions, as well as to Scripture, in confronting erroneous views in the various controversies that faced the church. For example, in regard to the Predestinarian Controversy Walther wrote: "This doctrine which is most wonderfully explained through the entire eleventh article of the Formula of Concord, is to us an exquisite, precious treasure, which we would not give up for all the world. To our opponents, however, who are completely governed by rationalistic and synergistic views, this doctrine is an abomination."[14] Missouri Synod's commitment to Scripture is strongly evidenced by the citation with full approval of this statement from *The Presbyterian* in the February 9, 1905 issue of *The Lutheran Witness:*

We are set for the defence of the truth. We are enjoined to "contend earnestly for the faith." We are to resist all onsets upon it. We would be false to God, to our vows and obligations, and to our generation if we did not oppose all inroads upon Scriptural doctrine and practice, and warn against all concessions which would weaken the force of Bible teaching, either in respect to what we are to believe, or what we are to practice. We have but one infallible rule of faith and practice. Whatsoever conflicts with it must be exposed and avoided. Those

especially whom God has appointed as guardians of His
Church, and the instructors of His people and the trainers of
the young in the home and in the school, must not be afraid
of controversy.[15]

Recognition of the dangerous inroads of higher criticism and its
challenge to Scripture as the infallible source of all teachings is
contained in the following statement from Rev. Dr. E. Fitch Burr:

The Higher Criticism has proceeded to cut out, with sharp
and hungry knife, the greater part in bulk and importance
of both Testaments, their histories, their prophecies, their
miracles, especially what the Christian ages have always considered to be fundamentals as to Christ, His miracles, His
infallibility as a teacher, His sinlessness, His atoning death,
His resurrection and ascension and deity. What a surgery
that was! The Book has been dismembered.[16]

Synod's strong adherence to Scripture, the Confessions, and orthodox writings came under severe criticism in the 1930s and 1940s.
Conservative Lutheranism was charged with teaching "canned theology." J. M. Moore charged conservative Lutherans with still thinking "in the dialectic of the Reformation."[17] But one of the strong
critics of the LC—MS's "backward stand in theology" is Edwin E.
Aubrey who wrote, "These churches became sects in America. . . .
This often meant that they became fixated in loyalty to an old faith
which was being modified and modernized in the old country. The
Missouri Synod Lutherans came to be more conservative than the
Lutheran Church in Germany and even sent missionaries back to
the old country to overcome 'defections' there."[18]

In late 1935 and early 1936 Dr. T. A. Kantonen, who taught
Systematic Theology at Hamma Divinity School in Springfield, Ohio,
wrote several articles in *The Lutheran* in which he charged the
teaching of verbal inspiration as being passé and obsolete in a new
era of scientific and historical methodology.[19] He contended for not
only a change in methodology but also for "new truth." In the concluding paragraph of the last of the four-part series, "The Need of
Lutheran Scholarship," Kantonen wrote, "I am convinced that the
highest kind of scholarship can flourish only in an institution as the
Lutheran Church, a fellowship of believers not content with ready-
made doctrine or institution, but ever searching the Scriptures for
new truth and ever receptive and obedient to the Spirit of the Living
God."[20] Dr. Kantonen was opposed to repristination theology which

he believed characterized the majority of immigrant Lutherans. His stinging criticism is clear in these words, "Its pastors dare not be satisfied with feeding souls hungering for the Bread of Life with the canned goods of past theology. Its theologians dare not use the Confessions of the Church as Gorgon heads upon which to stare with such fascination as to become petrified."[21]

In 1936 the *Journal of American Lutheran Conference* made this stinging criticism:

> Paradoxical as it may sound, nevertheless it is a fact that in a Lutheran Free Church in America a professor of theology is not permitted to be "free" to do original thinking and present views that are contrary to the accepted views of the Church. If he does, he will be shelved or compelled to close his mouth. We stifle theological thought development. Due to this method the Lutheran Church of America has not produced big theologians around whom have flourished "theological schools." Those that came nearest to do so were Walther of St. Louis and Sverdrup of Minneapolis; and the greater of these two is Walther. But both were products of the European system.[22]

More recently Carl E. Braaten notes, "If the Lutheran Church is a reality today, the question [What is Lutheranism?] is directed to us and must be answered by us, and it cannot be deferred to the text-book artist, who might discover what the Lutheran Church was in some past century."[23] He then proceeds to argue that the church today is governed by different historical factors which limits confessional subscription "not only *insofar* as they conform to the Sacred Scriptures, but also *insofar* as they are relevant to our time."[24] "The degree of the latter," he goes on to say, "must be determined by us."[25]

Thus, the traditional position of the LC—MS has always been what is characterized as repristination theology in the sense of drawing its theology primarily and exclusively from the Scriptures, the Confessions as clear expositions of the Bible, and the Fathers of the church insofar as they agree with the former. Dr. C. F. W. Walther is very clear on this point. In 1871 he wrote in *Lehre und Wehre:*

> Our Church has taken for the foundation on which she stands the Holy Scriptures, and on it she stands honest and squarely; from this foundation she will not depart one finger's breath (*"vel transversum, ut aiunt, unguem"*), that is her character, that is her charge, that makes her a blessing to all Christendom, that is her crown, of which she will not and cannot let herself be robbed.[26]

In addition to Scripture and the Confessions Walther una-
bashedly and quite proudly quoted the orthodox teachers of the
church. In 1882, at the cornerstone laying at Concordia Seminary
he proclaimed, "In this new Concordia the instructors and students
will indeed humbly sit at the feet of those blessed teachers of the
Church who have mined the priceless treasures of divine wisdom
and knowledge from the rich vein of Holy Scriptures. . . ."[27] In further
support of recourse to the Fathers of the Church Walther stated:
"Let no man despise the gifts which God bestowed during these 1800
years upon our godly teachers, the treasures stored up for us by
God's great goodness in their books. He that does so disobeys God,
God's explicit command laid down in Scripture. Such a man will not
grow in knowledge, but becomes increasingly blind."[28]

In 1897 Dr. F. Bente wrote:

> We occupy the very same doctrinal position as the Christians
> of the first century. What, for example, the congregation in
> Rome or Corinth knew in the year of our Lord 97, or should
> have known, just that and not one whit more Trinity Church
> in St. Louis in 1897 knows. . . . Holy Scripture sufficed for the
> Church in the past and will suffice for the church in the
> future.[29]

On this point Bente clearly echoes Luther's comments: "We are not
out to invent new things, but hold, and remain with the old Word
of God, as the ancient church held it."[30] And again, "We must confess
that the doctrine preached and confessed at Augsburg is the true
and pure Word of God, and that all who hold this doctrine are God's
children and will be saved—whether they believe it now or will come
to the understanding of it later. This confession will abide to the
end of the world, to the Last Day."[31]

Dr. Francis Pieper follows boldly in the footsteps of Walther in
resisting novelty of doctrine that emerges from the use of reason,
and he confirms that purity of doctrine is preserved when one limits
their source to Sacred Scriptures, ". . . the Christian doctrine given
to the Church by the Apostle is a finished product, complete and
perfect, fixed for all time."[32] Repristination theology is not a matter
of choice, as he says: "It is not left to our discretion whether we want
to abide by the doctrine of the Lutheran Church, as it is declared
in its Confession, or whether we should choose a different doctrine.
The doctrine of the Lutheran Church agrees perfectly with the doctrine of Christ as we have it in the Word of His Apostles and Prophets
. . . , and no other doctrine is permissible in the Christian Church

to the Last Day."[33] Pieper also said "The Church of the Reformation stands on the rock of Holy Scripture, on the *Sola Scriptura*."[34]

In the concluding paragraphs of his three-part article "No Development of Doctrine for Us!" Dr. Theodore Engelder follows in the footsteps of Walther, Pieper, et al., when he wrote, "First the Christian minister has no right to advance beyond what the Apostles and Prophets have said. . . . Second, it is a slander to designate the work of the Christian teacher as a mere 'phonographic' reproduction of the words of the holy writers and the creeds of Christendom."[35]

The LC—MS still holds to repristination theology in its commitment to the *sola Scriptura* foundation for all its teachings, the correct explication of Scripture in the Confessions, and to the role of the church in the preservation, explication, and proclamation of God's eternal truth. In its March 1975 report, "The Inspiration of Scripture," Synod's Commission on Theology and Church Relations maintains the centrality of Scripture in the words:

> The inspired Scriptures impart the Gospel without any distortion or any corruption because the Holy Spirit provided the terms for expressing the mystery of God's grace in Christ. The inspired Scriptures, then, provide us not merely with a model to guide us in our attempts to speak about God's redemptive purposes in a way that we regard as relevant to human needs as the world understands them. The Scriptures provide us with a *norm* for preaching the Gospel from which we dare not depart without invoking upon ourselves the apostolic curse (Gal. 1:8-9).[36]

On the role of the church the same document states, "God used the church to gather and preserve the holy writings in which He willed to give to mankind His saving Word until the end of the time."[37] Truth is fixed by Scripture, not by reason and modernized theologizing.

Adherence to the teachings of Scripture and the Confessions is in the very forefront of the Constitution of the LC—MS. Article II (immediately after the article which gives the body its name) states:

> The Synod, and every member of the Synod, accepts without reservation: 1. The Scriptures of the Old and the New Testament as the written Word of God and the only rule and norm of faith and of practice.
> 2. All the Symbolical Books of the Evangelical Lutheran Church as a true and unadulterated statement and exposition

of the Word of God, to wit: the three Ecumenical Creeds (the Apostles' Creed, the Nicene Creed, the Athanasian Creed), the Unaltered Augsburg Confession, the Apology of the Augsburg Confession, the Smalcald Articles, the Large Catechism of Luther, the Small Catechism of Luther, and the Formula of Concord.[38]

Concordia Seminary, St. Louis, in its Academic Catalog states that its function and purpose is to prepare men for the parish ministry in the LC—MS who "accept without reservation the Scriptures of the Old and New Testaments as the written Word of God and the only rule and norm of faith and practice and all the symbolic books of the evangelical Lutheran church contained in the Book of Concord as a true and unadulterated statement and exposition of the Word of God (Constitution of the LC—MS Article II, Sections 1 and 2)."[39]

Historically the LC—MS has never shied away from the characterization of its theological stance as repristination theology, but has worn it as a badge of honor when the term is employed in the positive sense as indicating loyalty to Scripture and the correct exposition of Scripture in the Confessions and orthodox teachers of the faith, whether ancient, Reformation, or post-Reformation. Scripture has made clear that whatever truth is necessary for man's salvation, a proper relationship with God, and God-pleasing fellowship with other humans, is contained within its pages. Man may explicate the Scriptures, as has been done in the Confessions and in other orthodox writings and teachings of God's ongoing church, but man may never add thereto or alter its substance. The church does not need new doctrine; it only needs the doctrines contained in Divine Revelation. The Smalcald Articles, Part II, Article II.15 says, "This means that the Word of God shall establish articles of faith and no one else, not even an angel."[40]

The LC—MS maintains that there can be no development of doctrine in the sense of additions derived from human reason when applied to theology, nor should the church seek "new truth" as an update to what is considered outmoded doctrine because of pressure to keep up with a world that rapidly changes in terms of science, fashion, and human learning.

If repristination theology is understood as establishing and maintaining correct doctrine merely by quoting in rote manner former theologians or historical documents, such as the Confessions, simply because of an antiquarian sentiment, fear of change, or ease of task, then LC—MS in not in favor of repristination theology in this sense.

Nor is it opposed to theological scholarship. This is evident from Synod's emphasis on an educated clergy, its operation of colleges and seminaries, graduate programs for advanced theological education, and provisions in its Bylaws for providing funding for advanced study by instructional and administrative personnel.[41] Scholarship, of course, is understood as having a servant role in plumbing the depths of the meaning of God's Word, not to enable man to contradict, stand in judgment over against it or redirect it to support human understanding.

Over the years and still today Missouri Synod stands by Holy Scriptures' claims for its own self-sufficiency in matters of doctrine, is in line with the view of the early church that we do not add to the Rule of Faith, and is heir to the Reformation principle of *sola Scriptura* and the Reformation's confessional legacy. Our church has stood, not always with ease, against the trends of modern theology to tamper with the Word of God and to rewrite God's agenda and teaching for His world. We are not ashamed to say with Melanchthon in the words of the Apology of the Augsburg Confession: "We know that what we have said agrees with the prophetic and apostolic Scriptures, with the holy Fathers Ambrose, Augustine, and many others, and with the whole church of Christ, which certainly confesses that Christ is the propitiator and the justifier."[42] If that is repristination theology, then we praise God that He has kept our beloved Synod a church of repristination theology.

Notes

[1] F. Pieper, *Christian Dogmatics* (St. Louis: Concordia, 1951), vol. 1, p. ix.

[2] Vincent of Lerins. *Commonitorium*, c. 2.

[3] Ignatius of Antioch, *Philadelphia* 8.2.

[4] Tertullian, *de virg. vel.* I. Also see Tertullian *de praescr. haeret.* 37, 44, 42, 14, 26, 36. Irenaeus *adv. haer.* i. 10.1,2; iii.4.1,2.

[5] O. W. Heick, *A History of Christian Thought* (Philadelphia: The Muhlenberg Press, 1946), vol. 2, p. 124.

[6] Men like Theodor Kliefoth and Gottfried Thomasius applied the Hegelian method to confessional Lutheranism. According to Thomasius the dogma that begins in Scripture unfolded in the teachings of the sixteenth-century Lutheran Reformation.

[7] E. Clifford Nelson, *The Lutherans in North America* (Philadelphia: Fortress, 1975), pp. 151-52.

[8] Carl S. Meyer, ed., *Moving Frontiers* (St. Louis: Concordia, 1964), p. 86.

[9] *Ibid.,* p. 110.

[10] *Ibid.,* p. 143.

[11] *Ibid.,* p. 149-50.

[12] *Ibid.,* p. 165-66.

[13] *Ibid.,* p. 167.

[14] *Ibid.,* p. 271.

[15] *Ibid.,* p. 362-63.

[16] *Ibid.,* p. 365.

[17] J. M. Moore, "No Change of Heart Yet!" *Christendom* II.4 (Autumn 1937), p. 575.

[18] E. E. Aubrey, *Living the Christian Faith* (New York: Macmillan, 1939), p. 97.

[19] The *Lutheran* in its December 12, 19, 26, 1935 and January 2, 1936 issues (vol. 18) carried a four-part series of articles on Lutheran scholarship by Dr. T. A. Kantonen.

[20] T. A. Kantonen, "The Need of Lutheran Scholarship," *Lutheran* 18 (Jan. 2, 1936) p. 8.

[21] *Ibid.,* (Dec. 12, 1935), p. 3.

[22] *Journal of The American Lutheran Conference* I. 6 (June 1936), p. 50.

[23] Carl E. Braaten, "The Crisis of Confessionalism," *Dialog* I.1 (Winter 1962) p. 39.

[24] *Ibid.,* p. 41.

[25] *Ibid.*

[26] C. F. W. Walther, "Foreword," *Lehre und Wehre* 17.1 (January 1871), p. 11.

[27] C. F. W. Walther, Address at 1882 cornerstone laying at Concordia Seminary, St. Louis.

[28] Proceedings, Synodical Conference, p. 11.

[29] Proceedings, Western District (1897), p. 31-32.

[30] Luther's Works, St. Louis ed., vol. 17, col. 1659.

[31] Luther's Works, St. Louis ed., vol. 16, col. 1538.

[32] Pieper, *Dogmatics,* p. 129.

[33] *Ibid.,* p. 184.

[34] Pieper, *Lehre und Wehre,* 1928. p. 14.

[35] Th. Engelder, "No Development of Doctrine for Us!," *Concordia Theological Monthly* 20.10 (October 1949) p. 726.

[36] "The Inspiration of Scripture," March 1975 report of the Commission on Theology and Church Relations, p. 17.

[37] *Ibid.,* p. 17.

[38] 1986 Handbook, The Lutheran Church—Missouri Synod, p. 9.

[39] 1989-1990 Academic Catalog of Concordia Seminary, p. 9.

[40] Theodore G. Tappert, trans. and ed., *Book of Concord* (Philadelphia: Fortress, 1959), p. 295.

[41] 1986 Handbook, p. 112, Bylaw 6.55.

[42] Tappert, *Book of Concord,* p. 166. (IV.389).

A Chapel, Worship, and Worship Instruction

WAYNE E. SCHMIDT

Time does not move forward in leaps and bounds but is, as a hymn writer has said, like an ever-rolling stream. Time does not stop, it moves silently and imperceptibly from one moment to the next and from one year to another. Each generation steps forward to the tasks and responsibilities presented to it and then proceeds quietly and gradually to hand over to the next generation both old and new assignments and challenges. With time, stopping points do not really exist, for time is a continuous course within which people live and events occur.

Some moments and events, however, deserve to be marked and celebrated in special ways as we live our lives under the grace of God in Christ Jesus. A 150th anniversary of the founding of a church institution is such an occasion. We can't stop the clock to celebrate an anniversary; we are compelled to keep on moving. But as we continue forward in our time we are able to take a quick glance backward to reflect on what took place before us. Such reflection helps us understand better what we might undertake to leave as a heritage for those who come after us.

Such a marking of time and accomplishments brings with it a variety of activities, projects, and celebrations. In Concordia Seminary's 150th year the planning for and designing of a free-standing chapel has surely been the major undertaking of the anniversary observance. The chapel venture is not only the costliest in terms of energy and financial resources but is also the fulfilling of hopes of the past and the stirring of excitement for the future. An inspiring chapel on campus will serve as an edifying place for the people of God at Concordia to come together for worship and will stand as a testimony to the centrality of worship in the life of Lutheran parishes and in the lifelong work of Lutheran pastors.

When the Apostle Paul addressed his congregation at Corinth,

WAYNE E. SCHMIDT is Chairman of the Department of Practical Theology at Concordia Seminary, St. Louis.

he spoke of their coming together. Coming together for spiritual engagement is a major activity in the Christian life, as the writer of the letter to the Hebrews makes clear when he urges us not to neglect meeting together (Heb. 10:25). The 150th anniversary chapel project, the building of a place for a Christian community to assemble for worship at Concordia Seminary, invites comments on the subject of worship, our coming together in the name of Jesus.

Defining Worship

Worship is not an easy concept to define. Some seek to arrive at a definition of the activity by examining those Hebrew or Greek words which are sometimes rendered in English Bibles with the term "worship." Thus the Hebrew *shachah,* to bow oneself down, or the Greek προσκυνέω, to prostrate oneself, have become major determiners of what it means to worship. Worship viewed from these etymological perspectives is seen as a man-to-God activity in which the creature acknowledges the absolute worth or sovereignty of the Divine Being. Etymological studies of this type can produce definitions such this: "Worship, in all its grades and kinds, is the response of the creature to the Eternal."[1]

That worship includes the humility, adoration, reverence, and praise implied in this kind of definition is well attested by both Biblical example and injunction. What the definition fails to express, however, is the emphasis of Holy Scripture on the importance of listening to God speak. Ancient Israel was called upon to hear the Word of the Lord. The Apostles were sent forth to tell. Groups and individuals in the Biblical record assembled to hear a message from God to His people. A serviceable definition of worship with which to guide those who lead and plan worship and with which to satisfy the expectations of those who come to worship must encompass more, therefore, than the actions of praise, adoration, and thanksgiving.

A striking thing about that which we generally refer to as worship in our ordinary conversation is that the Biblical writers use no single term for this activity. New Testament writers when speaking of what we might be inclined to subsume under the term "worship" seem scrupulously to avoid the common cultic terms which were available at the time. Instead, there is just the general repeated reference to the fact that Christians after the resurrection of Christ came together regularly and in their assemblies engaged in a number of different kinds of activities. There is no evidence of a single uniform format for these meetings, nor dare it be said that an assembled group felt obligated to include all religious rites and privileges in every meeting. Specific mention is made in 1 Corinthians 11, for example, of coming together to eat the Lord's Supper. In 1 Corinthians 14, on the other hand, no mention is made of the Supper in what is the most detailed description we have in the New Testament of a worship setting. The 1 Corinthians 14 gathering, which assumes the presence of outsiders, seems to be describing an outreach kind of assembly. In either case, however, coming together with the fellowship of believers is an assumed and expected phenomenon in the Christian way of life.

Predominant in the activity of the apostolic age, as well as in the days of the Old Testament for that matter, is proclamation. From Peter's incisive "Hear these words" (Acts 2:22) to the Lord's own message in Revelation, "I, Jesus, have sent my angel to you with this testimony for the churches" (Rev. 22:16), the New Testament is a book of telling and hearing. That is the starting point of worship, a starting point so simply and strikingly depicted in ancient Bethany where Mary sat at Jesus' feet and listened to what he said. Martin Luther understood it well when he said that in the house of God we gather that "our dear Lord himself may speak to us through His holy Word and we respond through prayer and praise."[2] We might say, then, that worship is the coming together of baptized Christians to hear the Word of God, to use the Sacraments of Holy Baptism and the Lord's Supper according to Christ's command, and in faith in Jesus as Savior to respond in prayer, thanksgiving, and praise to the Triune God who has redeemed His people. Worship is the service of God to us in Christ Jesus and the service of God which Christians render to their Lord in Christ's name. It is an activity uniquely comprehended in the German word for worship, *Gottesdienst* (service of God).

Planning Seminary Worship Space

Recognizing the importance of a Christian community's coming together regularly to hear God speak and to speak to him, the seminary's building committee of the 1920s included a chapel in the proposed De Mun Avenue seminary campus plan. "A chapel should be provided for in the block plan," the building committee minutes of April 7, 1922, matter-of-factly state.[3] The ambitious master plan for the campus being out of reach for the available financial resources, the committee proceeded, apparently without too much debate, to plan for the buildings essential to house and conduct classes at a boarding school. It was not that a separate chapel was considered unimportant, for Theodore Graebner, secretary of the building committee, writing in 1926 commented: "In modern college groups the significant feature is the chapel. These college 'chapels' are usually large and stately buildings, sometimes dominating the entire academic group. The architect's layout provides for a chapel to the southeast of the first Concordia group of buildings."[4]

The completed 1926 set of Concordia Seminary buildings did not include the free-standing chapel of the master plan. Provision, of course, was made for an assembly hall which could serve a variety of academic and student life functions and double as the gathering place for campus worship. The Word of God was heard in this hall, and God's people at Concordia practiced there faith's response of prayer, praise, and thanksgiving. True worship is not bound to a particular place or a specially designed place, as Jesus pointed out to the Samaritan woman at Jacob's well. When it is possible, however, to invest worship space with devotionally inspiring and reverent furnishings, not to do so leaves the worshipers who use such space with something of the feeling of King David: "I dwell in an house of cedar, but the ark of God dwelleth in a tent" (2 Sam. 7:2). Over the years modern conveniences and improvements came here and there at the seminary, but the make-do chapel remained basically the same.

It was not that no one felt a need to improve the situation. Seminary reports to the Synod in convention kept the issue alive and requested funding for a separate chapel facility. Things even seemed to move forward when in 1944 the Synod resolved in convention "that an appropriate chapel be built at Concordia Seminary; and that sufficient funds be appropriated from the proposed Peace Offering to symbolize our gratitude for peace."[5] The chapel which was to be erected was intended not only to be a place for worship but a facility for student "training in worship and liturgy."[6]

The convention action was not implemented, causing the Seminary's Board of Control to respond in 1947 with the following report and request:

> Attention is called to the fact that Synod assembled at Saginaw, Mich. (see *Proceedings,* 1944, p. 47), granted the request of the Board of Control of Concordia Seminary for a chapel for Concordia Seminary. No funds have been allocated for this purpose. We herewith request Synod to allocate funds for a chapel, for which funds were collected in the Thankoffering for Peace.[7]

No chapel building having been constructed by 1956, the synodical convention of that year was again informed of the need for such a facility which could seat one thousand and have "all the necessary facilities and equipment for worship and for instruction in liturgics and homiletics."[8] It was the conviction of those who wrote this report that a chapel together with several other needed structures would assist to supply the Synod with "properly educated pastors" and provide a campus "with an optimum capacity for service."[9]

The years continued to slip by, and hope had still not become reality. "We repeat our request . . . that funds be allocated for the construction of a new chapel" began a section of the Seminary's report to the Synod in convention in 1962.[10] The writers of the report seemed to feel, moreover, that it was time to summarize the whole story and to emphasize both the worship purpose and the educational function of a campus chapel.

A long history stands behind this request. No chapel was included among the buildings in the original complex dedicated in 1926. By 1945 the need for a chapel was so apparent that over $800,000 was collected for the erection of this building. However, inflation and building costs made that sum insufficient for the building in its original plan and material, and the Board of Directors of the Lutheran Church—Missouri Synod was compelled to divert the funds toward other projects caught in the inflation spiral. The assembly hall of the seminary has been adapted for the purposes of daily worship through the installation of a "chancel" and a movable altar in the platform area.

The proposed chapel will provide suitable worship facilities for the seminary campus community (faculty, students, and service staffs). Within 10 years it can be expected that 900 seatings will be necessary for the regular morning chapel services. Our plans include auxiliary space for 300 seats above the basic 900, because of the frequent services which attract a considerable number of visitors and the use of the building by the Western District of our Synod.

We consider a chapel a necessary educational building. A proper standard of architecture, conducive to worship, influences a very large portion of the ministers of the church as they worship, in this building during three of their most formative years. This chapel will provide classes in liturgics and homiletics with adequate facilities for instruction and practice in the conduct of worship and in preaching.[11]

Time, like an ever-rolling stream, has continued to move along. The seminary is in its 150th year, over sixty years on the De Mun campus. A free-standing chapel, requested so many times, still does not grace the campus and cannot be the gathering place for the anniversary celebrations of 1989. Anniversary energy has been harnessed, however, to try once more to accomplish the task. "It is not to be expected," wrote Theodore Graebner in 1926, "that this chapel can be built without the aid of wealthy friends of the institution who are willing to give in large amounts."[12] Such benefactors have been found and have been joined by appreciative alumni and other friends to push forward the project. Hope beaming in our eyes, we ask with more purposeful reason perhaps than others before us: "Precisely how will a separarate and distinctive chapel serve the particular needs of Concordia Seminary?"

The Seminary as a Worshiping Community

The first and primary use of the chapel is a daily one. Concordia Seminary is a Christian community devoted to the study of theology. Such theological study has a very specific focus, for the church has established Concordia "to prepare men for the holy ministry of Word and Sacraments in The Lutheran Church—Missouri Synod."[13] At Concordia Seminary men are preparing themselves to become pastors, men of God who like the apostles in Acts 6 have committed themselves in their life's work "to prayer and to the ministry of the Word." The study of theology at Concordia is not just an academic enterprise. Classroom activity has the parish ministry regularly in mind, and as men prepare themselves for that ministry they desire the opportunity to gather with fellow students and faculty in community worship, that activity, finally, around which all parish life centers.

Although theological study is a spiritually rewarding pursuit in and of itself, such study does carry with it the usual rigors and demands of academia. Papers, tests, reports, grades—these are not absent from student life at Concordia Seminary. Besides, faculty and students alike carry with them the daily burdens and effects of sin present in the life of all human-kind. Tragedy and pain, sickness and death, worries and anxiety come to the campus of Concordia Seminary as well as to any other community. The daily chapel service on campus provides the opportunity for the seminary community to put books and worries aside for a few moments in order to seek that refreshment which our Lord himself dispenses where two or three are gathered together in his name. Although the Lord is present wherever His Word is, a place set aside and specifically designed for worship assists mightily to remove those distractions which interfere with spiritual reflection and attention. A chapel on campus becomes the cathedral which an American poet once described when he wrote:

> Oft have I seen at some cathedral door
> A laborer, pausing in the dust and heat,
> Lay down his burden, and with reverent feet
> Enter, and cross himself, and on the floor
> Kneel to repeat his paternoster o'er;
> Far off the noises of the world retreat;
> The loud vociferations of the street
> Become an undistinguishable roar.[14]

Like any other church building, a seminary chapel is a place to use for corporate worship, a place of which one is able to say, "I was glad when they said unto me, 'Let us go into the house of the Lord' " (Ps. 122:1).

A seminary chapel, however, by its very presence on campus goes beyond the functional purpose of serving only to provide reverent space in which to conduct divine worship. The Synod in convention in 1944 resolved "that an appropriate chapel be built at Concordia Seminary; and that sufficient funds be appropriated from the proposed Peace Offering to symbolize our gratitude for peace."[15] A symbolic function was being assigned to the offering, to the chapel, or to both. The hope of 1944 to have a seminary chapel as a symbol of the Synod's gratitude for temporal peace was never realized. It must be said, however, that a chapel on the campus of Concordia Seminary will always be a symbol, a symbol which goes beyond any issue, focus, or concern of a given era or day. A chapel impressively and strikingly designed and situated among the academic and residential buildings on campus asserts that the study of theology at Concordia Seminary rises above the theoretical and finds expression in the worship life of God's people.

Since this goal can easily be lost sight of, a chapel building together with the daily use of it remains a constant testimony to a major focus in theological education. Faculty and students profit from the visual symbol of the chapel and are continually reminded of the source and goal of theological study. A building made to look like a church directs the attention of students and faculty to the life calling which the graduates of Concordia Seminary will be following, the calling of the parish pastor who weekly hears the summons to a similar kind of building in which to serve the people of God in Christ Jesus. To all who visit campus the seminary chapel is the silent yet articulate spokesman which gives expression to the purpose of the institution. As symbols with their quiet testimony interpret and give meaning to numerous areas and endeavors in human life, so a seminary chapel identifies the purpose and function of a school of the prophets. A God-pleasing institution for the study of theology understands theology, among other things, as a *habitus practicus,* a personal aptitude, attitude, and ability formed by the Holy Spirit through training in the word of God by which the pastor lives his own life under Christ and leads others in the way of salvation. The seminary chapel as the appointed place for corporate worship supports that concept of theological education and the concomitant practice of theology in the parish ministry.

Teaching Worship Leadership

To the utilitarian function of Concordia's chapel as a fittingly appointed place for the conduct of worship on campus and to the symbolic function of the building to indicate the ultimate purpose of theological education at the seminary must be added a third usage, namely, the pedagogical employment of the building. A major task and privilege of the pastoral office is the conduct of public worship in the parishes of the church. This is an awesome assignment which requires extensive seminary training. Recognizing this, Concordia Seminary's Board of Control when requesting funds from the Synod in 1944 remarked that there was "need for a chapel at Concordia Seminary for . . . training in leading in worship and liturgy."[16] The 1956 Board of Control request for a chapel which would seat one thousand stated the matter even more specifically when the Board's report expressed the desire to have a chapel "with all the necessary facilities and equipment for worship and for instruction in liturgics and homiletics."[17] Seminarians need adequate training in these practical areas of theology in order to be equipped to prepare for, plan, and lead Christian congregations in edifying worship.

A campus chapel assists in these areas of instruction in several ways. First, seminary professors especially competent in preaching and in the conduct of public worship become models for seminary students. Granted, campus worship is intended to address the spiritual needs of the worshipers and not to serve as the setting for a demonstration laboratory. It remains a fact, however, that those who are studying practical theology in the classroom cannot be oblivious to how preaching and liturgical conduct take place in the seminary chapel. In addition, students themselves have opportunities to participate in a variety of ways in campus worship. Students lead in devotions, may even preach upon occasion, sing in choirs, accompany worship with organ and other instrumental music, and get the chapel and things needed for worship services ready. Worship in a seminary chapel does assist in the education of seminarians.

The chapel being designed in the 150th anniversary year also includes a number of adjunct facilities in its lower level. A choir room, for example, provides rehearsal space for the choirs which sing at divine services conducted in the chapel and functions as well as a teaching station for classes in worship and church music. A very small chapel, equipped with audiovisual equipment for taping and recording student preaching and liturgical conduct, serves as a demonstration and practice area for classroom instruction, thus enhancing the quality of practical theology instruction on campus; for one learns also by doing.

A seminary campus chapel seeks first and foremost to provide adequate and reverent space for the seminary's corporate worship life. In doing that the chapel is also able to stand as a symbol of what theological education is about. The chapel being designed in Concordia Seminary's 150th anniversary year is intended, however, to serve one more purpose. The building is to become the place where future pastors will be trained for their role as worship leaders for the people of God gathered in congregations throughout the world.

Worship — A Major Subject in Practical Theology

A seminary curriculum adequate for the training of pastors addresses the subject of theology from several points of view. For the sake of convenience it is common for a seminary to divide itself into departments. At Concordia these departments bear the names exegetical, systematic, historical, and practical theology. Since the total curriculum has the aim of preparing men for the office of the holy ministry, the various departments are not independent disciplinary units but are complementary to each other and closely joined together. Good preaching and teaching, for example, do not take place without the support of exegetical, systematic, and historical study, and in the parish ministry a pastor's scholarly studies are of limited use if he is unable to communicate the fruits of his study to his parishioners for their spiritual upbuilding.

Curricular offerings in the Department of Practical Theology concern themselves extensively with the ways in which a pastor communicates and applies the saving truths of God's Word to those whom the pastor is called to serve. In his calling to care for human souls a pastor sometimes ministers to individuals and sometimes to groups. He has a message of Law and Gospel to preach and teach to confessing and committed Christians and, in keeping with Christ's command to make disciples of all nations, to those who do not know the saving Gospel of Jesus Christ or have become delinquent and careless in their faith-life. The young and the old come under the pastor's shepherding care; the sick and the healthy are his concern. To be able eventually to minister effectively in those situations it is helpful for seminarians to examine and understand some of the principles which underlie effective communication with various types and groups of people. Departmental offerings in practical theology include such fields, therefore, as preaching, worship, pastoral care and counseling, missions, and education.

The amount of time which a pastor devotes to each of his several activities varies according as circumstances and requirements present themselves in any given parish. The one thing, however, which remains constant in parish life is the regular routine of services of corporate worship. The gathering of people around Word and Sacraments is the *sine qua non* of congregational life. For that reason, indispensable in a seminary curriculum are those areas of practical theology which equip future pastors to lead corporate worship, the things, in other words, which are put into practice in a seminary chapel and conveniently taught within such specifically designed educational facilities as can be incorporated in a chapel building. Such an understanding is what lay behind the earlier requests for a chapel at Concordia Seminary, requests in which the formulators expressed the need for a facility suitable for the teaching of liturgics and homiletics.

This desire is consonant with what has been a major emphasis in practical theology in the seminary's curriculum. Recent academic catalogs list many more courses in practical theology than older catalogs, but common to both old and new catalogs are offerings in homiletics, liturgics, pastoral theology, and education. In fact, if homiletics and liturgics are considered one field because of their inseparable union in Lutheran worship practice, it is not incorrect to conclude that training for what takes place in the public assemblies of Christian congregations is seen as the single most important area in Concordia Seminary's Department of Practical Theology.

Such an emphasis has not been a mistake on the part of the designers of the seminary's practical theology curriculum, for, as was pointed out earlier, coming together to hear God speak and to speak to Him is a hallmark of the life of the church and a phenomenon clearly evident already in the time of the Apostles. The apostolic church, to be sure, is a story of outreach, but as disciples for Christ were made, these disciples came together regularly for what we call worship. In these assemblies the disciples grew and were strengthened in their spiritual lives through the use of Word and Sacraments and from these assemblies Christ's followers went forth empowered for their mission and dedicated to proclaiming Him who suffered, died, and rose again to make peace between God and man. On the contemporary American scene a seminary campus chapel bears testimony to the centrality of assembly in the life of the church, furnishes well-appointed space for the seminary community itself to come together, and by means of auxiliary rooms provides well-equipped space in which to teach students how to do those things which pertain to corporate worship in the life of Christian congregations. Three items are especially deserving of comment in this connection; namely, preaching, liturgical conduct, and music in worship.

Preaching in Public Worship

Throughout the history of Lutheranism the oral proclamation of God's Word has held center position in congregational worship. Luther himself spoke most emphatically on the matter when he said: "A Christian congregation should never gather together without the preaching of God's Word. . . . When God's Word is not preached, one had better neither sing nor read, nor even come together."[18] Luther was directing his remarks against the abuses which had become characteristic of worship in the Roman Catholic Mass of his day. Sermons were apparently not common, and when they did exist, they were more likely to deal with legends than with the Word of God. Worship, moreover, "was performed as a work whereby God's grace and salvation might be won."[19] Luther was convinced that the very nature of worship was misunderstood and that the content of the worship of the church in the sixteenth century was in need of reform. The exposition of Holy Scripture as this is done in sermons had to be restored to the church's public worship.

Such an emphasis is in harmony with what went on in the Christian assemblies portrayed in the New Testament. The inspired writers employ a number of words to describe the preaching activity of the New Testament church. They use the word κηρύσσω, for example, to proclaim as a herald, εὐαγγελίζομαι, to announce the good news, διδάσκω, to teach, and other words and expressions which denote oral communication. The church has a message to proclaim, as did the Incarnate Word himself whose public ministry Matthew described in the following way: "Jesus went about all Galilee, teaching in their synagogues, and preaching the gospel of the kingdom" (διδάσκων . . . καὶ κηρύσσων τὸ εὐαγγέλιον, Matt. 4:23). Having gained His resurrection victory and about to ascend to the right hand of His Father, the victorious Christ commissioned His apostles to make disciples of all nations by baptizing and teaching (διδάσκοντες, Matt. 28:20). The verbal activity embraced in the command to teach was not new to the twelve either, for they had once gone out two by two and preached (ἐκήρυξαν) that men should repent (Mark 6:12). The church moved forward with the spoken word.

The Apostles had no misunderstanding about their commission. In the house of Cornelius, for example, Peter declared that he and the other Apostles had been commanded to preach (κηρῦξαι) and to bear witness (διαμαρτύρασθαι) to the redemptive work of Jesus Christ (Acts 10:42). Added a bit later to the number of apostolic proclaimers, the Apostle Paul spoke of his call as a preacher (κῆρυξ) an apostle, and a teacher (διδάσκαλος) of the Gentiles (2 Tim. 2:11). Proclamation was at the center of Paul's energetic mission activity. He had been sent, he says in 1 Corinthians 1:17 to preach the Gospel (εὐαγγελίζεσθαι). Faith comes by hearing and hearing does not come about without a preacher (χωρὶς κηρύσσοντος, Rom. 10:14).

Aware of the necessity of proclamation in the life of the church for the nurture and strengthening of believers and for the conversion of those who do not know Christ, the Lutheran church has accorded preaching the highest priority in worship. The tightly organized discourse which we refer to as preaching in worship services today is not identical with what the New Testament was speaking about with the general terms referred above. The objective, however, is the same and the results are the same. In as much as the proclamation is normed by God's Word and is informed by the Gospel of Jesus Christ the preaching is the "sword of the Spirit" (Eph. 6:17) and the "power of God unto salvation" (Rom. 1:16). Such preaching is more than mere announcement of historical fact. It is a witness which effects and sustains saving faith.

Holy Scripture's stress upon the importance and necessity of oral proclamation has prompted Lutherans to speak about preaching in the strongest terms. Martin Luther, for example, remarked: "The preaching and teaching of God's Word is the most important part of divine service" (*Gottesdienst,* i.e., worship).[20] The German text of the Apology of the Augsburg Confession concludes: "There is nothing which keeps people with the church more readily than good preaching."[21] And in more recent times C. F. W. Walther added:

> To preach properly is difficult. For this reason a student of theology ought to make proper preaching his highest aim. For if he is unable to preach, he does not belong in the ministry. . . . The worth of a true minister of the Church lies exclusively in his ability to preach properly. If he has not this ability, the pulpit is not the place for him; for the pulpit is for preaching. Preaching is the central element of every divine service.[22]

Since preaching occupies such a central position in public worship the seminary addresses the practice of homiletics in several ways. First, the daily academic schedule is arranged so that faculty, students, and staff, have the opportunity to come together daily for chapel services. Although there is no set format for these daily services, preaching takes place regularly. Preaching in the seminary community has the same goal as the sermon in parish worship. The seminary community is in need of the proclamation of Law and Gospel as well as any other group of Christians. Preaching in the seminary chapel speaks to the issues of human sin and divine grace and in that way supports and sustains the Christian faith of chapel audiences. Something else, however, also takes place in a seminary chapel. Future pastors have the opportunity in their daily seminary community worship to become acquainted with various kinds of pulpit exposition and preaching styles. In this way seminarians learn for their own use what contributes to effective preaching. A chapel at the seminary combines homiletical learning with spiritual edification. As was said before, the pedagogical is not the primary purpose of chapel services, but the opportunity to teach in chapel should not be seen as inappropriate at a seminary, for students learn by what they see and hear as well as by what they are told. To attend chapel merely to be critical or to engage in intense analysis is admittedly improper, but to reflect constructively on how things are done and on what makes preaching particularly edifying or effective is to engage in a noble striving to make oneself "a workman who does not need to be ashamed and who correctly handles the word of truth" (2 Tim. 2:15).

The seminary classroom and not the chapel, however, is the primary teaching station for instruction in homiletics. Such instruction can go on at the theoretical level in almost any kind of classroom, but the time eventually comes when a student should step into a pulpit to preach a sermon. The miniature chapel planned for the lower level of the seminary's new chapel is intended to accommodate homiletical practice. The small chapel is to be equipped with the customary chancel furnishings so that the setting is similar to what one might find in a church. In addition, video recording equipment is to be moved from another campus location into a recording studio incorporated in the lower level chapel. Thus, this chapel, which is well appointed also to serve as a place where small groups may gather for worship, becomes a teaching and learning station, a facility designed and equipped to enhance the seminary's curricular instruction in the art and skill of preaching.

Liturgical Worship

Even as homiletics has been and still is seen as an important aspect of the seminary curriculum because of the essential role of preaching in public worship, so also instruction and practice in liturgical conduct has been a consistent offering in the seminary's Department of Practical Theology. The reason is not hard to detect. Public worship in the life of Lutheran congregations includes a number of elements in addition to preaching. Scriptures are read, hymns are sung, prayers are offered, and versicles and responses are spoken or sung in a setting which is commonly referred to as the liturgy. The rites used in Lutheran worship are the product of centuries of worship practices employed in the church catholic and have been set within a regular cycle of events and observances known as the church year.

Admittedly, rites and ceremonies are not the essence of worship as the Formula of Concord states: "We believe, teach, and confess unanimously that the ceremonies or church usages which are neither commanded nor forbidden in the Word of God . . . are in and for themselves no divine worship or even a part of it."[23] The rites and ceremonies have been introduced, however, "for the sake of good order and the general welfare"[24] and from that point of view rest on sound Biblical foundations. The Apostle Paul, for example, had felt it his responsibility to declare to the church of Ephesus "the whole counsel of God" (Acts 20:27). Pastors on the contemporary scene are aided in that very task by the rhythm of the liturgical year, an arrangement by which salient events in the life of our Lord and basic teachings of Holy Scripture are presented and regularly repeated for the upbuilding of the people of God. To give instruction in the various components of liturgical worship is to provide seminarians with an understanding of a structure which will enable pastors to teach, feed, and equip the saints of God well.

It is within the context of public worship, moreover, that the Apostle Paul issued his well-known directive, "Let all things be done decently and in order" (1 Cor. 14:40). Chaos was not to be tolerated because it interfered with clear communication and spiritual up-building. Well thought-out liturgical forms seek to invest corporate worship with substantive theological content and a spirit of reverence. Such forms can accomplish those aims if the worship leader understands what he is doing and how to do it. For that reason, Concordia Seminary has made liturgics an integral part of the training of future pastors. As with homiletics, classroom instruction in liturgics is also supplemented with opportunities for demonstration and practice. The lower level instructional facilities of the new anniversary chapel have been planned to accommodate that kind of teaching. In addition, daily services in a well-appointed chapel make it possible for the seminary community to acquaint itself with a variety of resources available for corporate worship as well as to employ such resources for the spiritual enrichment of those who worship in the seminary chapel. Liturgical forms are not ends in themselves but means which the Christian church has designed to order the proclamation of the Word, the administration of the Sacraments, the prayers, the doxologies, and the instruction which Christians engage in when they come together for worship.

Music in Worship

A third aspect of Christian worship which is not treated extensively in the seminary curriculum but which enhances chapel services at the seminary and which will be able to be demonstrated especially well in the new chapel is music. The use of music in worship should not be overlooked in seminary education, for music has contributed significantly to congregational worship life. It is not that congregations are attempting to make their church buildings concert halls. On the other hand, Christian worship without the use of music is almost inconceivable. Even those who maintain that they can't sing want hymns in worship.

The use of music, elaborate or simple, in congregational life is totally consistent with Biblical precedent and directive. From the song and dance of the Israelites after their deliverance at the Red Sea (Ex. 15) to the evening singing of a hymn prior to Gethsemane (Matt. 26:30) and the glorious choruses in the book of Revelation (e.g., Rev. 5:8-14), Holy Scripture is replete with references to music when God's people in Christ come together. The psalmist doesn't hesitate to use an imperative to urge song (Ps. 96), and the Apostle Paul exhorts both the Ephesians and the Colossians to employ "psalms and hymns and spiritual songs" (Eph. 5:19; Col. 3:16).

One is not surprised, therefore, that Martin Luther was encouraged to endorse the use of music in worship and in the training of pastors. Of music itself he said:

> Music is a beautiful and glorious gift of God and near to theology. I would not want to give up my limited knowledge of music for some great prize.[25]

Upon another occasion he commented: "I give music the place next to theology and the highest honor."[26] And with respect to the training of pastors the reformer did not hesitate to declare: "A schoolteacher must be able to sing; otherwise I do not hold him in esteem. Young men should also not be ordained into the public ministry unless they have had experience with music and have practiced it in school."[27]

The plans for the chapel drawn upon the occasion of Concordia Seminary's 150th anniversary have not overlooked the high position which music has held and still holds in the worship life of God's people. The chapel balcony is designed to provide ample space for choirs and instrumentalists. An organ suitable and adequate to accompany the hymn singing of both large and small groups of worshipers is also to be situated in the balcony. Choir and instrumental rehearsal space is to be included in the lower level of the building. All of this is planned so that seminarians might themselves sing to the Lord and at the same time gain insights into what can be done with song and music in Lutheran parishes.

Worship is coming together in the name of Christ to hear God speak, to receive the blessings of His Sacraments, and to turn to a gracious Lord in prayer, praise, song, and thanksgiving. Seminarians gather in worship while they are preparing themselves to become shepherds under Christ. So that these same seminarians might become competent to lead others in congregational worship, the seminary's Department of Practical Theology gives high priority to those understandings and skills which are so essential to have in order to serve God's people when they come together for worship. The seminary's new chapel is expected to contribute positively to edifying worship on campus and to be a center for training future pastors in the various aspects of congregational worship. The expectation is most fitting and appropriate, for the gathering of the people of God for corporate worship is at the center of the life of the church.

Notes

[1] Evelyn Underhill, *Worship* (London: Collins Clear-Type Press, 1936), p. 13.

[2] Martin Luther, "Sermon at the Dedication of Castle Church, Torgau" (1544), *Luther's Works,* American Edition, vol. 51, *Sermons I,* trans. and ed. John W. Dobberstein (Philadelphia: Muhlenberg, 1959), p. 333.

[3] Minutes of the Building Committee, April 7, 1922, Archives, Concordia Historical Institute, St. Louis, Missouri.

[4] Theodore Graebner, *Concordia Seminary: Its History, Architecture, and Symbolism* (St. Louis: Concordia, [1926]), p. 66.

[5] Ev. Lutheran Synod of Missouri, Ohio, and Other States, *Proceedings* (St. Louis: Concordia, 1944), p. 47.

[6] *Ibid.,* p. 46.

[7] Missouri Synod Synodical Centennial Convention, *Reports and Memorials* (St. Louis: Concordia, 1947), p. 10.

[8] The Lutheran Church-Missouri Synod, *Proceedings* (St. Louis: Concordia, 1956), p. 47.

[9] *Ibid.*

[10] The Lutheran Church-Missouri Synod, *Reports and Memorials* (St. Louis: Concordia, 1962), p. 4.

[11] *Ibid.,* pp. 4-5.

[12] Graebner, p. 66.

[13] Concordia Seminary, *Academic Catalog 1988-1989* (St. Louis: Concordia Seminary), p. 8.

[14] Henry Wadsworth Longfellow, *Divina Commedia,* Sonnet One.

[15] *Proceedings,* 1944, p. 47.

[16] *Ibid.,* p. 46.

[17] *Proceedings,* 1956, p. 47.

[18] Martin Luther, "Concerning the Order of Public Worship" (1523), *Luther's Works,* American Edition, vol. 53, *Liturgy and Hymns,* ed. Ulrich S. Leupold (Philadelphia: Fortress, 1965), p. 11.

[19] *Ibid.*

[20] *Ibid.,* p. 68.

[21] *Apology of the Augsburg Confession,* Article XXIV, section 51, German text, in *Concordia Triglotta: Die symbolischen Bücher der evangelisch-lutherischen Kirche* (St. Louis: Concordia, 1921), pp. 400-402.

[22] C. F. W. Walther, *The Proper Distinction Between Law and Gospel,* trans. W. H. T. Dau (St. Louis: Concordia, [1928]), p. 248.

[23] *Book of Concord, Formula of Concord,* trans. and ed. Theodore G. Tappert (Philadelphia: Fortress, 1959), Epitome X, 3, p. 493.

[24] *Ibid.*

[25] "Die Musica ist eine schöne herrliche Gabe Gottes, und nahe der Theologie. Ich wollt mich meiner geringen Musica nicht umb was Grosses verzeihen." Martin Luther, *Sämmtliche Werke* (Erlangen: Verlag von Heyder und Zimmer, 1854), 62:309.

[26] "Ich gebe nach der Theologie der Musica den nächsten Locum und höchste Ehre." Martin Luther, *Sämmtliche Schriften* (St. Louis: Lutherischer Concordia Verlag, 1887), XXII: 1541.

[27] "Ein Schulmeister muss singen, sonst sehe ich ihn nicht an. Man soll auch junge Gesellen zum Predigtampt nicht verordnen, sie haben sich denn in der Schule wohl versucht und geübet." Martin Luther, *Sämmtliche Werke* (Erlangen: Verlag von Heyder und Zimmer, 1854), 62:308-309.

Concordia Seminary, Theological Education and The Lutheran Church—Missouri Synod in the Twenty-first Century

J. A. O. PREUS

As Concordia Seminary, St. Louis, celebrates its 150th anniversary and as we thank God for His past blessings on this great school, it is most appropriate that we look into the future and try, by our poor human wisdom but under the promises which God in His Word grants us, to see what our church and our seminary will be like in the century now dawning upon us. A study of the past is always most helpful in evaluating the future, and the other essays in this volume are obviously dealing with this subject in various ways.

It is most significant that the first two articles deal with Concordia Seminary and *theological* education, for this establishes anew that the role of a seminary is exactly that—no more and no less—to provide theological education. It is equally significant that the third article deals with the seminary faculty in relationship to *the church*, because theological education in our modern age does not take place in isolation from or opposition to the church, but there must be the closest harmony and cooperation between the two. Theological education to be significant must take place within the confines of and for the benefit of the church. The church is educating theologians to serve the church in dozens of capacities, but always as theologians of the church.

It is in this context and on this background that we shall devote the next pages to this lively and interesting topic of Concordia Seminary, theological education and the LC—MS.

We must never forget that Concordia Seminary is several years older than the Synod which maintains it. This is not simply an accident of history. The founding fathers, Dr. C. F. W. Walther and

---

J. A. O. PREUS is the former President of The Lutheran Church—Missouri Synod.

those other young pastors with him, together with the dedicated and pious lay people who resolved to establish this seminary, had come to this country for theological reasons. Their departure from their homeland was a confessional act, and their establishment of the Perry County settlement was a confessional act; but the establishment in Perry County of the little log cabin seminary which ultimately blossomed into the world-famous Concordia Seminary of today was one of their greatest acts of confession. They were not seeking prestige or the plaudits of the world, but they were seeking to confess their Biblical and Lutheran faith and to perpetuate it for their posterity. And they were wise enough and farsighted enough to understand that without a seminary for the education of pastors they had no future, and their heroic confessional acts of leaving Germany and establishing a community in America would be soon forgotten, and all the benefits lost.

So we may say at the outset that the fathers of our Synod, together with the fathers of almost all other church bodies, recognized the vital and integral relationship between theological education and their beliefs, the future of their churchly endeavors and the achievements of their goals.

Likewise, at the outset, we may assert from our own synodical experience as well as the experience of other denominations, that the seminaries greatly influence the direction of the church. If a seminary gets to be out of step with its supporting church body, if the objectives of the two begin to deviate, both are in trouble. Almost every year we read of the diverging courses which the Southern Baptist seminaries and the Southern Baptist Convention (we would call it a denomination or church) are taking, and everyone wonders how long this can continue. But the bottom line is that both suffer, and confusion and mistrust hold sway.

As we enter the twenty-first century, certain gnawing questions become more acute. At the beginning of the twentieth century great optimism filled the air. Men like John R. Mott were calling for the conversion of the entire world during this century. Foreign missions were thriving, often under the flags of European nations with the power of empire and colonialism behind them. Things were really looking up for the church.

But then it all began to fall apart. The list of the calamities of the twentieth century is perhaps longer than that of any preceding century, at least since the fall of the Roman Empire or the end of the Thirty Years War. Even our vaunted scientific advances never seem to keep up with the miseries which come upon our fallen race.

In a century which has seemed to ridicule Satan more than any other, he has had his greatest field day. Secularism has been on the march. Our own nation has fought in four major wars in the lifetime of many people still living. Depressions, droughts, atmospheric catastrophes, atomic war, acid rain, AIDS, the break-up of the home, the soaring divorce rate, the abortion holocaust, not to mention Hitler's holocaust, the deluge of pornography, the bondage of half the world's population under the iron heel of Communism, the emphasis on personal liberty at the expense of society and the family, corruption in government and in business circles, the terrible problems of racism, poverty and homelessness, the decline of the public educational system, and worst of all the rise of Satanism and every kind of godless and anti-Christian secularism which have swept away almost the entire church in countries like France and Denmark, the rise of Darwinianism, Marxism—all these and a thousand more calamities have afflicted the church in the twentieth century. That the church exists at all after this ninety year onslaught is proof positive of Christ's statement, "The gates of hell shall not prevail against My church" (Matt. 16:18).

It hardly seems necessary to add to the list above the inner struggles of the churches in the twentieth century against existential philosophy, higher criticism, the misguided application of the women's liberation movement to the ordination question and of the entire liberation movement to theology itself to the detriment of both theology and the church, and an ecumenism which rolls through the churches like a loose cannon. Just as I was writing this article, I received the news on television that the United Church of Canada by a large majority had voted to ordain homosexuals of both genders. Of course, the usual split was predicted.

Carrying these burdens, the church and theological education enter the twenty-first century. And in the church we have a generation of people who have had more schooling, both men and women, than ever before. They may have no greater wisdom, but they have had more schooling. People in America are more liberal sociologically and politically than were their parents or grandparents; they are more affluent, they are more articulate, they are nearly all influenced by the sexual revolution, they come more and more from single parent homes. Homosexuality is discussed by five year olds, whose grandmothers (still living) never knew of the existence of such practices till they learned from their husbands, and then they did not learn much.

As a young pastor I once invited a young mother to bring her children and come to church. She said, "I will send my children, but I am not worthy to come to church myself. I murdered one of my own children by having an abortion." That sounds like it came right out of the Middle Ages.

Not long ago, at a meeting, I sat next to a Catholic priest who was in charge of recruiting young men for the priesthood. Since it is well known that the Roman Catholic church is having serious problems in this area, I asked how his efforts were going. He replied that recruitment was very difficult because of the celibacy requirement, and that the kind of young men they were getting were increasingly dependent psychologically, lacking in leadership ability, and not well suited for the office to which they were aspiring. All churches need to pay particular attention to the kind of people who are coming to seminaries and being recruited for the ministry. Leadership capabilities are more necessary than ever.

Our Synod is now almost an entirely American entity. We may have some German ethnicity and nostalgia, we may still think more like Germans than do others, but we are Americans. We live in this country, we work in this country, we serve American people who are influenced by the environment in which we all live and die. Thus all the problems listed above which beset our nation also beset our people, our churches, our parish schools, and the working and thinking of our pastors as they go about their daily round of duties. Moreover, these problems spill over into theological education and the seminaries which are preparing young American men for the ministry in twenty-first century America.

Now, having attempted to look squarely at the problems facing us and the situation in which the church must carry on its work in the twenty-first century, we must realize that the church has always labored under adversity. Even in times when things looked brighter, that in itself may have been the greatest adversity because then the church tended to relax, let down its guard and feel that ultimate success was just around the corner. As Lutherans, we must always remember Luther's theology of the cross. That is all that God has promised us, and we need to remember, as pastors and men dedicating themselves to becoming pastors, that church work was never easy, never a triumph, never more than one step away from failure. Yet the God whom we serve is never more than one step away either. He guides and protects His church and we must always be alert to His purposes and intentions.

This is why in the midst of all calamities we can face the future with confidence. As Luther says, "Stood we alone in our own might our striving would be losing, but for us the one true Man doth fight. . . ." This statement is just as true today as it was in Luther's calamitous time, or when Christ Himself, journeying to the cross, said to His oft-despairing disciples, "The gates of hell shall not prevail against My church."

The disciples on Easter morning were in despair, and even on the day of His ascension "some doubted" (Matt. 28:17). But our doubts and fears and anxieties, as we watch the slow dissolution of much that we hold sacred, must never blind us to the fact that the church is never built or preserved by our efforts but only by His Word and Spirit. The power and grace of God are greater than man's greatest achievements and also his greatest failures, greater also than Satan with all his snares or the world with all its glamor and and false promises.

It is with this realistic understanding of the situation in which we live that Concordia Seminary, in celebrating one hundred and fifty years of God's blessing and of His using us for His purposes, can together with our Synod move into the twenty-first century.

Synod and seminary together must constantly monitor the society in which we live, so that we may approach our task in the best possible way. This is best done by parish pastors and lay people who live and work at the cutting edge. District and synodical officials can also be extremely helpful, and every effort must be made by all parties to keep the lines of communication open. The seminary must listen to the field, and the field to the seminary, and the officials to both. The Board of Regents must be made up of people who spend at least part of their time in the so-called "real world." This applies also to the faculty, the students, the officials of the church and its districts.

The history of our Synod has not been notable in this matter of an open and helpful listening on the part of all parties. Faculties have tended to go determinedly in their own direction, followed often by unsure and confused students whose only certainty is that the faculty is right and whoever disagrees with them is wrong—particularly if the people disagreeing are church officials, the laity, and the congregations, as recent history in both our nation and our Synod testifies. But the church must also listen to the seminary, carefully and conscientiously.

But much more important than listening to or studying the "real world" around us, the seminary, faculty, administration, board, students, and synodical officials and the church-at-large must constantly listen to the voice of our God, as He addresses us in His

Word. We must enter the twenty-first century as we entered the nineteenth, as a Christ-centered and Biblical church, firm in our adherence to our Lutheran confessional position, our priceless theological heritage.

These are not mere words when used in connection with a discussion of a seminary, theological education and the church as we enter the twenty-first century. The longer I study theology, especially the writings of Luther and the early theologians of Lutheranism, the more I become convinced that Luther's theology is unique and as vital for the church of today as it was for his own time. What other church, even after the passage of four hundred years and thousands of hours of dialogue and ecumenical discussions, has really put Christ into the center of its theology, with the primary emphasis on the doctrine of justification, the proper distinction of Law and Gospel as the hermeneutical principle for all of its theology, the ontological and substantive role of Scripture as both the normative and the causative authority in the church, and the theological and essential role of the Sacraments the way historic Lutheran theology has done? Never has there been a greater need for sound Scriptural, confessional and orthodox Lutheran theology than right now. As we enter the twenty-first century, Concordia Seminary and The Lutheran Church—Missouri Synod must rededicate themselves and our program of theological education to a reassertion of our sound Biblical and confessional heritage.

Along with rededication to our theological heritage and our responsibility as church leaders, there must go also a rededication to our mission as a living part of the church of Jesus Christ who has commissioned His entire church to preach the Gospel of the forgiveness of sins and life everlasting to all the world, to minister to people in their need, to bring His love, comfort and help to every corner of the earth. In some circles it almost appears that the only aspect of the church's mission which is receiving any emphasis is the here-and-now. Sometimes the suggestion is even made that with the decline of church attendance and religious interest in Europe and the rise of secularism in the Third World, perhaps the total role of the church pertains only to the here-and-now, as if the transcendant and the eternal have somehow been relegated to the archives as no longer relevant. The dialogs with Marxists have fostered this line of thinking, as has Liberation Theology; but at the risk of sounding fundamentalistic, permit me to say that the Bible says that the eternal and the other-worldly aspects of the Christian religion (and for that matter of most other religions) play and must continue to play a vital role in our message and our mission, as well as in any kind of theological education which claims recognition as Christian. Theological education which de-emphasizes the transcendant and the eternal is not deserving of the name theological, but has merely become a somewhat moralistic form of sociology.

And since part of Christ's mission is "teaching them to observe all things whatsoever I have commanded you," we must continue to stress Christian morals, the third use of the law of God, and the concept of personal responsibility for our actions. While the media continue to treat drug addiction, AIDS and homosexuality along with most other human problems as only social problems for which society is responsible while the patient or the practitioner bears no guilt or sense of personal accountability, yet the church must be heard with its pronouncement that "Whatsoever a man soweth that shall he also reap." It is interesting to note that people who are dealing with alcoholics or drug addicts, if they really want to help these "patients" overcome the problem, do not lay the blame at the door of pappa or momma or big bad society but squarely on the back of the addict. They point out that the responsibility and the guilt are entirely his or hers, and no cure is to be expected for the "disease" without personal acceptance of the blame.

But it seems, as we enter a new century, that the eternal aspects of the Christian faith should receive new and greater rather than less emphasis in theological education and throughout the church. With an increasingly aging population, with the undertakers and cemetery owners doing a land office business, with the sicknesses of old age constantly reminding more and more of us that the end is coming, the church will be most relevant if it speaks in clear and certain terms about both heaven and hell, about dying in the faith, about pastoral care for the countless lonely and unchurched old people, and about eternal things. Pastors should receive new and better preparation for dealing with death, bereavement and grief among their people.

At the same time, because of the drug problem, broken homes, single parent families, and for many other reasons, the work among children and young people is both more difficult and more challenging than ever before. This is another aspect of the church's mission which the twenty-first century will compel us to re-examine. It will also lay an additional burden on our parochial schools but also give them an added opportunity.

One thing that has always bothered me during my years in office is the fact that so many pastors do not seem to be active readers, do not seem to be interested in continuing their education or polishing their professional skills. The twenty-first century will make this kind of activity even more necessary. Just as doctors, engineers and other professionals need constantly to keep abreast of developments in their fields, so the pastor must do the same; but his situation is even more urgent, because the whole world is his field, all people in all conditions are his concern. He needs to be the most general of generalists at the same time as he is a specialist in theology and a person who is able to divide Law and Gospel properly, to minister with the Gospel to people who are spiritually illiterate and often intend to remain that way.

All of this and much more compels us to assert that the seminary and the church in the twenty-first century, along with all aspects of theological education must be service-oriented rather than office or title-oriented or serve-me oriented. It may be important to me to be Reverend or Doctor or Professor so-and-so, but it is not very important to the average man or woman on the street. Respect for office, like respect for royalty is constantly eroding in America and in the world. Excellent surgeons are sued by ignorant and careless patients; governmental officials, even honorable ones, are stomped on by a hostile press, who in turn are ignored by a jaded public. Jim and Tammy Bakker, Jimmy Swaggert, and Oral Roberts are scoffed at. Church officials are fair game for free-lance journalists without credentials or credibility. University presidents, the CIA, professors and even students are mocked and ridiculed. Motherhood is despised and fatherhood is a joke on half the television shows our children watch. Children themselves are debauched by sales pitches, too much money, junkies and pornographers.

It is not strange then that pastors fail to evoke the respect they had a generation ago. And it is no help at all to conjure up visions of what the ministry was like in nineteenth century Perry County or among German Russians in Kansas in 1920, or in Luther's time, or even in twentieth century Europe. We are Americans and we live among Americans (like it or not) and the church, without compromising its Scriptural and confessional faith, must recognize that the twenty-first century is right around the corner. If we expect to do the job that we all went into the ministry to do, we must not and cannot take refuge in the past or behind a collar or in a chancel, but taking the armour of God and the sword of the Spirit, applying Law and Gospel, we must get into the homes of our people, into the lives of the unchurched, and into our secularized society, not with a pre-canned program designed perhaps more to enhance ourselves than serve our neighbor, but with a testimony and a witness to Jesus Christ, "the same yesterday, today and forever"—who speaks to our secularized age just as He did to the paganized and perverted ancient world, which like our own was dying in sin. Read a few chapters of Suetonius' "Lives of the Caesars," with their accounts of the imperial public homosexual partners, their depraved wives, their bloodthirstiness, and their debauching of everything that even antiquity called decent, if you think our generation is the first in human history to have problems. And when Suetonius jades you, try Tacitus. The Christian faith made great progress against this corrupt and perverse world, and it can do so again by the power of the Word and the Spirit. The church, its theological schools and its membership can enter the twenty-first century with the same confidence that the apostles had in facing the first century, for our power in not our own, nor is our message, but all comes from the One who has sent us on His mission and called upon us to serve Him and our neighbor.

Not that God hands out His blessings like a father giving Cracker Jack to his children; for it cost money, the money which He has entrusted to our people, to educate men for the ministry. Faculties need to be recruited, educated, paid and maintained. Students nearly always need financial aid, and this amount becomes greater as more and more of them are married. Buildings need to be maintained and libraries enlarged and better equipped. Thus, as we enter the twenty-first century there must be a call for increased support from our people for this very basic work of the church of the twenty-first century.

Both the church and the theological schools need to be aware of the rapidly changing image of the ministry, or the expectations and requirements of the office. Our Synodical Standing Committee on Pastoral Ministry, of which I have had the privilege of serving as a member for the past few years, is constantly discussing such topics as recruitment, seminary admission standards, the rising cost of financing theological education, the difficult problems of suitability for the ministry, the curriculum, and many other subjects of this kind. Recently our executive, Dr. Jonathan Grothe, himself until very recently a seminary professor, brought to our attention a very stimulating article entitled "Christian Identity and Theological Education," by Hough and Cobb, published in 1985. This treatise points out what I hope we have never forgotten; namely, that in the education of pastors the basic ingredient is *theologia*, the ingredient which unites all aspects of theological education, which gives it direction and purpose. They also point out that in recent years, under the influence of many conflicting theological trends, there is great debate among theologians and churchmen as to the purpose and goal of the church itself; and it is self-evident that when this problem is not clearly answered, theological education is at sea. What are we trying to produce? What educational program do we need? Where is the church going, and what kind of people are needed for its ministry? These are very important questions.

Hough and Cobb have a very interesting section on what they call ministerial "character," which means something like the word "image." Pastors have been viewed differently in different eras, and their education has been related to this, as well as the direction the church in general has been going. During the seventeenth and eighteenth centuries in America, among the Reformed particularly (who have set the pattern for the rest of American Protestantism and increasingly also for Catholicism), the dominant character or image was the Master, an authoritative figure, a man who knew his books, university-educated in the classics and Scripture. During the nineteenth century the churches were very much influenced by German *wissenschaffliche* concepts, the scholarly and highly disciplined type. In this period the so-called four-fold pattern of theological education emerged, which the Lutherans of this country also adopted and to some extent brought with them. This was a program of Scriptural studies, dogmatics, church history and practical theology. But, "despite the best efforts of theological schools to maintain the image of professional ministers as authoritative teachers, the actual social character changed." From this emerged a minister who carried on his work in a pluralistic society as we do today, and so-called authoritative traditions were under attack. No one has the right to assert his own rightness over against others—in our case particularly if the others happen to be Lutherans. The result of this shift from the authoritarian figure who proved his point from Scripture and other authoritative books to the pastor operating in the pluralistic environment was that the great operator became the dominant figure, the great evangelist, the pulpiteer. As Hough and Cobb put it, "Oratory replaced instruction as the dominant mode of clergy activity."

My father used to laugh about a conversation he once overheard between a husband and wife who were leaving an evening service at a neighborhood Methodist church. The woman said, "That preacher was not correct in his doctrine," to which the husband in a thick Swedish accent replied, "He vas not so good for doctrine, but he vas awfully good for talking."

We are in the last stages of this era. There are still some great preachers, but they are not significant as they once were, and the television evangelist has overshadowed and perhaps exterminated them.

Concurrent with the "prince of the pulpit" image was the so-called "builder" image, which actually described most pastors who were busy building congregations, sometimes as a result of the great revivalists and pulpiteers. During this period the churches grew rapidly and in some cases solidly.

This image was followed by what is called the professional image, which is current today. The professional is part manager and part therapist or counsellor. Preaching is not emphasized, nor is theological acumen or ability in languages, history or general culture, or even knowledge of Scripture. Since therapy is not an exact science, and since theology has become almost entirely a matter of personal opinion or doubt, since confessionalism and credalism are extremely unpopular, since few of us recognize any authority, not always even God's, and since the world has to a great extent turned off the church, we find the *wissenschaffliche Theologen* of Germany and elsewhere concentrating their efforts on what ultimately ends as destructive criticism of Scripture or what little remains of the confessional base of the churches. Or the more positively and less scholarly inclined take up therapy for home consumption or sociology for the wider consumption of the church-at-large, or in the case of those who want the truly fast track, ecumenism. Hough and Cobb continue:

> Ironically, however, it is precisely this confusion that has set the stage for the new dominant ministerial characters [images]. When there is no clear consensus on what the Builder is to build, when it is not clear just what the Master is to teach, and when the functions of the Pastoral Director are cut loose from their theological moorings, then what can be said about the purpose of the ministry?

A very pertinent question, it seems to me.

Again they say

> Theological consensus on the purpose of the church . . . did not emerge . . . and the theological climate now seems less conducive to consensus building. . . . Confusion about the ministry has increased. Reeling under the impact of post-Neo-orthodox theological criticism and the resulting cacophany of theological voices, and working in congregations with vastly

differing expectations, it is little wonder that ministers find no authoritative basis for their profession. . . . What conclusions can be drawn? Theological education is torn between academic norms, defined chiefly as excellence in the historical disciplines, and modern professional norms defined in terms of excellence in performing the functions church leaders are expected to perform. On the one hand is the character of the Master; on the other, that of the Manager. Partly as a result of this tension, theological schools do not succeed well by either standard.

This same tension exists in our LC—MS between the expectations of the church which supports the seminaries and the faculties who have devoted countless years to study, graduate work, parish work and teaching to perfect themselves for their craft, and yet fully regard themselves as servants of the church. The tension between what the seminaries often want to teach and what the churches and the Synod feel are needed is often great.

Yet it is my firm belief that if any organization can solve this problem which afflicts nearly all churches, Catholic and Protestant, including the Lutheran, it is our own dear LC—MS. Concordia Seminary is much beloved by or people and our pastors. Our Synod is committed to an educated ministry, to close cooperation and communication between Synod and seminary, to a lively interest on the part of our congregations to activities on our seminary campuses. Contributions by our people, while seemingly never sufficient, have been enormous. The ministry is held in high respect because of our pastors by and large proclaim the everlasting Gospel with power and conviction. We have been spared many of the incredible communication gaps which have plagued many mainline denominations, both liberal and conservative, between the theological school and the man in the pew. As we witness the moral, theological, financial and spiritual decline of the mainline churches we see the membership of these churches decline due to the pill, abortion, sociological pressures, the onward march of secularism and even governmental meddling, we can only pray that God will spare some, perhaps only the seven thousand in Israel, but some who will continue to bear witness to the truth of the Gospel, the great preaching of Law and Gospel, strict adherence to Scripture and our confessional basis. I like to believe that on the basis of one hundred and fifty years of faithful service, Concordia Seminary and our beloved LC—MS will continue to serve our heavenly Father with the strong and vital proclamation of the truth of the Gospel in the midst of this crooked and perverse world for another century and a half or as long as the world stands. May the God who has so richly blessed us hitherto continue to be with us as we prepare men to go forth proclaiming Christ!

Five Decades of Reflection

HERBERT M. KERN

My Seminary

I thank God for Concordia Seminary! I came to Concordia believing, "All Scripture is inspired by God" (2 Tim. 3:16). During seminary years my professors confirmed my God-given faith. "Thy Word is a lamp to my feet and a light to my path" (Ps. 119:105). My seminary education planted my feet firmly on this path. Praise God I have stayed on it. For the last well-nigh fifty years I have thought much about the work of the pastor and the training the seminary provides. I am grateful for the invitation to share my reflections as part of Concordia Seminary's 150th anniversary celebration.

Some of my professors were marvelous examples of faith and love. Their devotion to the truth left a lasting mark. They impressed on me that the pastor's calling is a high, noble profession and moved me to want to be the best God would enable me to be. A few of my professors were satisfied to have me merely parrot the information they handed out. Others made Scripture exciting. They gave me a good grasp of theological principles. They developed in me the desire to be a lifelong student of theology and to be acquainted with other fields of study as well.

I received good grades at the seminary. After graduation, I thought I knew a great deal. Soon I realized I was just a raw recruit with limited training. There was much to learn. Many pastors have told me they felt the same way.

It's easy to criticize a person or institution, for whatever is human is imperfect. My purpose in mentioning the following is motivated by the prayerful hope that our beloved seminary may be ever more effective in its task.

My professors properly stressed the importance of pure doctrine and consistently warned against aberrations from the truth. But as I recall, they placed more emphasis on knowing correct facts about the Lord than on the surpassing worth of knowing Christ Jesus

---

HERBERT M. KERN is Pastor Emeritus of Calvary Lutheran Church, East Meadow, New York.

(Phil. 3:8). This is always a danger whether in the seminary or a confirmation class. Teachers of the Word must beware lest a living faith be replaced by a book faith.

It was assumed students were honest. Yet I remember one person in our class who openly cheated during examinations. He later held a prominent position in one of our Concordia colleges. Others have told me of similar cheating that went on during their seminary years. Cadets of the United States Military Academy at West Point pledge they "will not lie, cheat, or steal or tolerate those who do." A seminary that trains men to be leaders in the war against the forces of evil should maintain a standard not only as high as that of a secular institution but as high as the expectations of the Scripture itself.

Two of us during our senior year preached each Sunday to a small congregation about sixty miles from St. Louis. We also did some house-to-house canvassing there. (I had spent my entire vicarage canvassing.) Once I was involved in some door-to-door visitation in the area around the seminary campus. Other than that I had no missionary or evangelistic experience as a seminarian.

Some of the most valuable training I had came from people outside our Synod. This included practical instruction in the following: congregational evangelism and Bible study, personal Bible study, public speaking, and personal evangelism and evangelistic preaching. (The latter by God's grace led to five summers of evangelistic tent ministry, thirty-one years on the Lutheran Hour sermon research committee, my assignment to start a mission congregation I served for thirty-two years, and training over one hundred seminary graduates in opening new churches.)

My Church

The Lutheran Church—Missouri Synod has been described as a sleeping giant. The majority of our people must be awakened. Many are committed to the Lord, but they need to be challenged and equipped to demonstrate their commitment. Our Lord has given us the precious treasure of the Good News. Yet vast numbers of our people do not openly confess their Savior (Matt. 10:32f.). I have observed that the one word Missouri Synod people hesitate to use in the proper way outside the church building is "Jesus."

For the last thirty years I have studied and lectured about those zealous slaves of Satan, the Jehovah's Witnesses. The average Jehovah's Witness spends 10 hours a month going from door to door peddling a false gospel. This "field service" is the only record the Kingdom Hall keeps of its membership. If we used a similar criterion for church membership, how many members would the Missouri Synod have?

In my involvement with a few dozen congregations besides my own I have discovered that about one-third of our Missouri Synod people when asked, "Are you a Christian? Are you sure you are going to heaven?" give the wrong answer. They reply along this line, "Yes. I believe in God. I was confirmed. I pray. I go to church. I live a good life. I work in the church. etc." A person, of course, is not saved by stating the right answer. Many who give a wrong answer no doubt truly trust in Jesus as their personal Savior. The point is that believers ought to be taught to express their faith in Jesus clearly and correctly.

My experience agrees with a national survey taken several years ago in which 46.3 percent of Missouri Synod laity expressed the belief that there are many religions in the world leading to the same God. Is this ignorance of the way of salvation and the failure to testify to the Savior due to their neglect to meet Him in His Word?

It is said that a congregation's spiritual level generally does not rise above that of its pastor. The relation of pastor and congregation is similar to that of husband and wife. In time one reflects the attitudes of the other. The spiritual depth of a pastor will be mirrored in his people. The same is true if his attitude is negative. Not all is well with our clergy. That is perhaps one reason for the spiritual lethargy of much of our laity. Surely this is of deep concern to our seminary professors and is an incentive to work even harder to mold our future pastors according to the divine pattern.

My fellow pastors

I respect most of the pastors who share with me the honor of serving Jesus in our Synod. They love the Lord, their work, and their church. I am ashamed of others. I hasten to add I am ashamed of certain things about myself, too.

Certain actions of our clergy are scandalous. For example, some estimates are that the divorce rate among our Missouri Synod pastors is as high as fifteen to twenty percent. One of the big disillusionments of my life was the unloving, unforgiving spirit shown by altogether too many clergy during the controversy of the 1970s. In that period of turmoil our leaders had a grand opportunity to show that Christianity works, that we can disagree with our brethren without being unChristian. We failed. Pastors slander the synodical president and district presidents. I know a few pastors who refuse to talk to their district president and won't allow him in their church.

I was told about a layman who went to his first synodical convention with great anticipation. He expected to be inspired and uplifted. He was disappointed. On his return he told his family, "I was shocked by the many dirty jokes the pastors told." It is not enough for our pastors to insist on sound doctrine and to tell their people to live godly lives. Pastors must practice what they preach.

My brothers on the Concordia Seminary faculty

What an awesome privilege and responsibility is yours! I thank God for what you do. Forgive me for not praying enough for you. I'm sure your task is more difficult and far-reaching than people realize. What an impact you have on your students' future! What headaches and turmoil you can spare them! What countless hours of wasted time you can save them in dealing with matters that detract from the main function of their ministry! You cannot work miracles. You can work only with the human material the church sends you. Those most qualified do not always enter the ministry. God give you faith, love, strength, wisdom, and joy. What follows is written with love for you and our church. Dozens of pastors—including those I've talked to in the preparation of this article—agree with my views. My earnest prayer is that eternal good may result from this article for God's glory.

My suggestions

May the Lord guide professors to observe the proper balance between doctrine and life, the theoretical and the practical, the intellectual and the devotional. Orthodox doctrine is basic. Constant emphasis must also be laid on clergy conduct. Pastors must be above reproach (1 Tim. 3:2). We must continue to pray with Walther, "Gott, gebe uns ein frommes Ministerium." God, give us a devout clergy. Many excellent pastors graduate from the seminary. Others cause much grief to congregations and district presidents. Not everybody who passes through the seminary has the faith or competence to serve as a pastor. In certifying graduates for ordination it might be well for the faculty to bear in mind the words of James 3:1, "Let not many become teachers."

Professors may take for granted that students entering the seminary know the Bible. Few do. Many do not go through our system of synodical colleges. They lack a through Bible background.

A parent of a student presently at the seminary told me, "I wish my son had gone to a Bible college first. It would have been good if he had learned more personal Bible study and been required to read through the whole Bible for a good understanding of God's message before reaching the seminary." A highly respected professor of Concordia Seminary said he wished that before students could start their seminary work, they would take a comprehensive course in the Bible. I suggest the faculty give prayerful thought to finding the best solution to this situation.

Students must know the Word. They must be encouraged to know Him Who is the living Word. It is important for students to become acquainted with what theologians have written. It is much more important they strive to reach the point where it can be said, ". . . they recognized that they had been with Jesus" (Acts 4:13).

Seminarians learn to proclaim Christ (Col. 1:28) to large and small groups. They must also be challenged to share their faith in Jesus on a one-to-one basis. Personal evangelism should not be just a program, a required subject, or an elective. It is to be a way of life for pastors and all God's saints. Students ought to leave the seminary not with a maintenance mentality but with a burning desire to make Jesus known. They must know more than how correctly to define evangelism and what is wrong with certain methods of evangelism. They must do it. They are to be encouraged to talk about their faith in Jesus with their fellow students and outside the seminary buildings with others.

Most of our pastors did not learn to be personal evangelists until years after they were in the parish ministry. A good many never learn to be zealous witnesses of Jesus.

Jesus teaches us, "Beware of false prophets" (Matt. 7:15). The seminary obeys this command. Our Lord also says, "Go make disciples" (Matt. 28:20). The seminary must do more than specialize in defensive teaching. Students need also to be taught to take the offensive, to reach out lovingly, aggressively with the truth.

The pastoral ministry falls into three areas: God (Scripture), society, and self. The seminary provides students with a rather through exegetical, doctrinal, etc. training. Sufficient attention must also be given to a clear understanding of the culture of our day and to personal dynamics. In my opinion the seminary curriculum has neglected the last two areas.

Too many seminary graduates are unequipped for much of the nitty-gritty work of the parish ministry. A fortunate few have had varied, valuable experience as vicars or field workers. Most know little, if anything, about stewardship and church finances. They have not learned how to prepare a Bible study and how to teach the Bible to adults and young people. They have had little or no experience with funerals and weddings. Some "bishops" have refused to let their vicar visit the sick or make evangelistic calls. A goodly number of us made no sick visits until after our graduation and ordination.

I suggest students in their field work each year be required to engage in the following: evangelistic calls, sick and shut-in calls, stewardship planning, Sunday School teacher training, church council meetings, Baptism, etc. Experiences that blend the academic with the practical prove most valuable.

Students should be encouraged to hear, meet, and work with pastors and others who have expertise in certain practical areas. They should be given a list of authors and materials dealing with such subjects as: church growth, personal evangelism, devotional life, adult membership instruction, confirmation of children, sick visitation, pre-marital and grief counseling, pastors' marriage, preaching, worship, youth work, cults, congregational Bible study, church administration, recruiting and training of Sunday School teachers, church finances, financial campaigns.

Congregations expect seminary graduates to have some skill in these areas. Students should be made aware of every possible resource so they know where to turn for help. A pastor who keeps learning will develop skills and gather useful information along the way. The earlier he learns such skills and knows what is available, the better he can serve people.

Our minds must be closed to every seduction. Yet students must not have spiritual blinders put on them so they can look only one way. When they get into the parish, they are exposed to different points of view. If they are unprepared, they are apt to make fools of themselves and fail to help people.

Students must not be instilled with a suspicion of everything that is non-Missouri. We have learned much from non-Missourians and non-Lutherans. The Church Growth movement has given us some valuable insights and direction. Synod's Dialogue Evangelism approach has drawn heavily from the Kennedy evangelism program. Our mission leaders are giving serious consideration to the business world's telemarketing method to begin new congregations. Our seminaries and colleges regularly use the secular procedure of the phonathon to raise money.

The renewal movement is not without its dangers. But we can learn much from it: the joy of worship, the expectancy of the living God to keep His promises, a personal relation with Jesus, and emphasis on the work of the Holy Spirit. In our warnings against the renewal movement let us beware lest we oppose God Himself.

We must not spend too much time discussing the restriction of female activities in our church body. Let's rejoice that many women are eager and competent to serve the Lord. Together with them let's do what Jesus tells us to do—proclaim His Gospel.

Luther's feet were planted firmly in both worlds. He was thoroughly at home in the Word, and he knew where people were at. So must also the present-day professor. He must love both books and people. He must, by his actions and disposition, be approachable. Students appreciate the professor with an open door policy, in whom they can confide in a climate of trust. A professor may do more good outside than in the classroom.

I taught at one of our synodical colleges and know how living in the ivory tower can insulate one from the outside world. I suggest that every professor be encouraged to take a sabbatical leave every seven years or so. The sabbatical ought not be a study leave, but a practical leave, if possible outside St. Louis. In the sabbatical the professor should strive to become acquainted first hand with the fears and hurts of people, to make calls on the unchurched, to comfort the grieved, meet with the church council, etc. Such an experience would help professors get in touch with the reality of parish life and understand the pressures and problems of the pastoral ministry. This would better equip professors to apply their teachings and theories to the day-to-day duties of the parish pastor.

How much seminary professors and all who teach can learn from Jesus! Our Savior lived close to people. For three years He taught His chosen messengers the truths of the kingdom. His preparation was not just for the future. During those three years He gave His apostles practical experience in the field. He sent them out to preach and work as they saw Him doing it.

Some will say: There is not enough time to do all these things at the seminary. For the eternal welfare of many inside and outside the Missouri Synod may earnest prayer be made to the Lord of the Church. May our seminary faculty inquire of Him whether they should take a fresh, bold look at our system, reshape our priorities, and make certain drastic changes in our traditional methods.

My ideal

What kind of pastor should our seminary faculty members under the direction of the Holy Spirit try to produce? What qualities should they seek to inculcate? A student does not come to the seminary with a full-blown faith. Professors can nurture that faith in whatever course they teach—whether it be systematics, hermeneutics, or homiletics. The following is a partial description of the ideal. It is my deep-felt hope that this ideal will influence faculty members as they train future pastors.

First, a living faith in Jesus ought to characterize a pastor. He should hold to pure doctrine. Above all, he must love the Savior. When people see a pastor, they should see some of Jesus in him. A pastor should be able to say with the apostle Paul, "Join in imitating me . . . live as you have an example in us" (Phil. 3:17).

Few occupations are as undisciplined as the parish ministry. When he receives program material from synodical and district headquarters, a pastor can say, "It won't work here" and throw the materials into the waste basket. As long as he does not rock the boat, he is safe. If his congregation meets the budget and his salary is paid, he can just coast lazily along. How essential it is that the pastor has a growing love for Jesus, loyalty to His church, and a deep sense of his accountability to the Lord!

Second, a pastor ought to love and respect his people. He must regard himself as a servant figure, not an authority figure. He should find out the real needs of his parishioners and strive to meet them in and outside the pulpit with the compassion of Christ.

A loving pastor is honest and levels with his people. He admits he has struggles and doubts and needs God's forgiveness like others. He is mindful he must live a consistent Christian life and that what he is at home is more important than what he is in public.

A pastor who loves God's saints will preach down-to-earth sermons that apply the forgiving, sustaining love of God to them. Recently while visiting out-of-state I heard one of our pastors preach a sermon that was doctrinally acceptable but dull and dry as dust. It had one poor illustration, no helpful applications to everyday life. It was an act of mercy when the preacher finally said "Amen." Thank God many Lutheran Church—Missouri Synod worship services exalt Jesus, emphasize correct doctrine and bring comfort and challenge to the churched and unchurched.

A pastor who loves people will, like the apostle Paul, be willing to become all things to all men (1 Cor. 9:22). While firm, he is flexible. A young seminary graduate came to a church in which a sizable number of people had no Missouri Synod background. The church had followed an open Communion policy for many years. On his first Sunday in the parish without any discussion or instruction of his people the new pastor announced, "From now on no one but a Missouri Synod Lutheran will receive the Sacrament at our altar." What tactlessness! How much permanent damage such insensitivity can cause to souls for whom Jesus died!

Over the years I have been troubled by the fact that pastors do not always speak highly of their congregation. The seminary can render a valuable service by encouraging students to develop patient, forgiving love in imitation of their Lord. The pastor and the congregation ought not to take a "you/me" but rather a "we" position. God calls them to be partners to serve Him with gladness and gratitude.

Some congregations have a long history of infighting. A layman told me there is more hatred in his church than outside it. Pastors need strength from the Lord to work with obnoxious people. Sometimes congregations need strength to deal with negligent and incompetent pastors. Those pastors who have learned something about interpersonal relationships before entering the parish have a big advantage. Some pastors never learn how to get along with people. Everybody suffers as a result.

The vast majority of our pastors do not work by the clock. They work up to seventy hours a week, even more at times. Some work too much. But not all are so conscientious. One pastor notified his members that his is a nine to five job. In another case a parishioner called the parsonage at 7 p.m., stating that a death had occurred in the family. The minister replied, "Call me again in the morning." A pastor who loves his people is willing to spend and be spent (2 Cor. 12:15). He does not feel sorry for himself, complain how tough his job is and how little he is paid. He loves what he is doing. He has a heart for the people he serves, and they sense it.

A shepherd of Jesus is to be kind and caring to his fellow pastors as well as to his people. He ought to accept both as they are. When a pastor is hurting, his fellow pastors at conferences and elsewhere should offer him fellowship and support and pray for his spiritual and emotional health. Brother pastors should feel free to share their doubts and fears in addition to their faith.

Third, a pastor ought to live his faith in a spirit of joy. The apostle Paul's joy often arose from conflict. Despite hard work, shipwreck, imprisonment, beating, and stoning he remained joyful. His was a joy of substance. Joy should be the hallmark of every pastor. He is a saved child of God headed for heaven. Through Jesus the victory is his. He is on the winning side. He can't lose. How exciting! Every call he makes, every prayer he offers, every Word of God he speaks— everything he does in the name of Jesus—has eternal value. A pastor

is to reflect this confident joy in leading worship, meetings, cate-
chetical classes, visiting the sick, and in his ministry to the dying
and grieved.

Joy in the Lord attracts people to Jesus, the church, and the
pastoral ministry. With joy in his heart the pastor is to "never flag
in zeal, be aglow with the Spirit, serve the Lord" (Rom. 12:11). God
make all of us—professors, pastors and people—such servants of
Jesus!

Luther's View of History:
A Theological Use of the Past

LEWIS W. SPITZ

"If the peasants but knew the subjects of our learned discourse," Luther observed, "they would hoot us and hiss us!" Our subject is one of gigantic proportions which can, however, be dealt with effectively only by paying meticulous attention to detail. I propose to conquer this subject or at least to attack it in three parts, like Caesar's Gaul, and then to draw upon those thoughts for some general conclusions regarding Luther and history.

I. Luther's knowledge of classical and humanist history may explain his approach to history on one level.

II. Luther's emphasis on God's involvement in history finds its corollary in man in history standing before God and before men or humankind.

III. Luther's special attention paid to the heroes of history on the one hand and to the lowliest of people on the other serves as a good test case of his view of history.

I

Luther's knowledge of classical and humanist history and its influence on his historical conceptions.

In his *Address to the Municipalities* Luther voiced his well-known lament:

How much I regret that we did not read more of the poets and the historians, and that nobody thought of teaching us these. Instead of such study I was compelled to read the devil's rubbish—the scholastic philosophers and sophists with such cost, labor and detriment, from which I have had trouble enough to rid myself.

If he felt the deprivation of his early years, was he able effectively to compensate for this deficiency in his later years? At the Leipzig

LEWIS W. SPITZ is William R. Kenan Professor of History at Stanford University, Stanford, California.

debate Dr. Johannes Eck expressed admiration for Luther's ability in Latin, and Peter Mosellanus (Schade) who presided at the debate, commented upon the excellence and precision of his Greek. Four months after Luther's death Melanchthon wrote in his *Vita* that Luther read many ancient Latin authors, Cicero, Virgil, Livy and others.[1] He read them, said Melanchthon, not as youths who make excerpts, but for teaching and images of human life, and with his firm and true memory he retained them and kept them before his eyes. He seems to imply that Luther did his basic reading of the classics in school and as an arts student.

Melanchthon, as usual, had it right, for in the *Table Talks* there are fifty-nine references to Cicero, fifty citations from Virgil, but the historian Livy fell to one side, and there are sixty-one references to Aristotle. In his writings and correspondence, Aristotle, Cicero and Virgil are most frequently cited, far more than any other classical authors, followed by Terence, Horace, Plato, Quintilian, Homer, and Ovid, roughly in that order. There are individual scattered references to Aesop, Plautus, Suetonius, Herodotus, Xenophon, Ammianus Marcellinus, Juvenal, Caesar, Aeschylus, Minucius Felix, Pliny, Tacitus, Demosthenes, Apuleius, Polycrates, Plutarch, Sulpetius, Severnus, Parmenides, Zeno, and a few others. Most of the authors whom Luther cited frequently had been published in Germany by 1520.[2]

Frequency of reference or quotation does not, of course, tell us everything, for the references to Aristotle are often pejorative. But it is obvious that the historians are less quotable than the philosophers and rhetoricians, which does not mean that their total impact on his thought was of less importance. Moreover, as E. Gordon Rupp observed in pointing out that there are many more classical references in Luther's *De Servo Arbitrio* than in Erasmus' *De Libero Arbitrio,* Luther's allusions were frequent but often very subtle and not used in an obvious or ostentatious manner.[3] It is not always possible to tell which allusions came from reading and which from conversations with colleagues.

Above all, Melanchthon had a formative influence on Luther's thought about history. Luther discussed the history of Tacitus with him, Melanchthon related, even on the journey to Torgau, on April 3, 1537. Melanchthon later on, between 1555 and 1560, gave lectures on world history.[4] A comparison of Melanchthon's *Introduction to the Chronicon* and Luther's prefaces to various historical works such as Hedio's *Chronicle* of 1539 or to Cuspinian's *Caesares* of 1541 reveals many similarities in their ideas about history. Twenty years after the Leipzig debate Luther commented that at that time he had not been well versed in history and had attacked the papacy *a priori* on the basis of the Scriptures, but that now he appreciated the correspondence of the histories and Scripture and could attack the papacy *a posteriori* from the histories.[5] In 1537, in fact, Luther wrote his own sharp attack on the monstrous fraud of the *Donatio Constantini*.[6] As a younger man he had been led by Hutten's edition done by Schöffer in 1520 of Lorenzo Valla's *De Donatione Constantini* to conclude that the papacy was the anti-Christ.

Luther did develop a deeper interest in history during the final three lustra of his life. He wrote prefaces to various "historical" works: *Vorrede zu Spalatin, magnifice consolatoria exempla et sententiae ex vitis et passionibus sanctorum . . . collectae; Vorrede zu Robert Barnes, Vitae Romanorum Pontificum; Vorede zu Epistola S. Hieronymus ad Evagrium de potestate, 1538; Vorrede zu Johannes Kymäus, Ein alt christlich Konzilium . . . zu Gangro; Vorrede zu Historia Galeatii Capellae, 1538; Vorrede zu Epistola S. Hieronymi ad Evagrium de potestat, 1538; Prefatio zu Georg Major Vitae Parrum, 1544; Vorrede zu Papstreue Hadrian IV. und Alexandrus III. gegen Kaiser Freidrich Barbarossa, 1545.* These prefaces show that Luther shared with the humanists a passionate interest in history, not merely like the annalists and chroniclers in particular events, but in the entire sweep of history. His writings were replete with historical reflections and judgments. The rising tide of cultural nationalism, which antedated the Reformation by a century and a half, increased the humanists' interest in their own people's history.[7] Histories should not be "cold and dead," Luther declared, but should serve useful moral purposes.[8] Good history requires good historians, men not afraid to write the truth, the "Lion-hearted."

Luther was fascinated also with the inner meaning and nature of history. God is active everywhere in history, though hidden, disguised as though concealed behind a mask (*larva*). Faith sees beyond fate and chance to the God whose Word reveals the true meaning and content of history. In the *Introduction* or *Preface* to *Galeatius Capella's History of the Reign of Francesco II Sforza, Duke of Milan,* who played a key role in the relations of Charles V and Francis I, Luther declares that "histories are a very precious thing," for "histories are nothing else than a demonstration, recollection, and sign of divine action and judgment, how He upholds, rules, obstructs, prospers, punishes, and honors the world, and especially men, each according to his just desert, evil or good." "The historians, therefore, are the most useful people," he commented, "and the best teachers, so that one can never honor, praise, and thank them enough."[9]

Arnold Berger argued that Luther saw history as a completion of the Bible, as a kind of *Weltbibel*.[10] That may be saying too much, but as Luther's interest in history grew, he did come to see the value of chronology as an aid to exegesis and for the light it shed on church history. He constructed his *Supputatio annorum mundi*, 1541, or *Reckoning of the Years of the World*, which was a chronological table so that, he explained, he

> could always have before his eyes and see the time and years
> of historical events which are described in Holy Scriptures
> and remind himself of how many years the patriarchs, judges,
> kings and princes lived and ruled or over how long a period
> of time one succeeded the other.

Possibly inspired by Eusebius, whose work he admired, he did three columns of events and dates for East, West, and German history and worked out parallel traditions of Biblical history and secular events. He projected the dates from creation to the year 1540, dividing the table up by millennia. He listed the Indulgences Controversy as a major event of the early sixteenth century! He drew on contemporary histories to fix dates, but where there was a conflict between the Scriptural data and that of some secular source, such as a chronology ascribed to Megasthenes, he opted for the reliability of the Scriptures. Although history was of great importance to the Wittenberg theology at the outset of the Reformation and Luther promoted it at the University, there is no real evidence that he sought to have chairs of history established in the university, as has been asserted, even though in the *Address to the Christian Nobility of the German Nation* in 1520 he declared such a step to be desirable.[11]

To return for a moment to Luther and the classical historians, it is instructive to note not just the frequency of citation, but also what he derived from them beyond their general pragmatic point of view. He regretted that so little remained of the total writings of his favorite historian, Livy.[12] The Italian humanist Sabellicus, who so maligned the Germans, imitated Livy, but nothing came of it.[13] Anticipating Leopold von Ranke, who wrote about both the Reformation and the Renaissance popes to prove that he was capable of impartiality, Luther commented that unfortunately Livy had written only the Roman side of the story and not that of Carthage as well.[14] Speaking of the story of Cain and Abel, Luther exclaimed: "What tragedies Cicero and Livy would have made of it."[15] He ascribes sayings to Livy such as: "The worst part befalls him who triumphs!"[16] He commented that he had previously read the history of Melchisedek and Abraham as though it were a story from Livy.[17] Mostly, he confessed, he missed in the ancients the majesty and glory of God's Word, for all that they relate is like the glorifying of man, but that is like straw that is "gone with the wind."[18]

The other Roman historians are met only in passing, Sallust, Suetonius, and Tacitus. Of these, like the German humanists, Luther is much preoccupied with Tacitus. Tacitus was the only literary source of note who wrote about the Germans between Julius Caesar and Ammianus Marcellinus. It has been said that his *Germania* is the most annotated text squeezed by the philologists and historians for all its meanings next to the text of the New Testament. Like the German humanists, Luther spoke of the picture of the early Germans, the noble savages, that Tacitus gives. They pulled together, helped each other, fed each other, and then moved on (*Germania* 21-23).[19] Tacitus preoccupied him frequently.[20] When in August, 1538, Melanchthon edited Tacitus' *Germania,* he included a Greek poem dedicated to Luther's son John.[21] In *Wider Hans Wurst* Luther commented that Tacitus had written of the drunkenness of the Germans and added that this problem had gotten much worse. In that same work he quoted Suetonius as reporting on a monstrous person who said, "I wish that after my death the world would be destroyed by fire," to which Emperor Nero replied: "Yes, I wish it would happen while I am still alive."[22]

Luther made virtually no use of the Greek historians, such as Herodotus, Thucydides, and Polybius. He does refer to Xenophon, but as a philosopher and a moralist, not as the historian of the *Anabasis.* On the other hand, he made good use of the ancient legists and applied their views of the law to contemporary problems, a subject deserving of further scholarly investigation. Where either tyrants or the unruly masses seize the government, the histories and lawyers tell us, evil befalls the state. He was at ease with the ancient historians and the world of classical antiquity. "If I were a youth," he exclaimed, "I would devote myself to Cicero, but with my judgment nevertheless confirmed in the Sacred Scriptures."[23] He hoped that God would be kind and merciful to Cicero and men like him, for he was the best, wisest and most diligent man.[24]

II

Luther's emphasis on God's involvement in history finds its corollary in man in history standing before God and before men or mankind (*coram deo; coram mundo*).

In his early writings up to 1518 Luther had been predominantly concerned with the position of man as he stands *coram deo,* the sinner standing in the presence of a righteous God and in need of conversion.[25] But from 1518 on, after the posting of the theses, he was forced to think explicitly about questions of law, ecclesiastical and worldly justice, society, man *coram mundo.*[26] He was forced next into using history as a weapon in controversy. After his experience at the Leipzig debate, when appeals to the history of the councils and the early church were made in order to refute the inerrancy of popes and councils and to point to doctrinal deviations, Luther called history "the mother of truth." His views of history are deeply imbedded in his strange dynamic theology. History, like nature, is indebted to the mystery of the creation.[27]

For Luther God is immanent in his creation and in history. God is omnipotent, omniscient, omnipresent. Reflecting the mystics he wrote that there is nothing so small but God is smaller, nothing so large but God is larger, etc., and He is in, with, and under all things.[28] "The World is full of God!"[29] "God is even to be found in the Cloaca," he explains to Erasmus in the *De Servo Arbitrio,* 1525.[30] Some of the most telling passages on God's rule over world history are to be found in his commentaries on the Psalms, on Genesis, and on the Sermon on the Mount. A few characteristic statements regarding the role of God as Lord of history will speak volumes, for Luther has a way of expressing ideas more effectively than most scholars.

"For no kingdom or government stands and functions of its own human power or cleverness, but it is God alone who gives it, establishes it, upholds it, rules it, protects it, preserves it, and also removes it. Everything is grasped by His hand and hangs suspended in His power," he wrote to John Frederick in his *Commentary on Daniel.*[31]

He described the course of history and especially the history of His saints as God's masquerades behind which He hides, ruling the world in which He strangely moves about and rumbles.[32] "The world is God's playground, for He has put down the mighty from their thrones and has exalted those of low degree" (Luke 1:52). *Ita Deus cum regnis ludit!* [33]

Why is it, Luther asked, that for twenty years the Empire had been taking measures against the Turks but without effect? It is because of internal corruption, he answered in his *Commentary on Psalm 2:5:* "Our sins have stirred up the wrath of God against us. Since He, therefore, wished to lay a punishment on us, He armed our enemies, the Turks, with anger and cruelty against us. But to us He sent fear, so that it is rightly thrown up to us that we have forgotten our valor and have degenerated from our ancestors. In this way He threw into disorder His own people the Jews, under Nebuchadnezzar, the Babylonians under Darius and Cyrus, the Persians under Alexander, the Greeks under the imperium of the Romans. For this little verse has always cast down and confused the enemies of Christ, and it will overthrow the Turk and Pope also. . . .[34]

Here are some representative expressions regarding God's immanent working in history. "God's guns are always loaded. He battered the Jews to pieces with the Romans, the Romans with the Vandals and the Goths, the Chaldeans with the Persians, the Greeks with the Turks. . . . Perhaps there will also be a bullet for us Germans which will not miss us; for we have conducted ourselves outrageously and still do."[35] "When God speaks, he casts one kingdom or four away. When he utters a sound, the whole world trembles. . . . His voice does not sound like other voices and instruments; with Him word and deed are identical. No sooner does He speak than it comes to pass."[36] A dynamic *translatio imperii* concept! What a giant, what a hero God is, Luther exclaimed, for when He says something, it is done.[37] *"Quando enim Deus verbum emittit, szo geets mit Gewalt."*[38] Like Hegel's "cunning reason," God works *e contrario,* (or *sub contraria specie*), not in a straight line.

It is time for a bit of analysis. Henri Strohl asserted that Luther's concept of an active and lively God, dispersing justice and immediately present, is new to the sixteenth century.[39] John Headley explains that "In his doctrine of the Word of God ontological and metaphysical categories disappear before religious and historical ones; the deed of God replaces the being of God as the central element of his theology."[40] "Luther's view of history," he continues, "was biblical rather than Augustinian; in every feature it imparted its scriptural origins, and in the reformer's doctrine of the Word of God it rested upon the substance of Scripture."[41] Martin Schmidt adds the thought that the Biblical origin of Luther's historical "categories" is to be seen more in terms of the realism and concreteness of these terms than in a literal implementation of them, for they are Biblical in spirit, not merely in letter.[42]

Some scholars have been misled by the fact that Luther was an Augustinian into believing that his church-state theory or the two kingdoms doctrine is in some way a repristination of Augustine's two kingdoms, really five kingdoms, as though in history man is caught "between God and Satan," an almost dualistic notion. While, as Helmar Junghans has pointed out, Luther owed something to

medieval patterns, specifically to Occam and Biel, what is striking
is that Luther was so different from them.[43] Certainly he owed little
or nothing to the *Via Gregorii*. Like Melanchthon, who told Luther
that he understood St. Paul better than did Augustine, Eric W.
Gritsch, in his brilliant and lively book, *Martin—God's Court Jester:
Luther in Retrospect* (Philadelphia, 1983), points to the difference
between Luther and Augustine, who, after all, wrote before the medieval institutionalization of the church. Gritsch cites Luther's approach to the Word in terms of Wilhelm Pauck's longtime distinction
between *Deus dicens,* God speaking in general, and *Deus loquens,*
God addressing Himself to me.[44] Gritsch stresses the Scriptures as
the source of Luther's historical thought. Yes, Heinrich Bornkamm
was correct when he wrote, "The pattern after which Luther models
his picture of history is the Old Testament."[45] God rules both realms,
the kingdom of the spirit and the kingdoms of this world. One result
was a transcendence of total pessimism, characteristic of much medieval thought. Luther, for example, concluded in his Genesis commentary, 1535-1545: "There is in the world, such as it is, more good
than evil."[46]

III

Luther's special attention paid to the heroes of history on the
one hand and to the lowliest of people on the other serves as a good
test case of his view of history.

God works within us, all men, but not without us; we are his
larvae or masks. Yet, God has special agents whom He uses to transform his "Word" into action.[47] These men of action Luther calls heroes, *Helden, Wundermänner, Wunderleute.* They serve God's purposes, sometimes unwittingly, and the result of their actions cannot
always be understood by reason. By wondrous wisdom and power
they help extend God's rule in the world and in the church. God
sometimes chooses unlikely candidates in order to demonstrate his
own power.[48] The hero is called by a sign, word, or direct movement
of the Holy Spirit. Some heroes have no idea they are designated
heroes until they have performed a great feat, such as David or
Samson. Real heroes are a gift of God to the people.[49] Luther distinguished religious and pagan heroes, both being instruments of
God, but the former doing the more important work (*opus proprium*).[50] God uses the *opus alienum* as a mask and as a vehicle for
the *opus proprium.* Luther created a "heroic" hierarchy by which he
ranked people in accordance with the amount of Spirit in them. The
degree of their humility and faith determines their position in his

pantheon.[51] Success is an indispensable sign of the hero's authenticity.

Who were Luther's heroes? The archetypal hero was, of course, Christ, a model for other heroes and for all men. Yet, he was not so much an *exemplum,* or example to be followed, as an *exemplar,* a demonstration of how God deals with all men. *Deus est heroicus sine regula!* God Himself had "the fear-inspiring, stern, strict spirit of a hero."[52] Christ was made in His Image. Luther applied to him the terms "warrior king," a medieval concept, and a giant.[53] Christ was a man of action and Luther compared him with Hercules and Achilles as the strong and unconquered man of war who led the battle against all who lacked hope and faith. Christ fights against all who are still "flesh," not yet filled with the Spirit.[54]

Next to Christ, Luther saw King David as the second greatest hero in history, for he was a man of action, who also had wisdom, faith, and humility. Only slightly below David was Abraham. He destroyed four armies almost single-handedly, a feat made possible only by divine intervention. Achilles, Agamemnon, Hannibal, and Scipio cannot be compared with Abraham in this heroic action.[55] God raised Abraham to such heights because he possessed the greatest virtue of all, following God absolutely.[56] Samson, less religiously unambiguous, was a kind of transition figure to Luther's pagan heroes. Although he was not notable for humility and faith, Samson was God's Word in action.[57]

It is difficult at times to discover Luther's criteria for choosing heathen heroes, the least common denominator being something similar to Hegel's idea that world-historical men are "the clear-sighted ones." After all, God knows, even if history remains enigmatic and obscure to us. Names occur such as Cicero, Cyrus, Themistocles, Alexander the Great, Augustus, Vespasian and Naaman, people directed by God. Hannibal had little specialized training and yet succeeded at war.[58] As Luther approaches his own times another criterion emerges, namely, whether a political leader or ecclesiastical personality was pro-papal or not. Emperor Maxmilian, King Sigismund of Poland, King Ladislaus of Hungary, Charles V, the Bishops of Würzburg and Cologne, and Andrea Doria are declared to be heroes of God.[59] Then, of course, there are anti-heroes, those such as Goliath, who had all the equipment and preparation, but who failed, and those such as Carlstadt, Müntzer, Zwingli, and "King Harry" (Henry VIII) of England who pretended to be heroes, but lacked the true calling. Of all the heroes of history, only Christ can deliver from sin and death and give to man eternal life.

Far more difficult is the problem of the way in which God uses unlikely persons and peoples to serve his purposes in history. Although the Old Testament is replete with examples of prophets such as Amos of lowly origin playing a major role in history, the prime example is the Virgin Mary in the New Testament. The primary document is Luther's commentary on the *Magnificat*.[60] Luther had written about a third of this commentary before he left for Worms, and completed it at the Wartburg by June, 1521. It is interesting to note that the most poignant discussions of God using the humble vessels surface during the two periods of Luther's "exile," while he was at the Wartburg and during his half year at the Coburg.

The *Magnificat* commentary is concerned with "inner" history primarily and an experiential way of observing God's working in history. It also demonstrates how God's lowly instruments are "used" for others. *Coram deo* and *coram mundo!* On the one hand, Luther insists that Mary is to be encountered just as one would encounter Peter, Paul, or Mary Magdalene, as an example which strengthens trust and faith in God.[61] On the other hand, he maintains that one should observe how "the infinite majesty of God is united with her utter poverty, the honor of God with her nothingness, the worthiness of God with her shamefulness, the greatness of God with her smallness. . . ."[62] Mary is a paradigm of how God works in people in the inner depths of history. Whether the person is a hero or of no great account in the eyes of the world, that person's true greatness depends upon his or her faith in God and humility. Mary sings "out of her own experience" in which "she has been illumined and instructed by the Holy Spirit."[63] Thus she teaches us that our speaking with God is made possible through His having first spoken to us; it is not a result of the *vita contemplativa*. Faith and event, not thought and being, are the categories proper to such discourse and conversation. Moreover, she speaks soteriologically and not psychologically nor merely religiously. She speaks of what she has not seen, but trusts Him in firm faith.[64] Mary teaches us that God is not magnified in His nature, but through our recognition, experience, and confession of His greatness, goodness, and grace. That is how He is truly magnified as God.[65] Mary's is a *fides explicita,* not a *fides implicita, fides historica,* nor a *fides traditionis.* One must believe that God both wishes and will perform great acts with one.[66] Faith is a one on one situation. Only the recognition of God's greatness and goodness in one's own life enables one to appreciate God as God in all life, in all creation. It is not one's wealth or wisdom, but God's grace and high regard that bring eternal reward. But the *coram mundo* is also there, for after the event which inspires trust the business of life itself becomes a *negotium cum deo,* lived for one's fellow man, for the whole world in Mary's case. In contrast to Mary, the haughty pope despoils and exploits the world. The lowly handmaiden of the Lord becomes the star of Christendom, the "head of Christendom" a star fallen from grace.

A longer report on Luther's *Commentary* and many analogous documents would bring out many complicated facets of this second approach to the question of God working in history. But space limitations forbid a fuller treatment and so a few words of analysis will have to suffice. Hermann Beyer, writing on God and history in Luther's exegesis of the *Magnificat* properly distinguished between "outer history," dealing with external goods of riches, wisdom, and power, and "inner history" or history within history, the real actuality, which transpires inside a person such as Mary, a relation between God and the human being.[67] He handles this distinction well, and yet he does not bring out a dimension that did not escape Luther, namely, the world historical importance of this inner history also for the external history of mankind. The implications of such faith for action in the outside world are tremendous.

A second analytical observation important for Luther's theological use of the past has to do with the concept of the *Deus absconditus.* In an early work the Lundensian theologian Gustav Aulen contrasted the *Deus absconditus* of nature and of history with the *Deus revelatus* of the Scriptures.[68] Luther's treatment of the *Magnificat* makes plain that for him God remains abscondite, hidden, also in revelation. That He would choose this lowly maiden, of a despised people, from an obscure town in lowly Galilee defies all reason. It is an affront also to "religion," it is a rebuff to *theologia gloriae,* it is the birth of the *theologia crucis!* There is no contradiction between the *Deus ipse* and the *Deus praedicatus* or the *Verbum Dei,* between God in His inner essence and God as He is proclaimed and revealed as the Incarnate Word. The key word for Luther's existential theology is *Dennoch,* nevertheless, not the *ergo,* therefore, of Thomas' sapiential theology.

Conclusions

1. The first part of this paper showed the extent of Luther's knowledge of classical history and his understanding of the value of history on a basic level. A knowledge of history does satisfy what Catherine Drinker Bowen has called "the Great Curiosity," the itch to know and the desire not to be or appear to be ignorant. On that

level, too, the questions of the *how* and the *why* are seen to be interrelated, there is a cause and effect thinking. Moreover, like the ancients and the Renaissance humanists, Luther adopts a pragmatic point of view. History is important for moral philosophy, for it is philosophy teaching by examples.

2. Luther believed that no one could comprehend the infinite subject matter of history and unlike some of the radicals he did not work out a set schema for all of history. In his *Supputatio* he merely followed a traditional outline of history and did not take that seriously, but viewed it as a useful device.

3. Luther did not think that the real meaning of history could be derived from a philosophy of history, but rather that a single theological insight, a conversion, a revelation from outside the closed circle of nature and history alone could offer a real grasp of the meaning of human history.

4. Luther has been criticized by some nineteenth and twentieth century historians for not being a historicist, a bit of anachronistic thinking on the part of disciples of historicism. But if Luther were alive today and had read Friedrich Meinecke's or other books on historicism, he would reject them even now, for he did not believe that the processes of history operate on their own nor that they have of themselves salvific powers or demonic powers.

5. Luther's understanding of how God relates dialectically to man in history allows for human freedom and responsibility in mundane matters.

6. History in terms of its real inner workings and meaning remains mysterious and God in a measure is still abscondite or hidden even in Biblical history.

7. History is to be taken seriously, for it is real and to be taken literally, not allegorically. We should take off our shoes, for the very ground upon which we stand is holy ground. It seems that the first *chair* of history at a modern university was established at Marburg University in Hesse (Philipp of Hesse's state) around 1528 under Melanchthon's influence. This puts Marburg ahead of all Roman Catholic universities including Italian Renaissance universities. This chair was occupied from 1536-1540 by Eobanus Hessus, who was considered to be the most outstanding Protestant poet. The formidable intellect of our times, H. Stuart Hughes has described history as a "work of art." In comparison with the trillions of dead planets and shining stars "out there," history is pure poetry!

Luther, though not himself a historian or even a church historian, did indeed have an important impact upon history, history as interpretation as well as history as "past actuality." The father of modern critical history, Leopold von Ranke, himself a Lutheran and not above adducing the name of Providence in a causal nexus, wrote of Luther:

"In no nation or age has a more . . . commanding and powerful writer appeared; and it would be difficult to find another who has so perfectly united popular and intelligent style and such downright homely good sense to so much originality, power and genius."[69]

Notes

[1] CR (*Corpus Reformatorum*), vol. VI, p. 157, no. 3478.

[2] Rudolph Hirsch provides a list of the classical authors and Italian humanists published in Germany between 1465 and 1500 and the classical and humanist authors published in German translations up to 1520, "Printing and the Spread of Humanism in Germany: The Example of Albrecht von Eyb," *Renaissance Men and Ideas,* Robert Schwoebel, ed. (New York, 1971), pp. 28, 31.

[3] E. Gordon Rupp, "Luther: Contemporary Image," *Kirche, Mystik, Heiligung und das Natürliche bei Luther,* Ivar Asheim, ed. (Göttingen, 1967), p. 13.

[4] See Myron P. Gilmore, *Humanists and Jurists: Six Studies in the Renaissance* (Cambridge, Mass, 1963), *"Fides et Eruditio: Erasmus and the Study of History,"* pp. 87-114.

[5] WA, L, 5. John M. Headley, *Luther's View of Church History* (New Haven, 1963), p. 51. See also Hans Freiherr von Campenhausen, "Reformatorisches Selbstbewusstsein und reformatorisches Geschichtsbewusstsein bei Luther 1517-22," *Archiv für Reformationsgeschichte,* 37 (1940), pp. 128-50. The classic work by Ernst Schäfer, *Luther als Kirchenhistoriker* (Gütersloh, 1987), is difficult to use, since it preceded the Weimar Ausgabe, but it was a great study. He documents Luther's amazing knowledge of patristic, conciliar, and medieval sources, historical annals and chronicles.

[6] *Einer aus den hohen Artikeln des päpstlichen Glaubens, genannt Donatio Constantin.*

[7] Heinz Zahrnt, *Luther deutet Geschichte: Erfolg und Misserfolg im Licht des Evangeliums,* (Munich, 1952) pp. 14ff., and the excellent recent work of Frank L. Borchardt, *German Antiquity in Renaissance Myth* (Baltimore, 1971). The old work by Paul Joachimsen, *Geschichtsauffassung und Geschichtsschreibung in Deutschland unter dem Einflusz des Humanismus* (Leipzig, 1910), remains a classic. Melanchthon in 1538 published *Arminius dialogus Huttenicus, continens res arminij in Germania gestas. P. Cornelii Taciti, de moribus et populis Germaniae libellus. Adiecta est brevis interpretatio appellationum partium Germaniae.* (Wittenburg, 1538), CR, vol. XVII, p. 611, which may have stirred up Luther's German pride at that moment. The most recent book on Hutten with an up-to-date bibliography is Eckhard Bernstein, *Ulrich von Hutten mit Selbstzeugnissen und Bilddokumenten* (Reinbeck Hamburg, 1988).

The literature on Renaissance humanist historiography and understanding of history is formidable in its extent from the magisterial volume of Eduard Fueter, *Geschichte der neueren Historiographie* (Munich and Berlin, 1911) down to the present time. Of the many recent books especially to be recommended are Eric Cochrane, *Historians and Historiography in the Italian Renaissance* (Chicago, 1981); Nancy S. Struever, *The Language of History in the Renaissance* (Princeton, 1970); Ronald Weiss, *The Renaissance Discovery of Classical Antiquity* (Oxford, 1969); Rüdiger Landfester, *Historia Magistra Vitae: Untersuchungen zur humanistischen Geschichtstheorie des 14. bis 16. Jahrhunderts* (Geneva, 1972); Donald R. Kelley, *Foundations of Modern Historical Scholarship: Language, Law, and History in the French Renaissance* (New York, 1970); and his most recent contribution, Donald R. Kelley, "Humanism and History," in Albert Rabil, Jr., ed., *Renaissance Humanism: Foundations, Forms, and Legacy,* vol. 3 (Philadelphia, 1988), pp. 236-270, an excellent statement. The humanist "pragmatic" view of history persisted into the Enlightenment and *Aufklärung.* See for example, Friedrich Schiller, "Was heisst und zu welchem Ende studiert man Universalgeschichte?" (1789), *Jenaer Reden und Schriften,* 2nd ed. (Jena,

1984), p. 2: "Fruchtbar und weit umfassend ist das Gebiet der Geschichte, in ihrem Kreise liegt die ganze moralische Welt." Johann Lorenz Mosheim, the so-called "father of modern church history," introduced the theme of lessons from and pragmatic uses of church history," after the polemical period in which historians such as Florimond de Raimond, Louis Maimbourg, and Veit Ludwig von Seckendorff used history as a weapon in controversy.

[8] WA, vol. 43, p. 418.

[9] WA, vol. 50, pp. 383-85. Preface to Galeatius Capella's History, 1538, *Luther's Works*, vol. 34, Lewis W. Spitz, ed. (Philadelphia, 1960), pp. 275-78.

[10] Arnold B. Berger, *Martin Luther in kulturgeschicht licher Darstellung* (Berlin, 1919), p. 553.

[11] Werner Elert, *Morphologie des Luthertums*, I (Munich, 1958), p. 426, note 2, discusses the question of whether Luther and then Melanchthon wished to establish chairs for historians, which would have been an advance over the Italian universities. See D. Karl Bauer, *Die Wittenberger Universitätstheologie und die Anfänge der Deutschen Reformation* (Tübingen, 1928), pp. 80-98: "Die Bereicherung der Wittenberger Theologie durch die Geschichte." See also the pioneering work of Ernst Schäfer, *Luther als Kirchenhistoriker* (Gütersloh, 1897), p. 84, in which he acknowledged that Luther wrote many works which required historical study and preparation, but held that his historical views were still always in the service of dogmatics and polemics. On Schäfer, see note 5 above.

[12] WA Tr, *(Tischreden)* IV, p. 598.

[13] WA Tr, III, p. 45, no. 3613.

[14] WA Tr, IV, p. 596.

[15] Op. ex., II, p. 15, compare VII, p. 314.

[16] Op. ex., XXI, p. 206, Pejor pars fere vincit.

[17] Op. ex., III, p. 265.

[18] WA 18, p. 400, 16-23; *Luther's Works*, Am. ed., vol. 46, pp. 83-84, "An Open Letter on the Harsh Book Against the Peasants," 1525.

[19] WA Tr, IV, p. 475.

[20] WA Tr, IV, p. 475. He discussed the *Germania* 18 and 22 with Melanchthon on the way to Torgau, April 13, 1537, and how Tacitus ascribed truthfulness and dependability to the ancient Germans, but then Luther complained that since then the words of "our people" have gotten worse. WA Tr, IV, p. 657. Compare p. 699, Lauterbach, p. 52.

[21] CR, vol. III, p. 565 ff., 568, 572; vol. X, p. 555; vol. XVII, p. 611 ff., 1141.

[22] Suetonius, *Ner.* 38:EA XXVI, p. 63.

[23] WA Tr, III, p. 612, no. 5012.

[24] WA Tr, IV, p. 14, no. 3925. Not yet superseded by a thorough modern work and thus still of value in Oswald Gottlob Schmidt, *Luther's Bekanntschaft mit den Alten Classikern: Ein Beitrag zur Lutherforschung* (Leipzig, 1883). See also Carl Gaenssle, "Luther's Knowledge of the Classics," pp. 206-229; E. G. Sihler, "Luther and the Classics," W. H. T. Dau, ed., *Four Hundred Years* (St. Louis, 1917), pp. 240-54.

[25] The most recent close study of Luther's exegetical work and his own experience is that of Marilyn J. Harran, *Luther on Conversion: The Early Years* (Ithaca, N.Y., 1983).

[26] F. Edward Cranz, *An Essay on the Development of Luther's Thought on Justice, Law and Society, Harvard Theological Studies*, XIX (Cambridge, Mass., 1959), pp. 20-21, *et passim*.

[27] See the excellent article by E. Thestrup Pedersen, "Schöpfung und Geschichte bei Luther," *Studia Theologica*, 3, fasc. I-II, (Lund, 1950-1951), pp. 5-33.

[28] WA, vol. 26, p. 339, *Bekenntnis vom Abendmahl Christi*, 1528.

[29] WA, vol. 26, p. 332.

[30] WA, vol. 18, p. 623. See Hans-Walter Krumwiede, *Glaube und Geschichte in der Theologie Luthers. Zur Entstehung des geschicht lichen Denkens in Deutschland* (Göttingen, 1952), pp. 16-17, 23. Written in 1948 this volume is the best treatment so far of the problem of theology and history in Luther. A second excellent book is that of Heinz Zahrnt, *Luther deutet Geschichte Erfolg und Misserfolg im Licht des Evangeliums* (Munich, 1952), cited in note 7 of above.

[31] *Luthers Sämmtliche Schriften*, VI, col. 895.

[32] For representative passages, see WA vol. 19, p. 360, no. 17 ff.; WA Tr, 6, No. 645; WA Tr, 2, No. 1810; WA 40, I, p. 174, 3: universa creatura eius est larva.

[33] WA vol. 19, p. 360, no. 6 ff.; WA Tr 5, No. 6156 (Lauterbach). One frequently encounters phrases such as *Sic enim ludit sapientia dei in orbe terrarum!* See WA vol. 15, p. 370, no. 20 ff., on Psalm 127 (1524). Hans-Henning Pflanz, "Geschichte und Eschatologie bei Martin Luther"

Deutsche Theologie, 5 (1938), pp. 246-290, finds that Luther's main interest in history was concerned with the progress of the Word through the ages in the struggle between the true and false churches.

[34] *Luther's Works,* Am. ed., vol. 2, p. 34.

[35] Commentary on Psalm 2 (1532), WA vol. 40, II, p. 12 ff. Luther returns to this theme frequently, e.g., WA vol. 19, p. 360, on Job 12:19, "He overthrows the mighty." See also WA vol. 31, I, p. 126, no. 29 ff., *Confetemini,* 1530.

[36] Enarr. Psalm II (1532), WA vol. 40, p. 229, no. 12 ff. God can, however, also chasten entire nations in a fatherly manner, WA vol. 3, pp. 334 and 340.

[37] *Luther's Works,* Am. ed., vol. 12, p. 33—God's only weapon is the "Word." *Sämmtliche Schriften,* XIII[b], col. 2628—God needs only words to transform the world.

[38] WA vol. 56, p. 422, no. 7.

[39] Henri Strohl, *L'Évolution religieuse de Luther* (Strasbourg, 1922), p. 161ff.

[40] John Headley, *Luther's View of Church History* (New Haven, 1963), p. 19f., 29.

[41] *Ibid.,* p. 267.

[42] Martin Schmidt, "Luthers Schau der Geschichte," *Luther-Jahrbuch,* XXX (1963), pp. 17-69, 33.

[43] Helmar Junghans, "Das mittelalterliche Vorbild für Luthers Lehre von den zwei Reichen," in *Vierhundertfünfzig Jahre Reformation, 1517-1967* (Göttingen, 1967), pp. 135-53. Ulrich Duchrow, *Two Kingdoms: the Use and Misuse of a Lutheran Theological Concept* (Geneva, 1977), points to the evolution and inversion of Luther's doctrine which developed during the 19th century. See Lewis W. Spitz, "The Christian in Church and State," in Manfred Hoffmann, *Martin Luther and the Modern Mind: Freedom, Conscience, Toleration, Rights* (New York and Toronto, 1985), pp. 125-161, and Lewis W. Spitz, "Impact of the Reformation on Church-State Issues," in Albert Huegli, ed., *Church and State Under God* (St. Louis, 1964), pp. 59-112, 459-472. John Tonkin, *The Church and the Secular Order in Reformation Thought* (New York and London, 1971), compares Luther's dialectical approach with Calvin's stress on salvation history, and with Menno Simon's consistent dualism.

[44] Gritsch, p. 109. In his pages on "Bible and History," pp. 98-103, Gritsch stresses the Scriptures as the major source of Luther's historical thought.

[45] Heinrich Bornkamm, *Luther und das Alte Testament* (Tübingen, 1948), pp. 54-68.

[46] WA vol. 44, p. 67. Franz Lau, "Äuszerlich Ordnung" und "weltlich Ding," in *Luthers Theologie* (Göttingen, 1933), p. 59, asserted that family, vocation, government, are a bulwark against chaos which is what Satan desires to create.

[47] *Sämmtliche Schriften,* XXII. (St. Louis, 1887), col. 1431. Because their calling is to translate the Word into action, these people are essentially men of action, *Sämmtliche Schriften,* (St. Louis, 1897) VI, col. 212 ff., XIII[b], col. 1050. On God's mummery, see Martin Schmidt, pp. 54-56. See the sprightly written chapter by Carl G. Gustavson, "Luther Hits the Jackpot: The Individual," *The Mansion of History* (New York, 1976), 167-175, p. 174. "Luther, as a Religious Man, was undoubtedly guided by a spiritual Hidden Hand but several non-religious factors greatly assisted Luther in hitting the jackpot, plus, of course, his own vigorous fist giving the machine some hard thumps to help matters along."

[48] *Luther's Works,* 3, p. 262.

[49] *Sämmtliche Schriften,* XXII, col. 1449, "Helden Gottes Gaben."

[50] *Sämmtliche Schriften,* XIX (St. Louis, 1907), col. 1481: "So hat Gott auch unter den undankbaren Heiden allezeit vortreffliche Gaben ausgestreut, und zwar solche die den Wundergaben gleich sind."

[51] Luther's Works, Am. ed., vol. 12, p. 226.

[52] *Ibid.,* vol. 13, p. 172.

[53] *Sämmtliche Schriften,* VI, cols. 212ff.

[54] *Ibid.,* VI, col. 213.

[55] Luther's Works, Am. ed., vol. 3, p. 322; *Sämmtliche Schriften* (St. Louis, 1880) I, cols. 889, 919.

[56] *Ibid.,* I, col. 1164.

[57] See the interesting monograph by R. Hermann, *Die Gestalt Simsons bei Luther* (Berlin, 1952). See also Ernst Kohlmeyer. "Die Geschichtsbetrachtung Luthers," *Archiv für Reformationsgeschichte* 37 (1940), pp. 150-69.

[58] Luther's Works, Am. ed., vol. 13, p. 154ff.

[59] *Sämmtliche Schriften,* XXII, cols. 1448 and 1450.

[60] *Das Magnificat verdeutschet und ausgelegt*, WA, vol. 7; English translation, Luther's Works, Am. ed., vol. 21, pp. 295-358. E. Thestrup Pedersen, p. 5: "Bezeichnend ist, dass Luthers Auslegung des 'Magnificat,' Marias Lobpreisung Gottes, ein der Hauptquellen seines Geschichtsverständnisses ist."

[61] WA, vol. 7, p. 569.

[62] *Ibid.*, p. 570.

[63] *Ibid.*, p. 546.

[64] *Ibid.*, p. 556.

[65] *Ibid.*, p. 554.

[66] *Ibid.*, p. 553.

[67] Hermann Wolfgang Beyer, "Gott und die Geschichte nach Luthers Auslegung des Magnificat," *Luther-Jahrbuch*, 1939, pp. 110-134. See also Gerhard Müller, "Evangelische Marienverehrung: Luther's Auslegung des Magnificat," *Luther: Zeitschrift der Luther-Gesellschaft* (1988, no. 1), 2-13, especially, 10-12: "Gottes Gnade und Werke."

[68] The concepts of the *Deus absconditus* or *Deus nudus* and the *Deus revelatus* or *Deus vestitus* are obviously most relevant for the question of Luther's views of God in history. Here you will find the central Biblical passage followed by two typical expressions by Luther of his views, and then references to some secondary materials chosen from a vast array of titles, as being the most basic and reliable, in the author's view. For the phrase, see one of Luther's favorite Hebrew prophets, Isaiah, cited from the *Biblia Vulgata*. It is Isaiah 45:15: *"Vere tu es Deus Absconditus, Deus Israel Salvator";* "Verily thou art a God that hidest thyself, O God of Israel, the Savior." See also analogous passages such as Exodus 20:21: "And the people stood afar off, and Moses drew near unto the thick darkness where God was." No one can behold God's face directly and live. Aristotle avowed that the *Primum Mobile* sees only itself. Thomas Aquinas, following Dionysius the Areopagite, wrote of the veils which cover the face of God. Luther wrote on this problem frequently. In his *Lectures on Genesis,* WA vol. 43, p. 460, 26, he wrote: *"Si credis in Deum revelatum et recipis verbum eius, paulatim etiam absconditum Deum revelatit."* (If you believe in the revealed God and accept his Word, he will little by little reveal the hidden God.) A similar statement is the following: WA vol. 3, p. 124, 33, *Dictata,* Ps. 17 [18] 12: *"Tertio potest intelligi mysterium incarnationis. Quia in humanitate absconditus latet, quae est tenebrae eius, in quibus videri non potuit, sed tantum audiri."* (In the humanity [of Christ], the hidden God is encapsulled. It is the darkness in which He cannot be seen but only heard.)

For secondary material on this problem see, Alfred Adam, "Der Begriff 'Deus absconditus' bei Luther nach Herkunft und Bedeutung," *Luther-Jahrbuch,* 30 (1963), 97-106; David C. Steinmetz, "Luther and the Hidden God," *Luther in Context* (Bloomington, IN, 1986), pp. 23-31; and David Löfgren, *Die Theologie der Schöpfung bei Luther* (Göttingen, 1960), pp. 193-240: *Deus nudus et vestitus* and *Deus absconditus et revelatus.* Gustaf Aulen, *Luthers Gudsbild en konturteckning* (Lund, 1926), which is incorporated into the fifth book of the larger German version *Das Christliche Gottesbild in Vergangenheit und Gegenwart: Eine Umrisszeichnung:* (Gütersloh, 1930), pp. 158-247, especially, 226-35. The second edition in Swedish is: *Den Kristna gudsbilden genom seklerna och i nutiden* (Stockholm-Uppsala, 1941).

[69] Leopold von Ranke, *Deutsche Geschichte im Zeitalter der Reformation,* II (6. Auflage, Leipzig, 1881), p. 56.

Is Faith Enough?

GOTTFRIED HOFFMANN

AN INQUIRY CONCERNING THE DOCTRINE OF JUSTIFICA-
TION DIRECTED TO THE ROMAN CATHOLIC CHURCH AND
THE EVANGELICAL CHURCH IN GERMANY

I

Published in 1985 by the German Bishops' Conference, the Catholic Adult Catechism says, "Many Catholics and Protestant theologians today are of the opinion that the Doctrine of Justification as
such need no longer separate the two churches, but that a consensus
on this question is possible."[1] The sentence is almost word for word
the same as a sentence in the Evangelical Adult Catechism, published by the United Evangelical Lutheran Church of Germany
(VELKD) in 1975.[2]

In the meantime this opinion of theologians has come to have
official importance. A commission consisting of representatives of
the German Bishops' Conference, of the Vatican Secretariat for the
Unity of Christians, and of the Council of the Evangelical Church
in Germany, the so-called Common Ecumenical Commission, requested the ecumenical work group (which has existed since 1946)
consisting of Evangelical and Catholic theologians, to examine the
accusations which were made on both sides in the Reformation Period. In the letter to the work group concerning this, it is stated,
"The so-called rejections or anathemas are no longer applicable to
our partners today according to general conviction. This can no longer
remain a matter of private conviction but must be concretely stated
by the churches."[3] The ecumenical work group met this quest and
published a study under the title of "Doctrinal Condemnations: Dividing the Church?" (Hereafter referred to as LV). This study was
received by the Common Ecumenical Commission and placed before

---

*GOTTFRIED HOFFMANN serves as Professor at the Theological
Seminary of the Selbststaendische Evangelische Lutherische Kirche
at Oberursel, West Germany. This article, written in German, was
translated by Roy A. Ledbetter.*

the German Bishops' Conference and the Council of the Evangelical Church for examination. At this time, the leaders of the churches concerned were asked to give concrete expression to the idea that "the condemnations of the sixteenth century no longer applied to the contemporary partners, in so far as their doctrine was not formed by the error which the rejection was to counteract."[4]

This examination process is now underway. The result has not yet been made known. If this should be positive, then one would have to be clear about two things: first of all, the basis of this decision is not the Confessions of the Reformation Period, but the interpretations which these confessions as well as their rejections have been subjected to in this study with which we are concerned. This the Common Ecumenical Council expresses clearly: "The churches, their teachers of theology and ministers shall explain the Evangelical Confessional writings and the official doctrinal expressions of the Roman Catholic Church in the light of the judgments formulated here."[5] The similarity to the Leuenberg Concord is unmistakable; this was to interpret the confessional writings of the Lutheran and Reformed churches in a binding way. Secondly, the study which is before us is concerned with the rejections of the Reformation time. It is not concerned with everything which still separates the churches, especially not with the new dogmas that have come to Rome since the Reformation concerning the Pope and Mary, and the theological developments which have arisen in the Protestant churches which question the validity of the Confessions. Certainly the ordination of women should also be considered a potentially divisive point. But from the Reformation Period there are also many questions that remain difficult; for example, in the doctrine of the ministry, the apostolic succession and the hierarchical structure of the ministry. If that document is accepted, it will only be a beginning, which in no way encompasses the goal of reaching full church fellowship.

Everyone who believes in Jesus Christ must be filled with thankfulness that such a serious discussion of doctrine between the Roman Catholic Church and the Evangelical Church of Germany was possible at all, much less with such a result. This means that one no longer looks at the other as someone who has strayed or even as a heretic who has to be persecuted but as a Christian for whom one has to struggle. It is true that this was not completely forgotten in the history of the Confessions, but it was often overlooked. Anyone familiar with the confrontations between the Confessions is familiar with what is meant, not only in the area of war, but also in the civil area and in the human area. It is indeed a matter of thanksgiving and praise that it is no longer the sword, or rejection, or enmity, or prejudice which characterizes the intercourse among adherents of a confession, but a reciprocal respect and recognition that what the other person does is Christian.

Our Thanksgiving for this change in the relationships between the churches does not, however, release us from the obligation to test the results which are laid before us. For the Lutheran Church, the doctrine of justification is that article by which the church of Christ stands or falls. The same care and thoroughness is befitting for the Lutheran Church as Martin Chemnitz showed in his examination of the Tridentine Council in the sixteenth century, even if this is only a partial or interim result. The following lines do not remove this condition. However, they should give an impulse for this by examining more closely the understanding and the meaning of justifying faith. At the same time, for the sake of brevity, this paper will not be concerned with whether or not these results are Scriptural or represent an accurate interpretation of the Confessions.

II

In the Reformation time and in the subsequent theological conflict, the justification of the sinner before God on the Lutheran side is represented by the phrase "by faith alone" and on the Roman side as "in the unity of faith, hope, and love."[7] The "Doctrinal Judgments —Dividing the Church?" (LV) explains that today and even to a large extent in the period of the Reformation, a difference in speaking and of accent was involved, through which basically the same thought was brought to expression. In one section, which contains the results of a longer explanation, it says if you take to heart all of this, then, when they say: "When it is translated from one mode of expression into another, then the Reformation language concerning justification by faith is similar to the Catholic Doctrine of Justification through grace and on the other side the Reformation Doctrine concerning the word faith includes also that which the Catholic doctrine contains in the context of I Corinthians 13:13 in the Triad of Faith, Hope and Love." Immediately before that, reference is made to a similar expression by Cardinal Willebrand in the plenary meeting of the Lutheran World Federation in Evian, "that the word 'faith,' in Luther's sense, is in no way intended to exclude either works or love or even hope. It is possible to say very correctly that Luther's concept of faith when it is considered completely probably means nothing more than that which we designate as love in the Catholic Church."[8]

In this way, the decisive assertion concerning justification involves basically the use of two different modes of expression in talking about one and the same thing. This assertion is grounded in two points: The Lutherans use the concept "faith" in a much broader sense than the Catholics, in that they use the word faith, justifying faith, to designate what the Catholics say is the unity of faith, hope and love, and sometimes designated only as "love." And what the Lutherans understand as justification by faith, the Catholics mean when they say justification through the saving grace (*gratia gratum faciens*). Certainly this statement is surprising, and in view of this, it becomes even more compelling to investigate what it really is that the Lutherans understand as faith and the Catholics understand as love and similarly what the Lutherans mean by justification through faith and the Catholics by saving grace that makes holy. In order to answer this question, it is necessary to look back upon some of the ways in which the LV came to their results.

The decisive starting point lies in the treatment of faith in the section of the essence of grace or righteousness before God. It is traditional to characterize the difference between the Protestant and Catholic understanding of justification in this way: that Lutherans understand righteousness before God or the grace of God as a reality outside of us in Christ, a reality which is promised to us in the forgiveness of sins and accounted unto us; Catholics, on the other hand, were said to understand it as a reality in the human soul, as an indwelling quality (*gratia inhaerens*). This indwelling quality or inherent quality comes about in a process by which human beings are changed. Now, however, New Testament studies have led to the recognition that this is not really a contradiction, at least not the kind which would force one to make a doctrinal condemnation.

> New Testament exegesis teaches us that the reformed way of speaking of righteousness which is "outside of us" and which works outside of us has its Biblical correctness. Christ Himself has been made our righteousness by God (I Corinthians 1:30). Therefore, only he is just before God who has been bound to Him through faith in baptism and whose sin and sinful self has died (compare Romans 6:6ff.; 7:4). Apparently, however, the thought of "infused" grace and "inherent" grace is also well-founded Biblically. For God's abiding love is also "outside of us" and at the same time is "poured out into our

hearts" (Romans 5:5). It is identical with the gift of the Holy
Spirit (Galatians 3:2-5; 5:6, Romans 8:23; II Corinthians 5:5)
and as such, unites us with Christ, fills us with trust and joy,
and empowers to a new life, which, since it is fellowship with
Christ in the gift of the Spirit, is not a life which we owe in
any way to ourselves.

New Testament exegesis has introduced progress which
cannot be too highly estimated, because it relaxes old controversial questions: It has brought to light the indissoluble
context of that which in Catholic tradition is called increate
and created grace (*gratia increata, gratia creata*) and that
which in the reformed tradition is called forensic and effective
justification. Systematic theologians on this side as well as
on that side have accepted this gift of exegesis.[9]

It is maintained, therefore, that both of the earlier positions in
this question of how a man can become righteous before God and
achieve salvation, are right in their own way and are valid together.
So the Catholics have learned that justification does not happen
internally but externally as well, and Lutherans have learned that
justification is not only external but also internal. There is an indissoluble connection between external and internal justification. At
the same time, the Biblical foundation makes plain what is to be
understood as external and internal justification. The external is
Christ made righteousness for us by God, the internal as inherent
grace or as grace which is poured out into our hearts is the love of
God, which is identified with the Holy Spirit. It is through this love
which is poured out into our hearts or through the Holy Spirit that
we are saved. This love unites us with Christ, fills us with trust and
empowers us to a new life.

Beginning with this understanding of justifying grace and righteousness, then, the contradiction which has existed until now between justification "through faith alone" and conversely justification
"in the unity of faith, hope and love" is dissolved. To this end, examination is made of what Lutherans understand as faith in the
act of justification. Justification by faith alone does not mean, as
the Council Fathers of Trent thought, simply the rational acceptance
of the contents of Scripture and the Creed, so that the effectiveness
of the Sacrament, the meaning of the good works, and the necessity
of a binding confession are excluded. What it does mean is trusting
the promise and with that, the forgiveness of sins and the fellowship
with Christ. "Even if such a faith of necessity makes the human

being new, the Christian does not put his confidence in his new life, but in God's gracious affirmation. Accepting this in faith is enough, if 'faith' is understood as 'trusting in the promise *(fides promissionis)*.' "[10]

At the same time, the Lutherans understood the difference and context of faith and works in this matter, even when the concepts of sanctification, new birth and regeneration could be used differently in the sense of the justification which follows a moral regeneration (Formula of Concord): as well as the basic new birth, which happens through Baptism (compare CA2 and the Large Catechism). For their part, Catholics understand regeneration, rebirth and sanctification as the working of Baptism through grace which sanctifies and with this mean apparently the unity of faith, hope and love. Both of these positions, then, are brought together from the New Testament:

> The New Testament witness does not only support the uniqueness of justifying faith, but also the theological unity of faith and love which is especially apparent in the proclamation of the Apostle Paul, this relationship between faith and confession (Romans 10:9), the love of God (I Corinthians 8:3) and the effect of faith in love of neighbor (Galatians 5:6). Faith does not exclude any of these things but includes all of these things.[11]

As a result of this, we read: "that which was decisive in the Reformation understanding of faith, the unconditional trust in the merciful God here and in the final judgment, is no longer a problem for Catholic theology," and again: "On the other hand, the reformers, in speaking of justification 'through faith,' express the Scholastic formulation of justification through '*gratia gratum faciens*' inasmuch as faith in God's mercy is grasped and received."[12]

Moreover, the concept of "faith" is explained very thoroughly in the proofs that follow and in their interpretation as the reception and apprehension of the mercy of God. This shows itself most clearly where the authors investigate Luther's rejection of the *fides caritate formata*. They understand this in this way, that he rejects a love which loves God above all things from its pure natural powers but not the love which flows from God Himself. The faith that justifies is not "simple naked faith," but a faith which includes love. In this sense, Luther is quoted from his commentary on the Galatians of 1531: "Indeed, if under formed faith they were to mean faith which is theological, or, as Paul said, unhypocritical faith, the faith which

God called believing, then their interpretation would not disturb me. Then faith would not struggle against love at all but would be in opposition to an empty opinion of faith; this is how we differentiate between the true and invented faith."[13] This quote from Luther, then, leads directly to the quote from Cardinal Willebrand which we had already mentioned and to the result which has already been cited, according to which Lutheran *justification through faith* agrees with the Roman *justification through grace* and the Lutheran word "faith" means, according to this, what the Roman "unity of faith, hope and love" says.

The same process was also used with the concept of justifying faith that had been used with righteousness: the two positions were brought together. In this process, of course, something important is noticeable. During the description of the Protestant position it is said that faith is "enough" when it is understood as trusting the promise. In the context of the examination, this can only be understood to mean that faith alone justifies. However, in the formulations of the results, this "alone" is never expressed. It does say that it is not a problem for contemporary Catholic theology to see the unconditional trusting in the merciful God, to hear it in the final judgment as decisive; but, at the same time, it is not said that this alone is enough for justification and therefore salvation before God. On the contrary, in saying that the Lutheran concept of justification "through faith" is understood in the sense of grace that makes holy and expanded to mean love in the Roman sense, we must understand that for the Roman side, faith as trusting in the forgiveness of sins and reception as God's child is not enough.[14] Even the Lutherans deviate from this.

Here it looks like even the authors of the LV themselves have noticed that for the Protestant side there is still a decisive question open. In one paragraph, which really forms a sort of appendix to the actual section that explains the agreement, they refer once again to the problem of differences which remain. Here we find sentences which contribute things of importance, perhaps decisive things, to the understanding of the whole. Let us cite them here:

With this the remaining difference of both formulations is to be neither denied nor reduced to an arbitrary selection of words; rather, different concerns and emphases express themselves again, upon which the Christian existence itself and some understanding of Protestant and Catholic Christians could depend. According to the Protestant understanding, faith, which clings to God's promise in Word and Sacrament unconditionally, is enough for justification or righteousness before God, so that the regeneration of a person, without which there can be no faith, does not contribute from its side to justification. The Catholic doctrine agrees with the Reformation concern that the regeneration of a person does not contribute to justification, certainly not one of which he can boast before God. . . . However, Catholic doctrine is compelled to see regeneration of humanity through the grace of justification for the sake of the confession of the power of God which renews freely, so that this regeneration in faith, hope and love is nothing more than an answer to the basic grace of God. It is only when we truly observe this difference that the following statement is valid: Catholic doctrine does not overlook that which is so important to the Protestant and vice-versa; and Catholic doctrine does not maintain that which Protestant doctrine fears and vice-versa.[15]

If the previous representation maintained the unity of content despite differing forms of speech, then in this place it is indicated that the different forms of speech also have to do with different concerns and emphases, emphases and concerns which involve not only obstacles for Protestants and Catholics but for all Christians. Here we have the task of clearly delineating the various emphases and concerns together with the common unity. The paragraph continues: ". . . by once again bringing up the decisive point of the Protestant understanding of justifying faith which holds fast to God's promise unconditionally in Word and Sacrament is enough for righteousness before God. Regeneration, without which there can be no faith, contributes nothing from its side to justification." Here, in Lutheran terminology, faith and regeneration (and that means love also) are distinguished from one another, and faith is defined as the holding fast to the promise of God in Christ. Here it is made clear that regeneration is inseparable from faith; that is, insofar as faith always brings about such regeneration and draws it after itself. But this regeneration makes no contribution to justification; it is its result. It is faith alone, in the sense of trusting the promise, through which man is made just before God, that is, is saved and brought into salvation. When faith is placed over against regeneration and is defined as trusting or holding fast to the promise, we see clearly the contrast to the representations of agreement saying that the concept of faith can be broadened to the unity of faith, hope and love.

The question is, then, how the Catholic position relates to this decisive point or concern. The normative sentence does not say plainly that Catholic doctrine does not agree with this concern, but does specify, "Catholic doctrine finds itself in agreement with the reformers' concern that the regeneration of the human being makes no contribution to justification. . . ." That means that they agree that there is no contribution of regeneration to justification. The question, however, is this: what about the statement "faith is enough"? A Lutheran reader is inclined so to understand the sentence "regeneration makes no contribution to justification" as meaning that faith (always trusting Christ and His Gospel) is enough by itself. He will then understand the Catholic emphasis on regeneration through justifying grace as emphasis on regeneration in the sense of the fruit of justifying faith.

But why is that not said? In fact the sentence closes thus, that regeneration makes no contribution to justification, certainly not in itself, but that faith alone is enough, if you look at the contribution as a ground for justification or as something that is earned. That, then, would not exclude regeneration as an essential part of justification. Likewise, the Catholic position emphasizes regeneration of human beings through justifying grace. If it is not something that is earned, then it is part of the justifying event as an "answer to God's boundless grace." Without it (this answer) it (justification) would never come about. Thus the question arises, whether the answer character of faith, hope, and love in the justification event—which is especially to secure the differences between justification and regeneration—is like that which the Lutheran confesses with the sentence, "Faith alone justifies."

It doesn't look that way. For faith, hope and love are understood in their unity as an answer to the grace of justification. Thus, love becomes a portion of the justification event, and the distinction which is so important to the Lutherans—that the fruit of faith not be brought into justification—is given up. By emphasizing that faith, hope, and love are an answer, the character of something that is earned is excluded, insofar as you do not see the answer itself as being an act of earning but you do not maintain the distinction between faith and love according to which only faith belongs to justification.

If the above is accurate, then the two positions have not reached agreement in a most decisive question. The moment of earning something is excluded, and that is truly not unimportant. But the actual problem still remains. Aside from the forgiveness of sins, the Catholics understand justification as the event in which grace works faith, hope, and love in the heart for Christ's sake and makes the human being just inside. Lutherans mean, however, that in the Gospel for Christ's sake, both the forgiveness of sins which is offered and reception as God's child are believed, and that this faith which He brings about with all love is enough. Bringing together faith and love, forensic and effective justification, proclamation of righteousness without clarifying what righteousness before God means and what it doesn't is not enough.

III

The following questions and observations are indispensible for the clarification that is proposed in which it is said that only words and formulas are involved and not the matter itself (but the matter is expressed in words!). They involve the understanding of faith and love as well as justification, in which both are bound up together, just like two tubes that are connected.

1. Luther and the Lutheran church have never argued that Christians do not live a new life, nor that the Holy Spirit does not dwell in them, nor that they must not resist the sinful desires which seek to gain the upper hand in them, nor that faith, hope, and love in Christians are simply empty words.[16] Christians truly are a new creation—even when they sin much daily and earn nothing but punishment. Therefore, in order to use the conceptualization of the LV, for Lutherans external and internal righteousness, righteousness as grace and as gift, forensic and effective justification, being declared just and made just or becoming just is not a problem as long as the second part of each pair of concepts indicates the new life of the one who has been justified. For them this is no new discovery of exegesis, since they have always spoken of a *nexus indivulsus*, an indissoluable context of faith and good works.[17] But they have never understood this new existence and life as something that brings them into salvation or preserves them in it.

Luther and the Lutheran Church are concerned about the question of how one comes into salvation before God. They are concerned about justification as the event of being saved, and not as the daily event of being renewed for those who have already been saved. They are concerned about the clear answer to the question of what it means for a human being to be able to comfort himself by saying: "I have been saved by God and am in salvation." That is the same as: "I am justified before God," because salvation and righteousness, which represents the revealed will of God, belong indivisibly together. He who is just before God has salvation and life, just as on the other side, there is no salvation or life before God without righteousness.

What does it really mean, then, for a human being truly to be able to say to himself, "I am just before God and am in salvation?" Of what does saving justification consist? Following Luther's lead,[18] the answer of the Lutheran church can be given with the three concepts which belong together—Christ, faith, and imputation through God.

Christ is God the Son, whom the Father has sent to be obedient. He fulfilled His will, which He had made known in the Law and suffered the death of sinners, which was threatened by the Law. He does not do that for Himself, but according to the will of the Father, He does it for our sake, and in our place. The human being, of course, knows nothing about this obedience of Christ. He learns about it through the Gospel, in Word and Sacrament. However, the Gospel does not only tell the story of Christ's obedience, but imputes to us the obedience and the suffering of Christ for our sake and in our place. Not only does it demand that we believe this, it even gives us this faith, which is nothing more than living trust. This faith is not only directed to the obedience and the suffering of Christ as an event of the past, but at the same time connects us with Him who is risen and present. For the Gospel not only bears witness to the death of Christ, but also to His resurrection, exaltation, and presence. It is not just a matter of course that through this faith the righteousness of Christ is imputed to the one who believes. It must be confirmed by the Father. Therefore, the imputation is necessary, that God recognizes my faith in Christ and His righteousness as my own righteousness: faith is counted or reckoned as righteousness.[19]

This means: the righteousness which a human being must have in order to be just before God is always and only the righteousness of Christ. Therefore, the Reformers called this the foreign righteousness, or the righteousness that is outside of us, which as saving righteousness, that is outside of us, which as saving righteousness always remains the foreign righteousness of Christ and only becomes ours through imputation, and never through our own fulfillment of the Law. Therefore, it can only be had through faith and no other way. For this reason, the Reformers rejected any understanding of the justification event, according to which anything more than faith as living trust has been present in a human being or at work in him without the saving event already being truly finished and the human being in salvation.[20] This "more," whether it is an internal right-

eousness or love or anything else, would then be an indispensible
part of the saving justification itself. Thus it makes no difference
whether this is ascribed only to God's doing, or partially to God and
a human being, or completely to the natural powers of the human
being. In each case, more or less righteousness in the human being
himself contributes to whether or not he is saved. In practice, this
means that I depend not only on Christ and His righteousness for
me, but also on that which has been done in me for righteousness.
For I am only saved, then, when some kind of righteousness has
been realized in me. In this case, the question immediately arises,
"How much righteousness has to be realized in me for salvation?"
a question which no human being can answer. The LV passes over
the fact that faith alone and living trust in Christ and nothing more
or additional belongs to saving justification. This can be noticed in
the way in which it speaks about forensic effective justification and
the broadening of the concept of faith that goes along with that. The
pair of concepts "forensic—effective" is used here for the *saving
justification*. According to this usage, then, to this belongs not only
that God declares the human being just, but also makes him just.
Here it is decisive how the making just or becoming just is understood: As an interior transformation, as a gift of a new, just being
and life, which reigns over sin. Justification, then, is an appropriation of the righteousness of God in the sense that it is realized in
the human being. This is not the way that the Reformation understood these concepts when it spoke of making just or becoming just
in the context of the saving justification!

This can be shown in the text from the Apology, which is always
used as proof for the effective justification according to the concept
customary today. Melanchthon distinguishes in Apology IV, paragraph 72, a different use of "becoming justified," once in the sense
of making a righteous person out of an unrighteous person, and, on
the other hand, a "having been proclaimed righteous." He explains
the first meaning himself, then, with the word that faith "accepts
the forgiveness of sin!"[21] Effective justification, then, for Melanchthon is *acceptance of the forgiveness of sins*; this is the same as being
born again: that is, the coming into being of the comforting, upright
and vivifying recognition that my sins have been forgiven.[22] The
coming into being of this recognition from the Gospel in the face of
the Law which condemns is nothing more than the coming into
being—not of the *fides otiosa* but of the justifying, living faith. The
fact that a righteous person is made out of an unrighteous person
means nothing more than that faith comes into being, which accepts

the forgiveness of sins. In the Lutheran sense, one can only speak of saving justification as forensic—effective, so that God's free proclamation brings about faith, which accepts this free proclamation.

Melanchthon explains the other meaning of the word "to become justified" in the sense of being proclaimed just, on the basis of Romans 2:13.[23] There it is not the unrighteous who were proclaimed righteous, but those who have done the Law, that is, those who are already righteous. The difference between these two concepts, therefore, does not lie in the fact that once one is proclaimed righteous and then again not, but that in one case, the proclamation of righteousness is connected with the acceptance of forgiveness (that is, going over from being lost to having been saved) and on the other hand, this is not the case. Effective justification, or rebirth, as the event of saving does not mean for Melanchthon, then, that in addition to justifying faith there has to be something else, whether it is love or any other new nature or even works;[24] but that the Holy Spirit brings about living faith through the Gospel, which proclaims the godless righteous and in this way the human being who is unjust is made righteous. It is precisely for this reason that Melanchthon can call this faith *gratia gratis faciens* and in this way specifically exclude love from it![25]

The Luther text also, which is quoted by the LV from Antilatomus, resists any interpretation in the comtemporary sense of forensic effective justification. The LV interprets that the righteousness of Christ is outside ours (that is, foreign righteousness) and becomes our own as a gift, insofar as grace addresses us and causes us to drive out the sin which is in us. In this way, grace is not just the favor of God. It can be understood in no other way than to mean that the righteousness of Christ goes over into us and becomes righteousness in us. Luther speaks quite differently here, because what he calls favor or inclination (in opposition to the grace of God, which he calls the gift in the human being), is not an internal righteousness but faith. This faith he calls righteousness, because we become righteous through it. That means that we have a gracious and not an angry God.[26] This faith, a deep and internal gift,[27] has nothing to do with justification as a saving event but works as a leaven against sin and thereby heals the destruction of sin, or that which is the same in the justified in the sense of daily increasing betterment. This involves only hanging on Christ or depending on Christ and being measured by Him, "because He is holy for you and righteous."[28] Luther also says that the *faith* which is given by God and has achieved grace, sweeps out sin.[29] Concerning the grace or righteousness of

God, he does not say that it addresses us,[30] or that it becomes our own or "makes" us into righteous people. The appropriation of the righteousness of Christ means that it avails for us, that we connect ourselves in faith to the obedience and suffering of Christ and hide ourselves in it.

2. The understanding of justification as "being made just" represents the broadening of the concept of faith into love as opposite. Now certainly Catholics and Lutherans both use faith and love with different meanings. When we try to explain this, we have to pay attention to whether or not that which the Lutherans want to exclude from the saving justification event when they say "only through faith" and thereby expressly exclude love is also excluded by the Catholics when they say "through love." What the Catholics and Lutherans understand as love would have to be something truly different.

For the Lutherans, faith is trusting in the forgiveness of sins through Christ, and with that, trusting Christ Himself as the reality which bears meaning. Faith is a living, comforting, supportive recognition of the heart, which is wrought or worked by the Gospel in the face of our guilt and of the Law of God which condemns us. Love is the movement of the heart which treasures God above all things and is inclined toward Him, serves Him gladly, and puts His will before all things. It is the answer to the love with which God in Christ has loved us and loves us, but an answer which does not arise from anything else but faith. Faith and love are characterized through the structure of receiving and giving, by which the giving grows out of the having received.

Now when the LV, in the context of saving justification take up the opinion of the Catholics and of the theological unity of faith and love, that is, faith, hope and love; and when they mean the relationship of faith, hope and love are included together; if the justifying faith (according to their understanding with Luther) is not a simple, naked faith and neither the works nor love nor even hope is excluded, then it is not to be recognized at all that the concept of love here in this matter means anything else than what the Lutherans mean, that is, the emotion of the heart with which the Christian is inclined toward Christ to treasure Him above all things, etc. This, because love here is understood with faith and hope as the answer of the human being. For the LV this answer in its theological unity belongs for broad stretches in the event of justification, in which it doesn't belong for the Lutherans. Of course, the Lutherans know about the theological unity of faith and love. Luther and the Reformers did not recognize any justifying faith at all which was not incarnated in love and good works. But this incarnation did not belong to the saving event itself. It depends, therefore, upon what sort of theological unity this is. Here we see that the formulation of the LV is not clear when it says, "Faith does not exclude works." This can mean that faith which justifies alone leads to love and good works, so that wherever faith is, there is also love and good works. But it can also mean that love and good works are taken up into faith and in this way belong also to saving justification.[31] Luther strictly rejects this last understanding. "Thus we cannot ascribe to this comforting form of faith shaped by charity, the power of justification, but only the faith which grasps Christ Jesus the Savior, and has Him in its heart. This faith justifies without love and before love."[32]

This is the customary interpretation and the interpretation which is represented by the LV concept, that Luther rejected the faith formed by love because he was concerned with "the nominalist doctrine that human beings could 'from their own natural powers' love God above all things, and that this ethical humanistic dimension could become decisive in the salvation process."[33] And in this way we see that this concept is a cardinal misconception and perversion of his thought. Where saving justification is concerned, there Luther rejects not only those works which are done without spirit and faith, but also all love and good works which the Christian does from God and as a gift of the Holy Spirit. This touches the Nominalist as well as Thomas Aquinas! Although the LV wants to interpret it that way, the passage in Luther's commentary on Galatians from 1531 does not regard love as part of justifying faith. When Luther insists on separating faith from love, this means that he rejects the understanding of faith as dead faith, which can only be made alive by love which is added to it. Instead of this he wants to make genuine faith clear, which is not a simple delusion, but which renews and changes the heart by comforting it and by supporting it. This faith produces love and good works, but it is faith alone which justifies, not love. From this we see a little later in the test: "Therefore faith justifies eternally and brings to life, and yet it does not remain alone, that means, at ease; not that it should always remain alone in its place and in its office, because it alone justifies eternally but it takes flesh and becomes human, that means faith is and does not remain at ease or without love."[34] Last but not least, Luther's understanding of the apposition of faith and love in justification can be seen clearly in the fact that the text Galatians 5:6 is not a text of justification, but of characterizing the Christian life in its totality.[35]

3. Now the analogy which the LV puts forward concerning faith and love must be investigated from another direction. This concerns the supposed agreement between justification through faith and justification through the grace which makes holy. Here we can see that a change apparently has taken place over against the traditional Catholic dogma.[36] In this the grace which makes holy is a supernatural state of being which is poured by God into the spirit and adheres to it constantly. This grace poured into the soul is the foundation, then, for participation in the divine nature,[37] it sanctifies the spirit in true righteousness and holiness, and bestows upon it a supernatural beauty and makes the justified person a friend of God and His child, and heir of heaven and a temple of the Holy Spirit. Distinguished from this are the three theological cardinal virtues of faith, hope and love, which are bestowed as a result of this grace and are of course inseparable from it.

Surely no one will seriously want to contend that this grace which makes holy is analogous to the Lutheran justification through faith alone. And indeed now, the LV identifies this grace which makes holy with the love of God, which is poured out into our hearts, and this, on the other hand, with the gift of the Holy Spirit.[38] A lot of other questions arise, even when in apposition to the traditional Catholic theology the supernatural state of being of the grace which makes holy[39] is identified with the Holy Spirit. What actually is this love of God which is poured out into our hearts? Is it the Holy Spirit which is gone into our hearts which makes us certain that God loves us? This truly would be close to the Lutherans, for they call faith the certainty that God loves us and forgives our sins in Christ. But they do not identify this certainty with the Holy Spirit which brings it about. Nor do they say that the Holy Spirit is only poured into the heart at first through the means of grace, and in this brings about the certainty that God loves one. This would mean that the Holy Spirit enters our heart before faith. Rather the Holy Spirit brings this certainty about through the Gospel and thus through faith enters the heart. Indeed, in the New Testament the gift of the Holy Spirit is placed after faith as the indwelling in the heart (Gal. 3:2-14 and 4:6; Eph. 1:13).

It is more important that the reference to Galatians 5:6 in LV (p. 54, 23) calls on us to understand the love of God which is poured into our hearts in such a way that we ourselves are loving ones. That even in this sense the spirit of love is in us, belongs essentially to the fact that we have been justified. In this we see clearly a decisive turning aside. Saving justification is not concerned with whether or not the Spirit is given to a human being or the personal power of love is poured out on it, whether it is the love of God for us or our love for God and our neighbor. The saving work of justification of the Spirit consists only in making us certain that the righteousness of Christ is ours and joins us to Him. The fact that the Spirit does not stop there, but does a great deal more, happens through and from this faith and is not part of the saving action itself.

In this way we can see clearly how important it is to understand Romans 5:5, which the LV does not explain: "The love of God is poured out into our hearts through the Holy Spirit which is given to us." The love which Paul means there is neither Augustine's love with which we love God, nor is it the Holy Spirit itself, but the love which God shows to us, that Christ died for us even when we were still sinners (v. 8). This is no other love than God's favor or His gracious inclination towards us. To say that it is poured out in our hearts through the Holy Spirit which is given to us[40] means that we recognize this love superabundantly in our hearts: God caused Christ to die for us while we were still sinners—how much more then, since we have been justified by his blood, that is, through faith in his blood (Rom. 3:25), how much more should we be blessed and able to withstand any difficulty!

Thus, in view of the grace which makes holy, we discern the same lack of clarity and differentiation in the context of faith as with the concept of justification. It all depends on the concept that faith alone is enough for saving justification; that is, in the sense of a trusting in the forgiveness of sins and reception as a child of God through the reckoning of Christ's righteousness to us through the power of the Holy Spirit. This faith is certainly something eschatologically new; that faith arises is God's new creation and a true rebirth of the person who before that had been dead before God. For the old person cannot believe and cannot recognize as a living reality that his sins have been forgiven and that he has been received as a child of God. Therefore this faith also brings about love and is active in good works and in this way is the beginning of the new life. But this love and this activity are not in the least a part of the activity through which the human being is justified before God. Only in this way can a human being truly be hidden in God without also having to ask about his condition before God. And only in this way, from out of the assurance of having been saved by God, can he give himself to God and the world.

The concern of this inquiry is that this decisive distinction between faith and love, with all of its consequences in view of saving justification, should be recognized and held fast. Otherwise the Reformation—and not only the Reformation—would be wasted.

Notes

[1] Katholischer Erwachsenen-Katechismus. Das Glaubensbekenntis der Kirche. Hrsg. von der Deutschen Bischofskonferenz, München [3]1985, p. 246. In general there are many almost complete agreements with the Evangelical Adult Catechism.

[2] Evangelischer Erwachsenenkatechismus. Kursbuch des Glaubens. Hrsg. im Auftrag der Katechismuskommission der VELKD von Werner Jensch u.a., Gütersloh 1975, p. 431.

[3] Cited from Lehrverurteilungen—kirchentrennend? I. Rechtfertigung, Sakramente und Amt im Zeitalter der Reformation und heute. Hrsg. von K. Lehmann und W. Pannenberg, Freiburg und Göttingen 1986, p. 179, 1-4 (Hereafter referred to as LV).

[4] LV, p. 195, 15-17.

[5] *Ibid.*, 25-27.

[6] *Ibid.*, pp. 56-59. Unfortunately volume 5 "Lehrverurteilungen—Kirchentrennend? II. Materialien zu den Lehrverurteilungen und zur Theologie der Rechtfertigung" has not yet appeared.

[7] *Ibid.*, p. 56, 4f.

[8] *Ibid.*, pp. 58, 28-59, 10.

[9] *Ibid.*, p. 54, 14-33.

[10] *Ibid.*, p. 56, 22-26.

[11] *Ibid.*, p. 57, 8-13.

[12] *Ibid.*, p. 57, 16-18; 29-33.

[13] *Ibid.*, p. 58, 22-27 with a reference to Luther's Works, Weimar edition (hereafter cited as WA), vol. 40, I, p. 421, 17-21.

[14] Compare for example the Catholic "Erwachsenen-Katechismus" p. 241: "Versteht man dagegen den Glauben im vollen und umfassenden biblischen Sinn, den Glauben also, der Umkehr, Hoffnung, Liebe einschliesst, dann hat diese Formel (scil. 'allein aus Glauben') *auch einen guten katholischen Sinn.*"

[15] LV, p. 59, 15-33.

[16] Martin Chemnitz already said this in his "Examen Councilii Tridentini" in his statement regarding the real difference: "Certum est, utrumque esse beneficium filii Dei Mediatoris, et remissionem peccatorum et renovationem, in qua spiritus sanctus in credentibus accendit novas virtutes." De Justificatione, Sectio I Articulus I Paragraph I. It is certain that there is both a gift of grace of the Son of God and agent of that gift just as there is forgiveness of sins and renewal in which the Holy Spirit arouses and implants new virtues in the believers.

[17] This is also the sense of the often misunderstood—and also unLutheran—"must" of good works in CA VI.

[18] WA, vol. 40, I, p. 233, 16ff.; W[2]9, 181.

[19] This justification is not a particular act of God which first occurs after a man has come to faith but is already present in the Gospel. Where faith has arisen there it has come to the individual.

[20] Compare Luther and Bugenhagen's reaction to Melanchthon's action in 1541 at Regensburg: "Ohne Zweifel ist, dass der, gerecht geworden ist, ohne Werke nicht bleibt, wie der Baum nicht ohne Früchte. Aber der Papisten Schalkheit ist diese . . . , dass man gerecht werde oder sei, nicht allein durch den Glauben, sondern auch durch die Werke, oder durch die Liebe und Gnade, die sie inhaerentem heissen (Welches alles gleich viel ist). Das ist alles falsch, und wo sie das haben, so haben sie es ganz und gar, und wir nichts." WA, Br. 9 Nr. 3616; W[2]17, 670.

[21] "Ideo primum volumus hoc ostendere, quod sola fides ex iniusto iustum efficiat, *hoc est*, accipiat remissionem peccatorum." BSLK, p. 174, 41-44.

[22] Here, the previous paragraphs (61-68) in which Melanchthon describes the manner of regeneration and the way of saving faith.

[23] Ap, IV, par. 251.

[24] We cannot overlook, as many Lutherans have, that Melanchthon's explanation in paragraph 72 has exactly the goal to demonstrate that faith is not only the beginning or foundation of justification but is exactly that by which we receive from God that whereby we are reconciled with God which means that we are justified.

[25] Compare LV, p. 58, 1-4.

[26] This is demonstrated by the Scriptural statement that Luther introduced as a foundation: Romans 3:21; 5:1; 3:28. Similarly: "Huic fidei et iustitiae comes est gratia seu misericordia, favor dei, contra iram, quae peccati comes est, ut omnis qui credit in Christum, habeat deum propitium." WA, vol. 8, p.106, 6-8. "Der Begleiter bei diesem Glauben und dieser Gerechtigkeit ist die Gnade oder Barmherzigkeit, die Gunst Gottes, gegen den Zorn, welcher der Begleiter der Sünde ist, sodass ein jeder, der an Christus glaubt, einen gnädigen Gott hat." W²18, 1162.

[27] Faith is the basic root the fruit of which good works are. Compare W² 18, 1159 and 1162.

[28] W²18, 1173. ". . . fidem esse scias, si ei adheseris, de ipso praesumpseris, quod tibi sanctus-iustusque sit." WA, vol. 8, p.112, 11f.

[29] "Ecce haec fides est donum dei, quae gratiam dei nobis obtinet et peccatum illud expurgat, et salvos certosque facit, non nostris, sed Christi operibus, ut subsistere et permanere in aeternum possimus, sicut scriptum est: 'Iustitia eius manet in seculum seculi'. " WA, vol. 8, p. 112, 12-15. "Siehe, dieser Glaube ist die Gabe Gottes, welcher uns die Gnade Gottes erlangt und jene Sünde auskehrt, und uns selig und gewiss macht, nicht durch unsere, sondern durch Christi Werke, dass wir bestehen und bleiben können in Ewigkeit wie geschrieben ist: Seine Gerechtigkeit bleibet in Ewigkeit." W²18, 1173.

[30] "Nam remissio peccatorum et pax proprie tribuitur gratiae dei, sed fidei tribuitur sanitas corruptionis." WA, vol, 8, p. 106, 18-20. "Denn Vergebung der Sünden und Friede wird eigentlich der *Gnade* Gottes zugeschrieben, aber dem *Glauben* die Heilung der Verderbnis." W⁹18, 1163 (Unterstreichungen vom Verf.).

[31] Paul does not mean that a man is only saved before God when he has expressed with his mouth a confession of faith but that the faith in the heart leads to the confession of the mouth (2 Cor. 4:13).

[32] W²9, 187. "Quare non isti formae gratificanti tribuenda est vis iustificandi, sed fidei quae apprehenditet possidet in corde ipsum Christum Salvatorem. Haec fides sine et ante charitatem iustificat." WA, vol. 40, I, p. 240, 14-16.

[33] LV, p. 58, 18-21.

[34] W²9, 363. "Quare fides perpetuo iustificat et vivificat, et tamen non manet sola, id est, otiosa. Non quod non sola in suo gradu et officio maneat, quia perpetuo sola iusificat, sed incarnatur et fit homo, hoc est, non est et manet otiosa vel sine charitate." WA, vol. 40, I, p. 427, 11-14.

[35] "Paulus enim hoc loco . . . non (inquam) de iustificatione disputat . . . sed brevi valut Epiphonemate concludit, quid sit ipsa Vita Christiana . . . Verum est sine operibus solam fidem iustificare, Sed de fide vera loquor, quae, postquam iustificaverit, non stertet ociosa, Sed est per Charitatem operosa." WA, vol. 40, II, p. 37, 8-25. "Denn Paulus . . . disputiert (sage ich) nicht von der Rechtfertigung . . . er beschliesst gleichsam mit einer kurzen Summa, was ein rechtes christliches Leben sei. . . . Es ist wahr, dass allein der Glaube ohne Werke rechtfertige, ich rede aber von dem wahren Glauben, welcher, nachdem er gerecht gemacht hat, nicht müssig schnarcht, sondern durch die Liebe tätig ist." W²9, 635.

[36] Compare Ludwig Ott, Grundriss der katholischen Dogmatik, ¹⁰1981, Freiburg p. 308ff.

[37] "Auch die Schrifttexte, welche die Rechtfertigung als Zeugung oder Geburt aus Gott darstellen. . .lehren die Teilnahme des Menschen an der göttlichen Natur, da die Zeugung in der Mitteilung der Natur vom Erzeuger an den Erzeugten besteht." Ott, p. 310.

[38] LV, p. 54, 19-23.

[39] That saving grace is truly different from love is sententia communior, compare Ott p. 309. For the distinction between grace and love by the Holy Spirit compare Ott p. 308: "Die tridentinische Bestimmung der Rechtfertigungsgnade . . . schliesst die Identität der heiligmachenden Gnade mit dem Hl. Geist aus . . . Nach Röm 5,5 . . . ist der Hl. Geist der Vermittler der Liebe Gottes zu uns, die uns bei der Rechtfertigung geschenkt wurde, und darum von der Rechtfertigungsgnade verschieden wie der Geber von der Gabe."

[40] Regarding the source of the Spirit Paul doesn't say anything here. From Galatians 3:2, 14 and 4:6 it is clear that it occurs through faith. Paul is saying that he is concerned here with justification and not with the way in which justification occurs.

The Lordship of Jesus Christ

RUDI ZIMMER

Introduction

There seems to be little doubt that one of the earliest Christian confessions was the Christological formula "Jesus Christ is Lord" (Κύριος 'Ιησοῦς Χριστός), if not the earliest.[1] It is, therefore, of great interest in determining what exactly it meant for the early Christian Church to confess Jesus Christ as "Lord," as well as what it means for today's Christians, who, with the early Christians, continue to confess Him as their "Lord."

In this study we will, in the first place, present a series of general observations regarding the use of the title "Lord" in connection with Jesus Christ in the New Testament. After this, following the clues indicated in these observations, we will proceed to determine the meaning of the Lordship of Jesus Christ. Finally, we will try to indicate some implications resulting from this study for modern Christianity.

Our sources for this study have mainly been the Scriptures of the New and Old Testaments. Although our topic points to the New Testament, the New Testament evidence itself required that the Old Testament be brought in to provide the key elements for the proper understanding of the Lordship of Jesus Christ.[2]

The use of κύριος as applied to Jesus, in the New Testament: General Observations

The following observations are based on a close examination of all New Testament passages in their contexts using the title "Lord" (κύριος) for Jesus. This examination began with the historical books because, although they were not the earliest writings, we find in them the earliest use of the title "Lord" as applied to Jesus, especially in those passages of direct address. The examination proceeded then to the Epistles up to the book of Revelation.

RUDOLPH ZIMMER is President of the Excola Superior de Teologia in Sao Paulo, Brazil.

The frequency of the use of κύριος *as applied to Jesus in the New Testament*

Κύριος is one of the most frequently used words in the New Testament.[3] It appears 717 times: 80 times in Matthew, 31 of them applied to Jesus; 18 times in Mark, 8 of them applied to Jesus; 210 times in the Lukan writings, 123 of them applied to Jesus; 522 times in John, 45 of them applied to Jesus; 14 times in James, 6 of them applied to Jesus; 275 times in Paul's Epistles, almost all of them applied to Jesus (in comparison, the name "Jesus" by itself appears only 17 times); 22 times in Peter's Epistles, 16 of them applied to Jesus; 7 times in Jude, 4 of them applied to Jesus; 16 times in Hebrews, 5 of them applied to Jesus; and 23 times in the book of Revelation, 8 of them applied to Jesus. The only New Testament writings in which κύριος does not appear are Titus and the three Epistles of John.

As this overview shows, the New Testament writers used the term κύριος not only as a designation for Jesus, but also for an "owner," or a "master," for an honorable "sir," and for the "Lord" God Himself. Our subject in this study, however, is the most common Christological use of κύριος.

The form of the title κύριος *as applied to Jesus*

Κύριος, as a Christological title, is used alone and in various types of combinations, in the New Testament literature: κύριος, κύριε, ὁ κύριος, ἐν κυρίῳ , [ὁ] κύριος [ἡμῶν] Ἰησοῦς, [ὁ] κύριος [ἡμῶν] Ἰησοῦς Χριστός, Χριστὸς Ἰησοῦς [ὁ] κύριος, Ἰησοῦς Χριστὸς κύριος ἡμῶν, Ἰησοῦς ὁ κύριος ἡμῶν, ὁ κύριος ἡμῶν Χριστός. In those passages in which Christological designations besides the title κύριος are used, their meanings are described too. That is why we assume that the uniqueness of the Christological meaning of κύριος is present above all in those passages in which this name appears alone, or as the only title qualifying the name "Jesus (Christ)."

The application of κύριος *to Jesus in Old Testament quotations*

The New Testament witness is unanimous in showing that, without any difficulty, Old Testament passages are applied to Jesus, in which κύριος translates mainly the Hebrew tetragrammaton YHWH (Yahweh). Jesus Himself and other people in the Gospel narratives and in the book of Acts, the evangelists, as well as the other New Testament authors, all see in the "Lord" Jesus Christ the fulfillment of a certain group of promises of the Old Testament with regard to Yahweh. Such an unanimous application of Old Testament passages to Jesus must receive special attention if we want to arrive at the Christological meaning contained in the name "Lord."

The relationship between the death and the resurrection of Jesus and His proclamation as "Lord"

We find several passages in which Jesus is called "Lord" during His earthly ministry (before His death and resurrection), especially through the vocative κύριε. Since this vocative is also used as a form of reverent address, similar to ἐπίστατα ("master," Luke 9:33) and ῥαββί ("master," Mark 9:5), one cannot always be sure whether the more profound Christological meaning is already present. However, there is a representative group of passages which maintain an intimate relationship between the death and the resurrection of Jesus and His proclamation as "Lord." Actually, His death and resurrection are considered the great event in which the Lordship of Jesus is plainly revealed. The apostle Paul, for example, declares: "For this very reason, Christ died and returned to life so that He might be the Lord (κυριεύσῃ) of both the dead and the living" (Rom. 14:9). This emphasis, too, cannot be forgotten as we establish the meaning of the Lordship of Christ.

The Lordship of Christ and the coming of the "Lord"

Again, beginning with Jesus, the New Testament witness abounds in showing the use of the title "Lord" in connection with Christ's coming on Judgment Day. In order to speak of this coming, the authors make use of a basic concept in Old Testament eschatology, namely the "day of the LORD" *(yom Yahweh)*. One cannot avoid the impression that the coming of the Lord "on that day" is seen as the final unfolding, the occasion in which the Lordship of Christ shall be universally revealed and recognized, when He alone will be exalted, and with Him all those who remain faithful to Him. In trying to establish the meaning of the Christological title "Lord," we also have to give due value to this evidence.

The origin and the development of the title "Lord" as a designation of Jesus

The confessional nature of the proclamation that Jesus is "Lord," so strongly present in some of the Pauline passages which point to an established liturgical use (1 Cor. 12:3; Rom. 10:9; Phil. 2:11), is already a clear indication that κύριος as a Christological title did not arise in the churches of the Hellenistic world.[4] As we already saw, two of the above conclusions force us to see the Christological meaning of κύριος as dependent on the Old Testament. In view of this, we have to conclude that "Lord," as a Christological title, arose and was used as soon as and to the extent that Jesus was seen as the fulfillment of those promises regarding a definite and final intervention of Yahweh in favor of His people and of all the nations of the world. This recognition is certainly present in the occasions in which Jesus applied this title to Himself, but even before that, in the words of Elizabeth (Luke 1:43). Above all, it came into general use among the faithful after His resurrection.

This conclusion is confirmed as we look at the issue from another angle. Gustaf Wingren says that "the confession of a particular belief is always related to the denial of that belief in the particular environment of the Church."[5] If this is true, as we think it is, then the recognition that Jesus is "Lord" arose precisely there where such a recognition was denied more than in any other place, namely, among the Jews. To illustrate this, let us recall the mocking of the Jews on the day of Pentecost (Acts 2:13). To them Peter answered: "Therefore let all Israel be assured of this: God has made this Jesus, whom you crucified, both Lord and Christ." (Acts 2:36).

Conclusive evidence in favor of this position is described by Vilson Scholz:

> However what demonstrates conclusively that the congregation of Jerusalem worshipped and confessed Jesus the Kyrios is the Aramaic expression Maran atha, which certainly is an echo of the liturgy of the church of Jerusalem, and whose preservation we owe to the apostle Paul (1 Cor. 16:22). Maranatha means "Come, our Lord" and appears translated into Greek in Rev. 22:20, erchou, Kyrie Iesou. The fact that this Aramaic formula attributes the Lordship to Christ indicates that Jesus was called Lord already in the church of Jerusalem.[6]

However, let us not forget one other bit of historical evidence. We know that, although Domitian (81-96 A.D.) was the first Roman Emperor who demanded worship as "Lord and God," already with Caligula and especially Nero, the title κύριος and the emperor cult had begun to be spread in the Roman Empire.[7] In Acts 25:26, Porcius Festus refers to the Emperor Nero calling him κύριος. Since Nero ruled from 54 to 68 A.D., when Paul wrote some of his most important Epistles, it may well be possible that, in passages like Philippians 2:11 and 1 Corinthians 8:5-6 where he proclaims Jesus Christ as the only "Lord," he may also be protesting against the blasphemy which was beginning to please the Roman emperors.[8] If in these passages such a protest is only a possibility, in John's Gospel and Revelation it is undoubted, for they were written at the time when, under the sponsorship of Domitian (81-96 A.D.) the emperor cult was propagated and its opponents persecuted. So, if at the beginning the confession that Jesus is "Lord" arose as a symbol of faith of the Christian church among the Jews, later it also became fit as a banner in the presence of a new challenge.

With these basic observations on the use of κύριος as applied to Jesus in the New Testament, especially as a Christological title, we believe that we are ready to go on to the next section in which we will try to establish the meaning of the Lordship of Jesus Christ.

The meaning of the Lordship of Jesus Christ

In the previous section we already perceived that the early church and the New Testament authors had a clear notion of what it meant to confess Jesus as "Lord." In this section, we will try to systematize in general lines this meaning.

When we want to know the meaning of a word, we look for its origin, for the situation in which it was and is used, and usually we reach its meaning. We saw in the above observations that "Lord" as a Christological title arose and was used when Jesus, in view of His life and work, was recognized as the fulfillment of that definite intervention of Yahweh on behalf of His people and all of humanity, which was announced throughout the Old Testament. This conclusion together with others showed us that the meaning of the Christological title "Lord" must be looked for both in the New Testament as well as in the Old Testament.

Jesus Christ as "Lord" is the Almighty Mediator and Ruler of the Universe

The recognition that the Lord Jesus was in control of nature must have emerged in the mind of Peter and his friends on the occasion of their great catch of fish (Luke 5). Peter's astonishment was so great that he stopped calling Jesus "Master," and fell on his knees at Jesus' feet and said: "Go away from me, *Lord,* I am a sinful man" (Luke 5:8). Later, Jesus Himself made an unequivocal statement about His universal Lordship in Matthew 28:18, although the title "Lord" is not used there. However, even though we stick only with those passages in which the title "Lord" is used, His Lordship over the universe is clearly defined. For as we study these passages we find that Christ's Lordship with regard to the created universe is presented as having two aspects: mediation and dominion.

The mediation of the Lord Jesus Christ with regard to the created universe is unmistakably stated by the apostle Paul in 1 Corinthians 8:6 "Yet for us there is but one God, the Father, from whom all things came and for whom we live; and there is but one Lord, Jesus Christ, through whom all things came and through whom we live (δι οὗ τὰ πάντα καὶ ἡμεῖς δι αὐτοῦ" (cf. Matt. 2:10, Prov. 8; Col. 1:16, 17). Similarly, the author of Hebrews speaks of the Lord Jesus as the One "through whom (δι οὗ)" God "made the universe" (Heb. 1:2), and he bases this statement on Psalm 102:26: "In the beginning, O *Lord,* you laid the foundations of the earth, and the heavens are the work of your hands" (Heb. 1:10). These statements show us that the Lord Jesus Christ is the Almighty Maker of the universe.

On the other hand, the Lordship of Jesus Christ with regard to the Universe goes beyond creation. It also includes the dominion, the ruling of the whole universe. The author of Hebrews states in the same context that the Lord Jesus is "sustaining all things (φέρων τε τὰ πάντα) by His powerful word" (Heb. 1:3). This sustenance is one side of his dominion. Besides this, His dominion includes the guidance of the universe, especially the history of mankind. When the apostle Paul was at Corinth, he had a vision in which the Lord Jesus said to him: "Do not be afraid; keep on speaking, do not be silent. For I am with you, and no one is going to attack and harm you, because I have many people in this city" (Acts 18:9,10). The statements of the Lord that "no one is going to attack and harm you" and "I have many people in this city" can only be understood if we recognize that Jesus was in control, conducting history. The idea of dominion, both in the sense of sustaining and governing, is certainly also present in those passages in which Jesus Christ is called "Lord of lords" (1 Tim. 6:15; Rev. 17:14; 19:16).[9] So, we can see that the Lord Jesus is also the Almighty Ruler of the universe.

The first impression which these passages give us is that the Biblical authors want to assert the divinity, or deity, of the Lord Jesus Christ through them. Evidently the recognition of the deity of the Lord Jesus is present, for the creation of all things as well as the dominion over them can only be attributed to someone who is true God. However, the contexts of these passages show us that the recognition of the deity of the Lord Jesus is rather always an established presupposition than an aim to be achieved.

Closer attention to the context of these passages shows us that in all of them the statements regarding the creation and the dominion of the Lord Jesus over the created universe lay the foundation of statements on redemption or on the Christian life resulting from that redemption. In Hebrews chapter 1, Christ's making and dominion over all of creation are mentioned and placed in such a way as to lay the foundation for statements on the decisive and superior character of the redemption revealed through our Lord Jesus Christ. In 1 Corinthians 8, the reference to Christ's involvement in the creation of "all things" was made in connection with the issue of food sacrificed to idols, which caused so much trouble among "weak" and "strong" brothers, "for whom Christ died." Similarly, the contexts of the other passages speak of redemption (see Matt. 28:18; Col. 1:16-17; Acts 18:9-10; 1 Tim. 6:15; Rev. 17:14; 19:16).

These findings force us to the conclusion that, much more than to prove the deity of Jesus, the aim of the Biblical authors was to place the Lordship of Jesus Christ over the created universe as the *foundation of particularity also in the redemption of the world,* both in stating that He alone has the *right* over all of creation, as in affirming that He alone has the power to guarantee its final and complete redemption.[10] In other words, through His Lordship over the universe, the Lord Jesus Christ establishes, on the one hand, His just claim on every creature of this great universe, above all, on man, and, on the other hand, He gives total guarantee that through His almighty power He can and does accomplish full and perfect redemption of those who come to believe in Him. So, in view of this, on those who reject His redemption His just claim remains up, to its execution on Judgment Day, but for those who come to believe in Him, His just claim gives room to justification and, at the end, to complete restoration, when they will not only be raised from the dead but will inhabit the new heavens and the new earth together with their Lord.

Jesus Christ as "Lord" is the Triumphant Personal Redeemer

The majority of passages containing the Christological title "Lord" speak of the redemption of mankind. These will occupy us now. Our conclusion that the meaning of κύριος has to be looked for starting with the Old Testament is to be followed especially at this point. However, since this involves so many quotations from and allusions to the Old Testament, we come to this question: Where should we begin? Besides this there comes another more difficult question: Should we stick only to the words of the quotations, or can we explore beyond them their Old Testament contexts?

Let us answer this last question first. Whereas the Old Testament was *the* Bible of the early Church and of the Lord Jesus Himself, we cannot take these quotations separately, but we have to take them as part of the wider context from which they were taken.[11] So, if we take the Old Testament quotations and allusions from this perspective, we note that all of them are connected in one way or the other with either one of two major events: the exodus from Egypt or the prophetic Day of the Lord.

In all of the Synoptic Gospels we find Jesus interpreting His Lordship on the basis of Psalm 110, (Matt. 22:43, 45; Mark 18:36; Luke 20:42, 44), which is also mentioned in Peter's sermon on Pentecost (Acts 2:34), and in Hebrews (7:17, 21). If one examines Psalm 110, it becomes evident that the exaltation of the King-Priest is related to His "day of battle" (v. 3) and "the day of his wrath" (v. 5). Jesus also speaks directly of Himself as being the "Lord" in connection with this concept. In two occasions Jesus pictures Himself on Judgment Day being addressed as "Lord" (Matt. 7:21-23; 25:37, 44). Especially in His eschatological discourse, (Matt. 25:37, 44), the judgment is entirely molded according to the themes of the Day of Yahweh (Matt. 24:29; cf. Is. 13:10; Ezek. 32:7; Joel 2:31).

Besides this, Jesus Himself states: "Therefore keep watch, because you do not know on what day your Lord will come (Matt. 24:42). Within the same concept fit Jesus' words when he said: "the Lord needs them" (Matt. 21:3; Mark 11:3; Luke 19:31, 34), spoken when He asked for the colt for His triumphal entry into Jerusalem, because they are connected with a prophecy of Zechariah (Zech. 9:9), which speaks of the "day of the Lord" (cf. Zech. 9:16).

Moreover, we must mention Elizabeth's words of astonishment when she received "the mother of my Lord" (Luke 1:43), and the words of the angel: "Today . . . a Savior has been born to you; he is Christ the Lord" (Luke 2:11). Both of these are connected with the "day of the Lord" (cf. Mal. 3: 1-2; 4:1-6). Finally, we have to add here the many other New Testament passages related to the "day of the Lord" (see Acts 2:20; 1 Thess. 5:2; 2 Thess. 2:2; 1 Cor. 1:8-9; 5:5; 2 Cor. 1:14; 2 Tim. 1:18; 2 Pet. 1:16; 3:10; James 5:7-8).

On the other hand, we have clear references to the exodus in passages that deal with Christ's Lordship. In all of the Gospels we find the quotation of Isaiah 40:3 as having been fulfilled by John the Baptist. He is the "voice of one calling in the desert, 'Prepare the way for the Lord' " (Matt. 3:3; Mark 1:3; Luke 3:4; John 1:23). Isaiah 40 is the great pericope of comfort entirely built on the themes of the exodus. It announces the advent of a new exodus for the people of God. Besides this, in three of the Gospels we find Jesus saying: "For the Son of Man is Lord of the Sabbath" (Matt. 12:8; Mark 2:22;

Luke 6:5). The Sabbath, as we know, was instituted at the exodus (Ex. 20:8-11; Deut. 5:12-15).

Going to the other New Testament literature, James speaks of the "Glory" as an appositive of the expression "our Lord Jesus Christ." It was at the exodus that the "glory of Yahweh" appeared for the first time as the gracious presence of God among His people (Ex. 16:10; 24:15-17; 40:34-35). The author of Hebrews speaks of the "great Shepherd of the sheep," identified as "our Lord Jesus" (Heb. 13:20). Through Isaiah 63:11 we see this, too, as an allusion to the exodus. Finally, in the book of Revelation the victorious "Lamb" is called "Lord of lords" (Rev. 17:14), which can only be understood as a reference to the paschal lamb of the exodus.

We have not mentioned all passages, but enough to show that they are related to either one of two major Old Testament events: the exodus or the prophetic Day of the Lord. However, a closer examination of the descriptions of the Day of the Lord in the Old Testament shows that this concept, too, has its origin in the exodus.[12] In view of this, we have to say that the Christological meaning of the title "Lord," as it is used to describe Christ's redemptive work, must be sought, above all, in the event of Israel's exodus from Egypt.

Κύριος *incarnandus*

As we saw, it is, above all, in the event of Israel's exodus that the meaning of Christ's Lordship in redemption is to be found. Therefore, if we follow the clues which the New Testament gives us by way of the Old Testament quotations in this connection, we come to several very significant and revealing occasions in the exodus event and in the further development of Israel's history.

One clue is the title κύριος itself, which is the Greek version of the Hebrew *yhwh* (Yahweh). This takes us to Exodus 6, where the name "Yahweh" is the central theme. Without going into details, one can say that the point of this text is not so much to make known the form of God's name "Yahweh," but rather the character and real meaning of this name. This becomes especially clear in verses 6 and 7. There it is said that as soon as Yahweh "will bring you out from under the yoke of the Egyptians," and "will free you from being slaves to them and will redeem you with an outstretched arm and with mighty acts of judgment," (Ex. 6:6) by which "I will take you as my own people, and I will be your God," then Israel "will know that I am the LORD (Yahweh) your God" (Ex. 6:7). So, the character and real meaning of the name "Yahweh" is associated with this great deliverance of Israel from the tyranny of Egyptian enslavement.

In this connection, it is important to say that the book of Exodus has enough evidence to show that the Egyptian enslavement was not merely political but above all religious and spiritual. This becomes apparent when we see Egypt being referred to as a personified being (cf. Ex. 3:8), the common understanding of the Pharaohs as being sons of the gods, and especially the statement that Israel's liberation constituted a victory over "all the gods of Egypt" (Ex. 12:12; cf. 15:11; 18:11).[13]

To be noted, too, is Yahweh's personal involvement in Israel's liberation. From birth He prepared Moses as His personal mediator, whom He later made "like God to Pharaoh" (Ex. 7:1), and gave him as a guide and victorious leader to Israel (Ex. 3:10, 16-18; cf. Is. 63:11; Num. 27:17). Besides this, Yahweh Himself "descended" (Ex. 19:18) in His "glory" into the middle of His people, on a cloud (Ex. 16:10; 24:15-16; 40:34), from which He spoke to them through Moses. All this is summed up in His personal name "Yahweh." So, the personal God "Yahweh" reached out personally to His people, leading them to victory and salvation.

One other clue associated with the Christological title "Lord" is the Sabbath. At Mount Sinai, Yahweh instituted the "Sabbath day" (Ex. 20:8-11). The first reason given for it is linked to creation. However, as Moses recalled the institution of the Sabbath day, he pointed to a second reason: "Observe the Sabbath day by keeping it holy . . . the seventh day is a Sabbath to the LORD your God. . . . Remember that you were slaves in Egypt and that the LORD your God brought you out of there with a mighty hand and an outstretched arm. Therefore the LORD your God has commanded you to observe the Sabbath day" (Deut. 5:12, 15). So the celebration of the Sabbath was a perpetual sign that Yahweh was the Redeemer of Israel, who separated them as His "treasured possession" (Ex. 19:5; cf. 31:16, 17; Ezek. 20:12).

However, since the Sabbath was also a celebration of creation, we have here what we already saw before: Yahweh performed Israel's redemption because He is Lord over all creation. Beyond the Sabbath day, however, Yahweh instituted a Sabbath year, the Year of Jubilee (Lev. 25:8-54), which was to be celebrated every fiftieth year. On this occasion all the debts were to be cancelled and all the slaves set at liberty. This was to be the greatest celebration of the people's liberation from Egypt.[14]

As time passed, though, it became clear that the release from the power of Egypt in the exodus was not yet the definite and decisive liberation of mankind from Satanic slavery. The people of Israel,

instead of truly being a "kingdom of priests" before the other nations
(Ex. 19:5-6), rather prostituted themselves with their gods and were
slowly absorbed by those nations. That is when the prophets "saw"
(Is. 1:1; Amos 1:1; etc.) that the liberation from Egypt was really
the "shadow" (Col. 2:17) of a definite and final liberation which
Yahweh was yet to realize. So they started to announce the advent
of a "Day of Yahweh" (Is. 13:6, 9; Joel 1:15; 2:1, 11, 31; Amos 5:18,
20; Zeph. 1:7, 14; etc.).

That is where the next clue from the New Testament passages
on the Lordship of Christ points. The terminology and the figures
used to describe "that day" derived mainly from the exodus, but the
proportions of that "Day of Yahweh" were to be greater than anything that had happened so far: "That day" would be a day of cosmic
changes (Amos 5:18, 20; Zech. 14:4-5), of universal devastation (Is.
13:9), of slaughter and destruction of the enemies (Is. 34:2), of lam-
entation and terror (Zeph. 1:18; Is. 13:7-8); but also of releasing a
"remnant" (Is. 10:20), of fertility (Is. 4:2), of pouring out the Spirit
(Joel 2:28-29), of praise and celebration (Zeph. 3:15), and of universal
peace (Is. 11:6-9).

With the proclamation of this "Day of Yahweh" it also became
clear that the first day which was consecrated to Yahweh, the Sabbath, as well as the Year of Jubilee, as they celebrated the liberation
from Egypt, they proclaimed at the same time the advent of another
Sabbath, an eschatological Jubilee, when Yahweh would come to
deliver definitely and decisively all of humanity from the slavery of
the Evil One (cf. Is. 58:13; 61:1-3).

Above all we need to emphasize that "on that day" Yahweh would
accomplish redemption personally. This is already implicit in the
expression "Day of Yahweh." Moreover, although the prophets announced that Yahweh would visit His people "on that day" as the
Davidic King (Is. 11:10; Jer. 30:9), or as the King-Priest (Ps. 110),
they also stated that, Yahweh Himself would come and tend His
flock "like a shepherd" (Is. 40:11; Ezek. 34:11-31).

This is, in summary, the background which we have to view the
coming of the Lord Jesus Christ. And it is starting with this background that we shall understand what it means to confess Jesus
Christ as "Lord" (κύριος).

Κύριος *incarnatus*

Luke informs us about the impact which the visit of the pregnant
Virgin Mary had on the pregnant Elizabeth. As she heard Mary's
salutation, "Elizabeth was filled with the Holy Spirit" (Luke 1:41)

and exclaimed in a loud voice: "Blessed are you among women, and blessed is the child you will bear! But why am I so favored, that the mother of my Lord should come to me?" (Luke 1:42-43). Elizabeth perceived that she was at the brink of the decisive redemptive manifestation of God. Finally, the angels on the fields of Bethlehem announced the good news: "Today in the town of David a Savior has been born to you; he is Christ the Lord" (Luke 2:11). The great "day of the LORD" had dawned on enslaved mankind. It is evident that the "day" cannot be understood here as an ordinary day, but as the whole period of God's redemptive intervention in Christ. However, few people had become aware of this manifestation yet.

A clear indication that the "Day of the Lord" had arrived is Jesus' insistence on working on the Sabbath day. According to the law of the Jews, all of the work which Jesus did on the Sabbath should have waited for the next day. Why did He not wait? Being the definite and incarnated manifestation of the redemption promised by God, Jesus wanted to demonstrate to the people His right to deliver on the Sabbath day, for it was this liberation that the Sabbath had been announcing. Jesus certainly was "the Lord of the Sabbath" (Matt. 12:8; Mark 2:28). That is why He did so many healings on the Sabbath, including the casting out of demons (Matt. 12:9-13; Luke 4:31-37, 38-39; 13:10-17; John 5:1-10; 9:1-41; etc.). In doing these miracles on the Sabbath, Jesus was proclaiming a specific message: Behold, here is the Triumphant Redeemer personally performing the final and decisive liberation, by which He is setting mankind free from the demonic enslaving powers.

All of this is emphatically presented in Luke 4:16-21: Jesus was in a synagogue at Nazareth on a Sabbath day. After He read the text from Isaiah, which speaks of "the year of the Lord's favor," He said: "Today this scripture is fulfilled in your hearing." Since the expression "the year of the Lord's favor" is a reference to the Year of Jubilee, Jesus was announcing the beginning of the great jubilee of the eschatological last days in which freedom and rest would be established definitely. The "shadow" was being absorbed by the "body" (Col. 2:17). The promise of redemption was giving way to redemption itself.

Even so, only very few people recognized that Jesus was the great Redeemer sent by God. His external form was a scandal for the people. Nazareth! Can anything good come from there?" some said (John 1:46). Others shouted: "You are demon-possessed" (John 7:20). Still others stated: "By Beelzebub, the prince of demons, he is driving out demons" (Luke 11:15). And the crowd shouted: "Crucify him!"

(Mark 15:13). According to them, this humble man could not be the Triumphant Redeemer. However, it is precisely in this that we find the key by which the work of Jesus came to reach universal significance.

As we spoke of the exodus, we observed that Yahweh in various different ways emphasized that He was personally involved in the liberation of the people of Israel. Now all of this was being fulfilled in the PERSON of the man Jesus. At first sight, which was also the impression of many of Jesus' contemporaries, the deliverance undertaken by a man seems to be inferior to a liberation undertaken by a whole nation (Israel in the exodus). However, we have to recognize that a liberation accomplished by a man is not inferior, but on the contrary infinitely superior if this man is at the same time the Almighty Mediator and Ruler of the Universe, and if, on the other hand, this Lord of the Universe chooses to become man precisely to meet the enemy on his own ground, so that He may be able to strike that enemy at the spot of fatal vulnerability.

In the fall narrative, in Genesis 3, we discover the fatal spot of Satan. There we perceive that it was through the way of exaltation, of wanting to "be like God" (Gen. 3:5), that the devil conducted first man to disobedience, to sin, and, as its consequence, to death, which enslaved all of mankind. Therefore, the chains of sin and death which hold mankind captive under Satan's claws can only be torn through the way of humiliation and total obedience to the justice of God (which is impossible to any human being). That is why, by the supreme grace of God (Rom. 5:15, 20), the Lord of the Universe became man in order to confront the devil in the decisive battle, in the name and in the place of every human being. So He met Satan in all types of temptations, but without sin (Heb. 2:18), and, in total obedience to the justice of God, took upon Himself the sins and guilt of all human beings and proceeded on the way of humiliation up to the accursed and heinous death on the cross.

This, however, was the only way to strike the devil at his spot of fatal vulnerability without, at the same time, destroying man, but rather liberating him from enslavement. And there was no danger of Jesus being defeated, for as Lord of the Universe His victory was guaranteed beforehand, so that even on the day of His human birth He was called "the Lord" (Luke 2:11). This was confirmed when three days after His death Jesus rose up as the Triumphant Redeemer, establishing publicly the defeat of Satan and his hosts. It is in this, then, that the Lordship of Jesus consists: In His victory over the power which was enslaving and destroying mankind.[15]

The unanimous witness of the New Testament writings confirms this conclusion, for it identifies precisely the death and resurrection of Christ as the establishing event of His Lordship. Here we see the intimate connection between the revelation of the meaning of the name "Yahweh" in the exodus and the revelation of the meaning of the title "Lord" in the event of the death and resurrection of Christ, a connection of type and antitype, in which, however, the latter entirely absorbs and supersedes the former recapitulating and consummating it much beyond its own perspective. As Thomas saw the risen Christ, he exclaimed: "My Lord and my God!" (John 20:28). Peter, in his Pentecost sermon, said: "This man . . . you, with the help of wicked men, put to death by nailing Him to the cross. But God raised Him from the dead, freeing Him from the agony of death, because it was impossible for death to keep its hold on Him . . . Therefore let all Israel be assured of this: God has made this Jesus, whom you crucified, both Lord and Christ" (Acts 2:23-24, 36; cf. Rom. 14:9). Also in his first Epistle, Peter writes: "Praise be to the God and Father of our Lord Jesus Christ! In His great mercy he has given us new birth into a living hope through the resurrection of Jesus Christ from the dead" (1 Pet. 1:3). The cosmic manifestations associated with Jesus' death and resurrection gave further assurance that the final liberation had occurred, as the prophets had foreseen (cf. Amos 5:18; Is. 13:10; Zeph. 1:15; Ezek. 38:19).

So, what did it mean to confess Jesus Christ as "Lord"? It meant and still means to recognize, acclaim and proclaim Him as the personal Triumphant Redeemer. "Triumphant Redeemer"—because He, in great victory, has torn apart the chains that held us prisoners of Satan, namely, sin and death, as we hear from the apostle Paul: "Where, O death, is your victory? Where, O death, is your sting? The sting of death is sin, and the power of sin is the law. But thanks be to God! He gives us the victory through our Lord Jesus Christ" (1 Cor. 15:55-57). "Personal Redeemer"—because Jesus Christ, although being true God and the Lord of the Universe, personally took upon Himself our fight, became man, and offered Himself like a Lamb without defect, in total obedience to the justice of God, as a sacrifice in the place and for the sake of every one of us human beings. Thus, Christians do not follow a principle, they also do not worship a far distant god, neither do they submit themselves to an enslaving tyrant, but they have as their Lord the person Jesus Christ who identified Himself with them in their greatest personal need. Certainly this, too, was being put before the Corinthians when Paul said: "For even if there are so-called gods, whether in heaven or on

earth (as indeed there are many 'gods' and many 'lords'), yet for us
there is but one God, the Father, from whom all things came and
for whom we live; and there is but one Lord, Jesus Christ, through
whom all things came and through whom we live" . . . but, Paul
continues saying that even for the "weaker brother" he "died" (1 Cor.
8:5, 6, 11).

However, if we go back for a moment to the prophets' words on
the "Day of the Yahweh," we have to recognize that even with the
death and the resurrection of Christ the ultimate consummation of
the redemptive work seems not to have occurred. For, where are the
radical cosmic changes of universal range (Is. 13:10; cf. Zeph. 1:15;
Joel 3:15)? Where is the universal devastation with the destruction
of the sinners (Is. 13:9; cf. 34:2; Joel 2:3)? Where is the universal
terror and anguish (Is. 5:30; cf. 8:22)? And where is, on the other
hand, the universal peace (Is. 11:6, 9; cf. Hos. 2:18; Joel 2:3)? At
last, where is the total restoration, the complete reversal (*shuv shev-
oth*, Zeph. 3:20)? In fact, the New Testament itself recognizes this
situation: while on the one hand it states categorically that the
liberation of mankind from the dominion of Satan was definitely
accomplished through the death and the resurrection of Jesus Christ,
on the other hand it places with the same emphasis the consummation of this deliverance in the future, "when our Lord Jesus comes
with all his holy ones" (1 Thess. 3:13), namely, at His Second Coming.

Is this delay of the consummation a sign of weakness of the Lord
Jesus? Are those who put their hope in Him being deceived? St.
Peter, in his second Epistle, mentions people who thought like that.
He showed them that, on the contrary, the delay is rather a confirmation of God's love for all men. As he said: "The Lord is not slow
in keeping his promise, as some understand slowness. He is patient
with you, not wanting anyone to perish, but everyone to come to
repentance" (2 Pet. 3:9). In other words, the Lord Jesus wants the
blessing of His great redemption to come to all men that no one may
perish.

However, when the Gospel, which announces the good news of
freedom, is preached in the whole world (Matt. 24:14), then the Lord
shall certainly come, but at that time "like a thief in the night" (1
Thess. 5:2; 2 Pet. 3:10). Then those prophecies of universal range
connected with the "Day of Yahweh" will also be fulfilled. That is
why, in the New Testament, the theme of the "Day of the Lord" is
continued and deepened (Matt. 24:42; 1 Thess. 2:2; 2 Thess. 2:2; 1
Cor. 1:8-9; 5:5; 2 Cor. 1:14; 2 Tim. 1:18; 2 Pet. 3:10, 12). One of its
main emphases is that the patience of the Lord Jesus will not go

beyond "that day." For on that day "at the name of Jesus every knee" shall "bow, in heaven and on earth and under the earth, and every tongue confess that Jesus Christ is Lord, to the glory of God the Father" (Phil. 2:10, 11). Many will do it voluntarily and as victors (Matt. 25:34-40; Rev. 17:14), but so many others will do it as "cursed," about to be thrown into "eternal punishment" (Matt. 25:41-46; cf. Rom. 14:10, 11). This takes us ahead to the next part.

Jesus Christ as "Lord" is the Enabling and Defending Guide of those made free

We saw that the Lord delays His return because He does not want anyone to perish (2 Pet. 3:9). This means that those who do not recognize Jesus as the Personal Triumphant Redeemer and believe in Him continue as prisoners of the devil, so that unless they, too, come to this recognition they shall have the same destiny of the enslaver. That is why, in order to take to them the message of victory, the Lord Jesus established the church, which is the communion of those made free. To this church, whose task is to proclaim liberty to the captives, Jesus Christ comes as the Enabling and Defending Guide. We think that this designation synthesizes what the New Testament speaks of Jesus as "Lord" in those passages related to the Church and its task. He is the "Enabling Guide" because He bestows gifts on the Church for the accomplishment of its task (Luke 24:34; Acts 1:24; 9:15; 10:14; 20:24, 32; 2 Cor. 8:5, 9; etc.), and guides it with His commandments (John 13:14; Acts 21:14; 1 Cor. 1:10; 9:14; 1 Pet. 2:13; 3:15; Heb. 13:20; etc.). He is the "Defending Guide" because He defends the church from all of its enemies and assists it with His power up to His coming on the "Day of the Lord" (Acts 7:59, 60; 12:11; 2 Tim. 3:11; 1 Thess. 4:6; 2 Thess. 1:8; 2:8, 9; Rev. 17:14; 19:16; etc.).

In view of the limits of this study, let us only consider the commandments and imperatives spoken by the Lord Jesus Christ or given in His name. John tells us that, after Jesus washed the disciples' feet, he told them: "Now that I, your Lord and Teacher, have washed your feet, you also should wash one another's feet" (John 13:14). If we look closely at the second part of this verse, we see Jesus giving the disciples a command. This poses the question: Is the Triumphant Redeemer, and the Enabling and Defending Guide also a legislator? Similar commandments appear in the Epistles, given "in the name of the Lord Jesus." The apostle Paul, for example, at the beginning of his first Epistle to the Corinthians, says: "I appeal to you, brothers, in the name of our Lord Jesus Christ, that all of you agree with one another so that there be no divisions among you . . . " (1 Cor. 1:10). In Ephesians we read: "Therefore do not be foolish, but understand what the Lord's will is. Do not get drunk on wine, which leads to debauchery. Instead be filled with the Spirit" (Eph. 5:17-18). Or that other commandment: "In the same way, the Lord has commanded that those who preach the gospel should receive their living from the gospel" (1 Cor. 9:14). Should we understand these passages in the sense that Jesus first sets us free from the power of Satan and his associates, and then He Himself becomes a new tyrant for us?

In order to understand this question, let us go back again to Exodus. As the people came to Mount Sinai, Yahweh "descended" upon the mountain and gave Moses the Ten Commandments (Ex. 20). If we look at the Hebrew, we will see that the verbs in the Commandments are indicatives and not imperatives. Actually, the Ten Commandments are statements of that which the redeemed Israelite, who proved God's grace, will voluntarily do, and not "commandments" of what he must do to merit God's love. On the other hand, these same statements will become law to him as soon as he falls into sin, because they are the summary of God's holy will.

Similarly the question of Jesus' commands must be treated. We live in the end time, waiting for His final return. His commandments are the expression of what the Christian will do as one that was completely delivered from slavery. However, since, at the same time, we remain being sinners, these commandments condemn our best efforts. Richard N. Longenecker shows how the Christian is motivated to do what he is expected to do by such commands: "Also, the imperatives find their motivation in the indicative of the Gospel. Christian ethic is motivated by love and not impelled by a desire to gain righteousness."[16] In view of this, the attempt to divide our Savior and Lord Jesus Christ into a Savior who redeemed us from sin and, at the same time, into an enslaving tyrant is totally contrary to the witness of the New Testament.

Conclusion

Dr. Martin Luther has nicely summarized most of our subject in the explanation of the Second Article of the Creed, in his Large Catechism:

> What is it to "become a Lord?" It means that He has redeemed me from sin, from the devil, from death, and from all evil. Before this I had no Lord and King but was captive under

the power of the devil. I was condemned to death and entangled in sin and blindness.

When we were created by God the Father and had received from Him all kinds of good things, the devil came and led us into disobedience, sin, death, and all evil. We lay under God's wrath and displeasure, doomed to eternal damnation, as we had deserved. There was no counsel, no help for us until this only eternal Son of God, in His unfathomable goodness, had mercy on our misery and wretchedness and came from heaven to help us. Those tyrants and jailers now have been routed, and their place has been taken by Jesus Christ, the Lord of life and righteousness and every good and blessing. He has snatched us, poor lost creatures, from the jaws of hell, won us, made us free, and restored us to the Father's favor and grace. He has taken us as His own, under His protection, in order that He may rule us by His righteousness, wisdom, power, life and blessedness.

Let this be the summary of this article, that the little word "Lord" simply means the same as Redeemer, that is, he who has brought us back from the devil to God, from death to life, from sin to righteousness, and now keeps us safe there. . . .[17]

However, I would like to suggest some implications of this study for us today:

(a) The Lordship of Jesus Christ requires the unquestionable reaffirmation of the "scandal of particularity."

(b) The Lordship of Jesus Christ is an affirmation of the decisive character of our liberation from the chains which held us captive to Satan.

(c) The Lordship of Jesus Christ is a death sentence for all types of "lords" who attempt to undermine the decisive character of our Lord's work.

(d) The Lordship of Jesus Christ constitutes a rejection and condemnation of all types of arrogance and pride, and a powerful invitation to humility.

(e) The Lordship of Jesus Christ calls everyone of us and the Christian church as a whole for an urgent missionary activity that receives priority over all other activities. Although other activities may appear being important, if, however, they take the place of that activity, or if they do not support it, then they come under the Lord's judgment.

(f) The Lordship of Jesus Christ requires, on the one hand, that we reveal the true nature of sin and death, namely, their enslaving power which places mankind under Satan's feet and, on the other hand, that we proclaim total deliverance through the redemption of our Lord Jesus Christ, dead and risen.

(g) The Lordship of Jesus Christ calls us to a personal ministry in which even death is not too high a sacrifice to be rendered for the deliverance of but one captive of Satan.

(h) The confession of the Lordship of Jesus Christ gives security to the child, to the youth, to the adult, as well as to the old person, in the midst of the frightening world of today.

(i) The message of the Lordship of Jesus Christ is the only one capable of empowering us to live a consecrated life that is modeled according to the perfection for which we have already been conquered by our Lord.

(j) The confession of the Lordship of Jesus Christ is impregnated with the expectation of the Lord's imminent return on the day of final revenge against His and the Christians' enemies, and of final liberation of the faithful.

(k) The confession of the Lordship of Jesus Christ commissions every theologian and pastor of today with the permanent theological task of articulating the Christian faith in such a way as to meet our present challenges, so that through the power of the Holy Spirit it be recognized as relevant to the most basic human needs.

Notes

[1] The confessional character of this expression can be seen in the use of the verb "to confess" (ὁμολογέω, ἐχομολογέω) in Romans 10:9, Philippians 2:11, and 1 Corinthians 12:3. See also Gustaf Wingren, *Creation and Law* (Edinburgh and London: Oliver and Boyd, 1961), p. 3.

[2] One can find a similar approach in Wingren, *Creation and Law,* pp. 6-17.

[3] W. F. Moulton and A. S. Genden, eds., *A Concordance to the Greek Testament,* rev. H. K. Moulton (4th ed., Edinburgh: T. and T. Clark, 1963), pp. 565-74.

[4] Cf. Werner Kramer, *Christ, Lord, Son of God,* Studies in Biblical Theology 50, trans. Brian Hardy (London: SCM Press Ltd., 1966), pp. 65-66; Richard N. Longenecker, *The Christology of Early Jewish Christianity,* Studies in Biblical Theology—17 (London: SCM Press Ltd., 1970), p. 125.

[5] Wingren, *Creation and Law,* p. 4.

[6] Vilson Scholz, "KYRIOS IESOUS CHRISTOS: Jesus Cristo é Senhor," *Igreja Luterana* (30. Trimestre de 1981), 41, 3:6.

[7] Adolf Deissmann, *Licht vom Osten: Das Neue Testament und die neuentdeckten Texte der dellenistisch-römischen Weit* (Vierte Auflage; Tubingen: Verlag von J.C.B. Mohr—Paul Siebeck, 1923), pp. 300-301; cf. Ferdinand Hahn, *The Titles of Jesus in Christology: Their History in Early Christianity,* trans. Harold Knight and George Ogg (London: Lutterworth Press, 1969), pp. 69-70.

[8] Cf. Deissmann, *Licht vom Osten,* p. 302.

[9] One clearly perceives in these passages that the Lord Jesus does not depend on the conversion of men in order to exercise His Lordship over them and over creation. Rather, He retains His divine liberty not only to sustain the universe, but also to take even His enemies into His service.

This is in perfect agreement with the Old Testament revelation (cf. Gen. 45:5-8; 50:20; Is. 10:5-27), which was *the* Bible of early Christianity.

[10] Therefore, when we say that the New Testament teaches the "scandal of particularity" (John 4:22; Acts 4:11-12), this already has as its foundation the Lordship of Christ over the universe.

[11] Wingren, *Creation and Law,* p. 7.

[12] Rudi Zimmer, "The Day of Yahweh and the Latter Days in the Old Testament and the Qumran Literature" (Unpublished Research Paper, Concordia Seminary, St. Louis, 1976), pp. 11-12.

[13] Rudi Zimmer, "The Toledoth-Formula in Genesis" (Unpublished Th.D. Thesis, Concordia Seminary, St. Louis, 1980), p. 238.

[14] Robert D. Brinsmead, "Jesus and the Sabbath," *Verdict: A Journal of Theology* (September 1981) 4:6-16.

[15] See also Wingren, *Creation and Law,* p. 29.

[16] Richard N. Longenecker, *Paul, Apostle of Liberty* (Grand Rapids: Baker, 1964), p. 179.

[17] Theodore G. Tappert, trans. and ed., *The Book of Concord* (Philadelphia: Fortress, 1959), p. 414.

Real Life Ministry: Definition and Appraisal

HOWARD W. KRAMER

"Real-life ministry" is a term being heard more frequently in seminary circles and throughout the church. The term is often used in conversations which stress the need for major changes in the training programs of prospective pastors. The conclusion reached in many discussions is that current seminary students are not being adequately prepared for "real-life ministry."

In Lutheran Church—Missouri Synod circles, the term "real-life ministry" surfaced quite prominently in a February, 1986 Planning Conference held in St. Louis. Present at the meeting were representatives of all the districts of The Lutheran Church—Missouri Synod, normally the president and full-time executives; the presidents of the colleges and seminaries of the Synod; a generous sampling of elected officials and executives of the Synod; and a variety of other guests. Although a number of topics were treated by various units of the conference, it was Planning Unit III (Higher Education) which summed up its recommendations under the title: "Training Clergy for Real-Life Ministry." We will refer to the recommendations of this unit later; the point is that the term "real-life ministry" assumed meaning for many Lutheran Church—Missouri Synod leaders on the occasion of this conference, especially in the report of the Higher Education Unit.

I. Defining Terms

The report of the unit which produced the statement on "real-life ministry" gives only indirect information on the meaning of the term. Thus, the first purpose of this study is to define the term as precisely as possible.

We begin with the word "ministry" and face the first problem, the fact that "ministry" means different things to different people.

HOWARD W. KRAMER is President of Concordia Lutheran Theological Seminary, St. Catharines, Ontario.

It is not our purpose to debate the relative merits of the several popular views of the ministry. Because the Planning Council Unit entitled its report "Training *Clergy* for Real-Life Ministry," we will assume that "ministry" means the Office of the Holy Ministry and not some other or broader definition of the term. This, then, is "ministry" in the traditional Lutheran sense, a ministry ordained by God and with authority in spiritual matters only. The minister in this case is a pastor or shepherd in the spirit of the term "Seelsorger." His primary purpose is to lead people to the Chief Shepherd and keep them in the fold by the use of the means of grace.

The practical implications of this definition of "ministry" are significant in view of the wrong impressions of ministry in society. The media are not helpful. In many movies, television programs, books and magazines the pastor is depicted as a bumbling fool who tries to act important and officious, but who really looks quite silly as he attempts to make ancient rituals and beliefs applicable to twentieth century life. There is obviously no concept of "shepherd" in this image of the ministry.

There is also a general tendency to see the pastor as one who ignores principles and beliefs in the interest of gaining and keeping a following. Oswald Hoffmann, long-time speaker on "The Lutheran Hour," stated in one of his sermons that there may be a crisis in theology today because

> too many people expect a minister to be a carbon copy of the sweet-talking, unctuous, confidence man—a sort of corporate vice-president in charge of public relations, whose job it is to know what people want to hear, and then offer it to them in the most attractive package possible. The idea is to please as many people as possible and the worst possible thing is to rock the boat.[1]

This mistaken idea of "ministry" also omits the meaningful quality of spiritual service devoted to the use of our Lord's means of grace.

Next comes the real challenge of this study, that is, a definition of the term "real-life." The use of the term in reference to pastoral education suggests that there is training for something less, or other than, "real-life." If this is the case, then there is also a suggestion that either: 1) the church never really trained pastors for "real-life"; or that 2) "real-life" has changed and the church has failed to adjust its pastoral training to the changes. Assuming that no one would try to prove that the church has always failed to prepare pastors for "real-life," we assume that the real accusation in urging preparation for "real-life" ministry is that the church has failed to adapt its pastoral training to fit the changes in the world over recent decades or centuries.

As we list examples of change in the world, we are not suggesting that anyone claims that the Holy Spirit is powerless to do His work under the changed conditions; there is simply a recognition that the devil has some powerful and different tools with which to work. These indisputable changes will influence the manner in which the Christian message is preached and perceived.

Compared with the period of one hundred and fifty years ago, we now have the materialism, secularism, hedonism and violence of the world introduced into our family rooms through color television. Average children and adults spend long hours daily digesting what is offered there. Materialism, secularism, hedonism and violence were evident one hundred and fifty years ago as well, but they can hardly be said to have been so graphically and attractively packaged and so continuously presented.

The skyrocketing divorce rate, the number of single parent families, and the increasing acceptance of unmarried mothers are symptoms of some significant changes in society. When teachers in parochial schools and Sunday Schools can no longer assume that the majority of the children in classes are living with their natural father and/or mother we have obviously undergone some kind of environmental change in our church and society. The situation may call for new and innovative approaches to such segments of our audience. Symptoms of the change in the make-up and attitude of the younger generation include the great increase in the use of drugs among young people. While alcohol has been around for a long time and has been abused just as long as it has been around, the wide use of drugs like marijuana, heroin and cocaine in Western culture is a new phenomenon. Apparently, too, young people become sexually active at younger and younger ages and illicit sex is almost taken for granted among many. With contraceptives easily available and abortion not difficult to obtain, we are facing a new challenge in even discussing moral issues with the members of the younger generation.

An additional change in society, one which no pastor may ignore, is the changing role of women in our society. Women, who make up over fifty percent of congregational membership, properly are enjoying a new sense of independence and confidence in recent years; women have also been given new opportunities for service in our church. Further, many mothers work outside the home and more and more have careers of their own. If a pastor ministers as if he is still dealing with the role of women as it was in Walther's day, he may find himself ineffective in that area of the ministry.

Another change in the make-up of present-day congregations is the fact that a larger percentage of the members are as well educated as or better educated than the pastor. This situation is very different from that of one hundred and fifty years ago when the pastor was often the most highly-educated person in the parish. The pastor will recognize that his parishioners may be influenced in their view of life by the philosophy of the art, music, drama and literature which is part of their education and life. The pastor may also recognize that such educated individuals may be "turned off" by traditional jargon and presentations, especially if accompanied by the pastor's "Sunday only" voice. The point is simply that the educational level of the audience has changed and the pastor needs to be aware of it.

The complexion of the audience has changed in other ways. In the age of Walther, non-Caucasians were extremely rare in congregations. Today, minorities, for example blacks and Hispanics, are a significant feature of North American society. They live in the community of the church building, and they may be part of the audience on any given Sunday. "Real-life" ministry will not think only in terms of white Anglo-Saxon Protestants, but it will include constituencies which are not necessarily comfortable with Western European culture and thinking. The church has become aware of unique cultures in foreign mission fields and has adapted to them; it must recognize and adapt to the new and unique cultures represented in North American audiences. The point is that the change in the audience which the church seeks to reach constitutes a change in the "real-life" situation.

The audience has changed in other perceptible ways. More people are living longer and the average age of many congregations is significantly higher than it was. Add the fact that the birth rate is down significantly from what it was one hundred and fifty years ago and this "higher average age" becomes even more important.

The number of single adults of all ages is another consideration. Unmarried singles, divorced singles and bereaved singles are said to constitute a very significant portion of our society and of our churches. A pastor who speaks and preaches as if everyone lives in a family setting in which a father, mother and four children live happily together will eventually alienate the singles in his audience.

Summary: The term "real-life ministry" is the subject of this study. One's definition of "ministry" may affect one's approach to the discussion. We define "ministry" in the traditional Lutheran sense. The average critic of current ministerial training and practice seems to believe that seminarians are not receiving "real-life" ministerial training because the Church has not adapted to a society which has undergone significant changes in the last century or two. "Real-life" is different today in some respects because of the changes in our environment.

II. "Real-Life" Ministry Means "Relevant" Ministry

In analyzing what the members of The Lutheran Church—Missouri Synod Planning Council meant by "real-life" ministry, we find that it means that a ministry must be "relevant." What follows is the earlier-mentioned report of Planning Unit III:

"Training Clergy for Real-Life Ministry"

The Image We See: A clergy model that has increased awareness of, sensitivity for and ability to apply Law and Gospel effectively to the wide range of human needs found in the parish and community through an inter-personal ministry.

Recommendations:

1. A total program of identifying, cultivating and screening those who have the interest and aptitude for pastoral ministry.

2. The activation of an even more exhaustive process of ongoing evaluation of the seminarian throughout the seminary experience.

3. A comprehensive internship supervised by approved pastors that would build on exposure to practical aspects of ministry including lay involvement in the evaluation process.

4. A greater articulation of college/seminary curricula to emphasize programs that enhance interpersonal ministry skills (including various tracks to accommodate background, abilities and interest).

5. Required participation in continuing education experience that emphasizes interpersonal ministry for all clergy, using an ongoing certification process for recognition and encouragement.

6. The selection and employment of evaluation instruments to assist student selection, screening, exposure, experience, placement, orientation and professional support.[2]

In analyzing portions of this report, we wish to choose three areas of emphasis to support the thesis that "real-life" means "relevant" ministry. They are:

1. Pastors must be effective in their "interpersonal" activity (Careful screening will make certain that pastors without "interpersonal" skills are not permitted in the ministry);

2. The internship (vicarage) experience must be strengthened in its practical aspects;

3. Seminary curricula must be adjusted to enhance "interpersonal" ministry skills.

Treating these emphases individually, it becomes evident that each is concerned with some aspect of the "relevant" ministry concept.

1. Interpersonal Ministry Needed

The term "interpersonal" occurs three times in the report of the planning unit. In the general introductory statement we read that the ideal clergy model envisioned for the future is to be achieved "through an interpersonal ministry." The references to "interpersonal ministry" in the recommendations which follow include one at the seminary level to encourage curricula emphasizing programs that enhance interpersonal ministry skills, and, at the pastoral level, continuing education programs which accomplish the same purpose.

What is this "interpersonal" ministry? As one reads the pages of raw data from the questionnaires of the hundreds who attended the sessions, it is evident that "interpersonal" ministry refers to a caring, "Seelsorger" kind of ministry which treats individuals with compassion and Christian love no matter who and where they are. Since that is what is meant, we discover that we are not facing a new concept at all. We often speak about our Lord's ministry as being one of compassion and true love. We note His concern for the lost sheep, the prodigal son, the woman taken in adultery and the Samaritan woman. The Gospels often reveal Jesus in a "one-on-one" situation. Today, too, most people will agree that a good pastor should be a caring, concerned individual who can speak meaningfully to a despairing teenager, a lonely widow, a bereaved mother, or an unemployed adult. The pastor who fits this concept of the ministry is one who knows where his people live and has seen their homes. He reasonably well understands their working and living environments. To be a "relevant" pastor, he must often deal with people on a personal basis as an understanding, warm, caring individual. "Real-life" ministry will certainly be made difficult if the pastor is deficient in this quality.

Apparently, there are those who see their pastors as ill-suited to an interpersonal ministry. A warm smile and a firm handshake do not in themselves make a good pastor, but people believe that they symbolize something necessary. Parishioners may expect the pastor to spend a fair amount of time reading the Bible in the original languages, preparing his sermons carefully, writing monthly newsletters, attending meetings in the congregation and in the community, running the office, etc., but they want the pastor to relate effectively to the successes and failures they experience as human beings in a sinful world. In their view, he must not be so engrossed in his studies and other activities that he cannot relate to the situation of a junior executive who has just lost his job, an alcoholic struggling to control his habit, a woman considering an abortion, or the host of individuals being swallowed up in a materialistic philosophy. He must be able to convey the message of the Law and Gospel in all such situations and do it in a meaningful way. He must be thoroughly human.

The recommendation is not to "while away" countless hours in idle conversation in order to get close to people. Quality rather than quantity is required. Neither are we speaking of those who are very effective in their interpersonal relationships but who actually have an insincere motive. Interpersonal relationships of the type which affect "real-life" ministry will not be mere attempts to win friends and influence people. They will not be mere attempts to bring personal success to the congregation in which a pastor has been placed. Winning people to the pastor of the organization is quite a different matter from helping people by winning and keeping them for the Savior.

While present-day seminarians may have an inadequate concept of interpersonal ministry, and while the church may be concerned that it takes too long for them to be educated to "real-life ministry," a study conducted twenty-five years ago suggested that pastors at that time rated as more satisfying "those activities which involve the minister existentially with people . . . than those which are relatively routine, administrative, and regarded as peripheral to . . . [their] main function as mediator of Word and Sacraments."[3] The specific activities which rated highest in satisfaction among those polled were adult confirmation classes, preaching, personal study and private prayer, communion, sick calls, Baptisms, and calls for comfort or counseling.[4] This study also found that "clergymen . . .

tend to value professional adeptness in a fellow minister, but think that laymen would value personality skills more."[5] Lutheran pastors in the study recognized the importance of personality skills and interpersonal ministry, and they received great satisfaction from those activities which permitted them to deal with people directly, even if not on a "one-on-one" basis.

A more recent study by Dr. David Schuller of the Association of Theological Schools, listed significant weaknesses which have been identified among some clergy of various denominations. Among the top ten weaknesses identified were: 1) The pastor blames others; 2) he cannot delegate properly; 3) he cannot develop commitments and loyalties; 4) he is divisive; 5) he does not support others emotionally while disagreeing with them intellectually; 6) he needs constant approval and support from others; and 7) he treats differentness as a threat. President Karl Barth of Concordia Seminary, St. Louis, who quoted the results of this study in a recent *Concordia Journal* article, notes that "six of the ten clergy weaknesses have to do with interpersonal relationships, including relationships with those who, like the pastor, have been divinely called into the service of the Lord."[6]

While there may be somewhat different emphases in studies of the type referred to above, it appears that the Missouri Synod Planning Council's emphasis on "interpersonal" ministry echoes a theme of many articles and studies over the years. Not everyone will agree with Lyle Schaller's claim that in ministry "people skills are more important than technical skills,"[7] but it is clear that the point about the importance of interpersonal relationships is a way of emphasizing that a pastor who does not relate well to people on a personal basis may not have a "relevant" ministry even if he is well-versed in theology.

The Planning Council Unit also recommends that "careful screening must be done to make certain that pastors without 'interpersonal' skills are not permitted in the ministry." This emphasis puts teeth into that which the statement on "interpersonal" ministry introduces. If the church takes the argument for "interpersonal" ministry seriously, it is asked to screen out those who do not show promise in this area. This may mean that an applicant for seminary study never begins his study at all or that the admitted student who later shows lack of promise will be asked to discontinue.

Screening is simply a euphemism for "denial of enrollment" or for "disenrollment." That is a process with which we have not been comfortable. Because one cannot predict with absolute certainty how

effective a pastor will be, seminary faculties are generally torn between: 1) the desire to treat prospective students charitably; and 2)
the desire to produce the most able candidates for the office of the
ministry. Pastors and laypersons asked to write letters of reference
for prospective seminary students are troubled with the same tension. The fear of dealing uncharitably with someone whom the Lord
may be able to use in the ministry definitely deters admissions
councils, screening committees and others from doing their duty at
times.

The Planning Unit's treatment of the screening function is, then,
essentially a statement to the effect that the church has failed to be
firm enough in its screening of prospective pastors. It must now face
the fact that, without adequate and firm screening programs, additional unsuitable candidates will be placed into the ministry and
will be permitted to remain in the ministry unless the church also
improves its method of counseling ineffective pastors out of the ministry after they have been ordained. The major flaw of these unsuitable candidates and pastors, according to the report, is their
inability to deal with people on an "interpersonal" basis, that is, in
a "relevant" manner.

2. Strengthen the Vicarage Experience

The second emphasis to consider states that "the internship (vicarage) experience must be strengthened in its practical aspects."

The inclusion of this point in recommendations urging concern
for "relevant" ministry training may surprise some. If there is any
period of training on which the church and the seminary depend to
complete the student's education in practical ministry, it is the vicarage period. What has happened? If the vicarage is not doing an
adequate job of training, where is the problem? Three possibilities
suggest themselves. Either:

1. The church is so ineffective in "real-life" or "relevant" ministry
that a student vicar will not presently be able to learn it in a vicarage;
or

2. The church is not carefully choosing the locations for vicarage
assignments; or

3. The seminaries are doing an inadequate job of supervising the
vicarage experience.

Assuming that the first point involves the basic question which
is being addressed throughout this study and will have to be solved
by a general change in attitude, we turn to the latter two possibilities. We are dealing with a mechanism for: 1) choosing vicarage

assignments more carefully, making certain that the supervising pastor is "approved," namely, a successful practitioner of "real-life" or "relevant" ministry; and 2) improving the system of seminary supervision during the vicarage experience.

On the matter of choosing vicarage assignments more carefully, we face a formidable problem. The church presently depends on congregations to request vicars. Thus the Placement Committee is limited in the number and type of requests. The committee cannot choose a good place for a vicar and offer the congregation the equivalent of the vicar's salary for a year. If there is an insufficient number of requests for vicarages, the Placement Committee is helpless. How can the committee select only parishes or situations which are known to offer "real-life" experiences?

This brings up the question of why congregations request vicars in the first place. The answer clearly varies. A congregation may want a vicar so that it may be part of the pastoral education program of the church. In this ideal situation the congregation provides a setting in which the student can experience ministry as it is practiced today. In such an ideal situation, the congregation may also participate in an evaluation of the student's progress. The pastor of the congregation will clearly see himself as part of the seminary faculty.

Contrast the preceding with the situation as it is sometimes described. Vicars are requested primarily because they will be a help to the pastor, perhaps in an area which the pastor cannot do well. Congregations and pastors with this view may fail to see the vicarage as an educational experience for the vicar. Further, some vicars are placed in charge of parishes which are supervised, perhaps distantly and indirectly, by the pastor of the neighboring or mother congregation. Such situations may provide some training for the vicar, but, unless the supervising pastor is extremely diligent, it is not likely to be the quality educational experience for which the seminary hopes. We continue to hear horror stories from former vicars who had hardly any supervision and basically no constructive learning sessions with supervising pastors.

The seminaries may also be at fault in their failure to supervise a vicar adequately and aggressively during the vicarage year. While a reasonable amount of such supervision can be done by letter and telephone, it would be desirable to have the seminary vicarage supervisor drop in on the vicar several times during the year for a "face to face" evaluation. Present seminary funding budgets do not generally permit the staffing necessary for such supervision.

The suggestion that the "vicarage experience be strengthened in its practical aspects" presents the church with quite a challenge. The Planning Council Unit has hit on a valid concern if we expect to have pastors who minister in "relevant" ways. Even if there were only a very few inferior vicarage experiences (and we affirm that there are many excellent vicarage experiences and many perceptive, patient and able supervising pastors and congregations) we should work for improvement.

3. Adjust the Seminary Curriculum

The third point for us to consider is the recommendation that seminary curricula be adjusted to enhance "interpersonal ministry skills." This recommendation reflects another very important facet of the concern for "real-life" or "relevant" ministry.

As seminary curricula are structured in our circles, we generally find four departments: Exegetical Theology, Systematic Theology, Historical Theology and Practical Theology. (The claim that everything in the seminary curriculum must be "practical" in some sense will provide material for another article.) Seminaries tend to require fewer hours in Historical Theology than in the other areas, and they tend to require more hours in Practical Theology than in any other single area. If the vicarage is counted as Practical Theology, the portion of pastoral education devoted to Practical Theology is easily twice the total of that in any other field. The increasing emphasis on Practical Theology appears to result from an already-accepted belief that pastors need more training in areas like preaching, pastoral counseling, administration, parish education and evangelism. Whatever one's definition of Practical Theology may be, it is apparent that the subject areas of the average Practical Theology Department include those in which a pastor deals with people on an interpersonal basis. The recommendation that seminary curricula be adjusted to enhance "interpersonal ministry skills" means that students should be taught to be relevant in their preaching, counseling, admonishing, teaching and administration. It is in these areas that a pastor deals with others in small groups or on a "one-on-one" basis, and he should be comfortable and reasonably personable in his interaction with others in such settings.

It is possible to enhance the "interpersonal ministry skills" in a curriculum by spending more time on certain subjects and/or by improving the quality of the instruction. We have already stated that there are many ways by which the vicarage experience can be improved; no one has recommended lengthening it. If we add more requirements in the area of Practical Theology, we may have to consider adding a year to the pastoral education program.

Another alternative is to substitute "practical" courses for some of those which have been taught in the Exegetical, Systematic and Historical departments. Such suggestions generally bring a violent negative response. Most people say that the four-year program for the pastoral ministry is long enough already. Further, many will argue that we cannot cut back at all on the exegetical, systematic and historical requirements because many graduates are also weak in these areas. If we cannot add a year to the training program of pastors and if we cannot substitute additional Practical Theology courses for courses in other areas, we will have to seek another answer.

It should be possible to achieve the goal of preparing students for "real-life" or "relevant" ministry by improving the quality of the educational experience. To accomplish this we need to look at the courses in Practical Theology and attempt to strengthen them. For example, take the area of preaching, considered by many to be the single most important activity of the pastor. Relevant preaching has a decided effect on the church-going habits of church members. Are our students hearing "relevant" sermons from their pastors and from their seminary professors? Is the problem partly that the professors who teach seminary students how to preach fail to help them address "real-life" situations? The problem which Kierkegaard saw one hundred and fifty years ago is still a problem today. Kierkegaard commented about the sermon he heard from Bishop Mynster in Copenhagen on May 19, 1850: "Today, Whitsunday, Mynster preached against monks and hermits—Good God, to want to play that tune in the 19th century, in order to be rewarded with applause. He did not attack a single one of the forms of evil prevalent in our day— ugh, God forbid, that might easily have become too serious, no, he preached against the monasteries."[8]

Kierkegaard's complaint is one that present-day pastors and seminarians might well heed. What is the point of preaching, perhaps even eloquently, on some subject that concerns no one in the congregation? One parishioner said about his pastor's sermons, "The trouble with my pastor's sermons is that he scratches where he itches, not where I itch."[9] The parishioner was simply describing his pastor's failure to address "real-life" issues. There was a day when the subject of monasteries was relevant, but it was not relevant in the Denmark of 1850, and it is not relevant in the North America of 1989.

What seminarians need to be taught as far as possible is that what is said in the pulpit must bear a relationship to daily living. One parishioner summed up the concept of "relevant" preaching when she said to her pastor, "As I listened to your sermon this morning, it seemed as though you had been peeking through the keyhole of our home this past week."[10] The woman who said this felt that the sermon contained a message for her; it was not a sermon directed at some nebulous audience from another age.

We are not speaking of a "relevancy" which might ignore the basic spiritual needs of people of all ages. Law and Gospel are always preached in order to answer those basic spiritual needs of the hearer. An illustration of such "relevant" preaching is described by the woman who said, "I like a sermon that stabs me awake, that prods and pulls me toward the impossible, and then shows me Christ, with Whom all things are possible."[11] The seminarian who is taught to understand meaningful preaching of this sort will realize that there is nothing new about the basic needs of people today. Sin and forgiveness are the same as ever. He will, however, make it obvious that he knows he is living in the present rather than in 1839, 1530 or 1054. "Real-life" preaching means that God's eternal truths are applied to the circumstances and environments in which we find ourselves now.

We have used preaching as an example. Sermon preparation and delivery are features of Practical Theology that everyone considers important. The need for "relevancy" in preaching is obvious. What we might say about the areas of worship, pastoral practice, pastoral counseling, evangelism and administration would simply apply the same principle to those areas. It takes little imagination to conjure up the interesting topics one might introduce on the subject of "relevant worship." Someone might ask how, for example, chanting by the pastor is meaningful for a generation which in "real-life" uses public address systems to make a speaker's words audible? Similarly, lively discussions would result from the introduction of "real-life" ministry dimensions to the areas of pastoral practice, counseling, evangelism and administration. All subject areas should include and apply the basic, solid components which are part of our Christian and Lutheran convictions. Those who fail to make the message of sin and grace basic and meaningful in their work are ineffective pastors. "Real-life" ministry asks that we make certain that our message is relevant for the age in which we live.

Admittedly, we can never teach everything in the classroom, and we cannot anticipate all the challenges which will face a pastor thirty years after certification. Nor can we solve the dilemma of the district president who must counsel with a pastor whose work is obviously ineffective. We can, however, improve the teaching which is done in seminary classrooms so as to give it a more "relevant" dimension.

Summary: The emphasis of Unit III of the Planning Council was on "interpersonal" ministry skills among prospective pastors. "Interpersonal" skills are those which make for a "relevant" ministry. They are the skills which assist the pastor in serving as a sincere, understanding, warm, caring individual who relates to the circumstances and environment, that is the "real-life" situation, of his people. Screening is the device by which unsuitable students are prevented from enrolling, or continuing enrollment, in the seminary. Vicarage assignments and vicarage supervisors should be carefully chosen so as to provide the best possible "interpersonal" and "real-life" experiences for the student. While seminary curricula probably cannot increase the number of courses in Practical Theology, the seminaries can emphasize the "interpersonal" and "real-life" features of present coursework. Preaching, worship, education, evangelism, counseling and administration should all be taught with concern for "relevancy."

In conclusion, the Planning Council of 1986 did the church a favor by highlighting a concern which has troubled it for a long time, in fact from the very beginning. Our Lord's preaching was recognized as different; it had meaning for His audiences. The disciples of our Lord had to try hard to be "relevant" in their dealings with Jewish and Gentile audiences. We note St. Paul's sermon on Mar's Hill which was very conscious of a philosophically-oriented audience. By bringing the challenge of relevancy to our attention, the conference brought some leaders, and especially the seminary personnel, to consider again the basic concern of the church: How does one relate Law and Gospel in such a way that people see them as having meaning for life in these last years of the twentieth century? To rephrase the question we might ask: How does one relate Law and Gospel in such a manner that people do not automatically tune out the message? Since conversion and strengthening of faith come through the means of grace and the operation of the Holy Spirit, we will never assume that human beings do what only God can do. However, we have been given talents to discern that some people are repelled by God's message because they do not see it as meaningful. Since no one wants to stand in God's way, the church and the seminaries will encourage the most "relevant" approaches to ministry. That is what "real-life" ministry was about in 1839 and that is what it is about in 1989.

Notes

[1] Oswald Hoffmann, "On Being a Minister," in a Lutheran Hour sermon delivered August 3, 1969.

[2] Report of Unit III (Higher Education), Luthern Church—Missouri Synod Planning Council, St. Louis, Missouri, February 18-20, 1986.

[3] Ross P. Scherer, "The Lutheran Ministry: Origins, Careers, Self-Appraisal," *The Cresset,* January 1963, p. 13.

[4] *Ibid.*

[5] *Ibid.*

[6] David Schuller in an article by Karl Barth, "The Doctrine of the Ministry: Some Practical Dimensions," *Concordia Journal,* vol. 14, no. 3 (July 1988), p. 212.

[7] Lyle Schaller as quoted by H. Armin Moellering, "Some New Testament Aspects of the Ministry Identified and Applied," *Concordia Journal,* vol. 14, no. 3 (July 1988), p. 240.

[8] Soren Kierkegaard in Alexander Dru, ed., *The Journals of Kierkegaard* (New York: Harper and Row, 1959), p. 192.

[9] Roland Wiederaenders, *A Joyful Ministry* (St. Louis: Faith Forward Committee, 1962), p. 4

[10] *Ibid.*

[11] Hoffmann.

Albert H. Schwermann Pioneer Canadian Pastor, Educator and Churchman

NORMAN J. THREINEN

The year 1913 was a good one for the church in western Canada. Nineteen seminary graduates were assigned that year to man the growing number of Missouri Synod mission stations which were being started over the vast region of the Canadian West, fifteen of them from St. Louis. These graduates represented an increase in 1913 of twenty percent in missionary strength.

Among the 1913 graduates from St. Louis was a man who had been considered by the faculty for placement as a missionary in India. Upon his entreaties that he could not stand the heat, however, he was assigned to the Synod's northern-most post in Mellowdale, Alberta. His name was Albert H. Schwermann, a man who was destined to play a very important role in the development of the Canadian church, particularly in western Canada.

The Molding of the Man

Albert Henry Schwermann was born into a Missouri Synod pastor's family on June 13, 1891, in Jefferson City, Missouri. By coincidence, he was born about three months before the Synod's first resident missionary arrived in western Canada, where Schwermann was to spend his entire ministry. Young Albert later attended the Christian day school at Covington, Illinois where the family had moved in 1894. There his father served not only as pastor but also as teacher in the school. In addition to teaching him the normal school subjects, the elder Schwermann instilled in his son a life-long love of music, giving him organ lessons and advancing him to the point that Albert was able to serve as the church organist.[1]

Despite young Albert's inclination to enter the business world, his father insisted that he study for the ministry. Consequently, he

NORMAN J. THREINEN is Associate Professor of Historical Theology at Concordia Lutheran Seminary, Edmonton, Alberta, Canada.

enrolled at Concordia College in Fort Wayne, Indiana following his confirmation at age fourteen in 1905. Although he had not been particularly outstanding as a student, Albert advanced through sexta and quinta (grades 9 and 10) in one year with the help of tutors, so that he completed the six-year pre-seminary program in 1910.[2]

In 1906, while Schwermann was in attendance, the college introduced military training under the direction of a captain from the United States War Department. While some of the students regarded the "40-minute drills, summer or winter," and other military activities as "idiocy," Schwermann considered them "a new and exciting adventure, something to break the monotony of college life." According to Schwermann's later assessment, military training produced in the students a lifestyle characterized by neatness, promptness, and cleanliness.[3]

In 1910, Schwermann entered Concordia Seminary, St. Louis, one of two hundred ninety-seven students enrolled that year. The large number of students overtaxed the capacity of the seminary which had been designed to accommodate two hundred. The students endured cramped quarters, large classes, lack of adequate library and music facilities, and the outside disturbances of city noises.[4] Yet Schwermann's recollections of his seminary days were of sitting at the feet of Franz Pieper and Georg Stoeckhardt. He recalled how each of his professors "stressed the supreme importance of the Bible as the foundation for all theological studies because it is the verbally inspired and altogether inerrant Word of God."[5] His recollections are in line with a historian of the seminary who depicts the years of the Pieper presidency as "The Period of Conservation."[6]

In addition to the emphasis which all of his seminary mentors placed on the inspiration and inerrancy of the Scriptures, two things made a lasting impression on Schwermann at the seminary. One was the death of Georg Stoeckhardt; the other was the 1911 synodical convention at which the English Synod became the English District of the Missouri Synod.

With this background of parsonage home, college military discipline, and conservative seminary training, Schwermann was thrust out into the frontier of Western Canada.

Pioneer Missionary

In some respects, parts of the Canadian prairies had begun to pass out of the pioneering stage by the time Schwermann arrived in 1913. In older rural settlements and in the cities, the church was often well established; congregations of the Missouri Synod had in some instances already existed for more than twenty years. Yet on the fringe of the older areas, new settlements were continually growing up as immigrants kept pouring into the land. It was to one of these frontier areas that Schwermann was called as a missionary.

Schwermann's call was to "Mellowdale and vicinity." When he received his call, he knew only that it was north of Edmonton; Mellowdale itself was not on the map. His parish, which had been established two years earlier, was approximately sixty miles wide and one hundred miles long. It was a sparsely-settled area which had just been opened for homesteading. There were no roads and even trails were often non-existent. To serve the people in his six thousand square mile parish, Schwermann was constantly on the move, sleeping in the homes of hospitable settlers, braving swollen streams in the spring, traversing mud-holes in summer, and facing sub-zero weather in winter. Much of his travel was on horseback.

The people to whom Schwermann ministered had diverse backgrounds. A few, from Ontario and the United States, were accustomed to church life in North America. Most were from an Eastern European country and had a very different church background. Especially among the latter, liturgy was generally suspect as being too "Catholic." Strife and petty quarrels among neighbors were common. Patience, indoctrination and much tact was required of the pastor in such a situation.

With no public school in the community, Schwermann started a Christian day school which he taught four days a week for a year in spite of his heavy schedule of travel throughout his parish.

One of the things which Schwermann missed was the close association with brethren in the ministry and their seasoned counsel as he faced new challenges. To be sure, things were not as bad as they had been nineteen years earlier when Emil Eberhardt arrived in Stony Plain as the first resident missionary in Alberta; Eberhardt's closest brother in the ministry for a number of years was five hundred miles away in Montana. Schwermann's neighboring pastor was closer by, but the conditions of travel meant that he was still three days away from Schwermann's base of operation in Mellowdale. Fortunately for Schwermann, Eberhardt was the neighboring pastor; his lengthy tenure in the area made him a seasoned veteran. Yet opportunities to consult with him were normally limited to three times a year when pastoral conferences were held.

Western Canada was still part of the vast mission field of the Minnesota District in 1913. Its development was guided by C. F. Walter, the District's Secretary for Canadian Missions, who kept in

212 Norman J. Threinen

constant touch with every missionary, giving them sound advice, and often sizing up the situation in a given parish better than the missionary himself.

By the time Schwermann accepted a call to a more-established Alberta parish in Wetaskiwin in 1916, significant physical progress had been made in the frontier settlements which he had served. Telephones, roads and the railway had all appeared. In the Mellowdale church, too, physical progress was evident in the form of a new organ.

The Mellowdale call, which had been viewed by his friends and relatives as the "worst call" given by the Board of Assignments in 1913, was regarded by Schwermann as the "best one." He loved the work, the country, the people, and the climate. He loved pioneering. It gave Schwermann a feel of the church at its most basic grass-roots level. And, it gave him an experience in pioneering which would, with some modification, be useful as he entered into other new areas of ministry.

A College is Born

The new parish to which Schwermann had been called and to which he brought his bride only months after his installation was located in Wetaskiwin, one of the older settlements of the province. The five years which Schwermann spent there gave him hands-on experience with a more traditional, well-established congregation and brought him into the broader life of the church. It was while he was at Wetaskiwin that Schwermann became involved with the movement to found a college in western Canada.

The need for a college on the Canadian prairies which could begin to train pastors from western Canada for the mission field out of which they came had been recognized for some time. Those who recognized the need most keenly were pastors who had committed themselves to ministry in western Canada but who saw many of their co-workers leave to return to the United States after only two or three years of service in Canada. The need for a college had formally surfaced in two different pastoral conferences in 1913 just prior to the time that Schwermann arrived on the scene; one in Winnipeg and the other in Calgary. World War I had caused an abatement of the enthusiasm but immediately after the war the flame was rekindled. At the 1919 convention of the Minnesota District, at which the representatives of western Canada requested and were readily granted permission to form two separate synodical districts, western Canadians were also given approval to petition the synod for an educational institution in western Canada. The formation of two separate synodical districts was a natural outgrowth of what had become two distinct mission fields, but the question of where the college should be located was to become a contentious issue.

Schwermann's leadership role in having the college located in Edmonton may have come about somewhat by circumstance. In 1918 Schwermann had been elected secretary of the conference of pastors and lay representatives from Alberta and British Columbia which had met annually since 1917 to plan for the new District. When the Minnesota District gave approval to western Canadians to petition the Synod for a college, it became the responsibility of the elected executive of the conference to gather the information needed to present the case to the Synod in 1920. John E. Herzer, the chairman of the conference, was located in Calgary, a considerable distance from Schwermann, and the college fact-finding committee was located in the Edmonton area reasonably close to where Schwermann lived. As a result, Schwermann became the key person to carry the ball on the college issue for the Alberta and British Columbia District conference.

Reporting to Herzer on February 4, 1920, Schwermann said, "Abe [Emil Eberhardt] and I threshed thru [sic] the whole college matter last week and found that we had a mountain of work before us if we are to get the college to Alta."[7] An attempt to arrange a meeting of the Alberta and British Columbia conference with its counterpart in Manitoba and Saskatchewan to meld their efforts in presenting the college cause to the Missouri Synod was unsuccessful because they could not agree to the best time for the joint meeting. However, it is quite clear that Schwermann and the rest of the Alberta and British Columbia conference had already determined that there was no more suitable location for the college in western Canada than Edmonton.

Another factor which propelled Schwermann into the leadership of the movement to found a college in western Canada was his election as the pastoral delegate from the Alberta and British Columbia Conference to the Synodical convention in Detroit in 1920. Although the conference of pastors and lay representatives from Alberta and British Columbia which met on February 10, 1920, to deal largely with the school issue decided to also send Eberhardt to Detroit and although two additional pastors from the Edmonton area (A. Rehwinkel and S. Thies) attended the convention as well, Schwermann's position as a voting delegate was pivotal. It was a jubilant Schwermann who wrote Herzer from Detroit, "The Lord has crowned our humble efforts with success. College was granted; to be opened in Sept. 1921 with sexta [grade 9] and teachers and buildings provided as needs arise."[8]

While the 1920 Detroit convention resolved to establish a college in western Canada and appropriated funds for this purpose, it did not decide on its location; this decision was left to the Synod's Board of Directors. After the convention, the Manitoba and Saskatchewan conference invited the Alberta and British Columbia conference to a joint gathering in Saskatoon, the city which they favored as the location of the new college. Aware that Synodical President Pfotenhauer, who would have considerable influence on the final decision of the Board of Directors, would be present, the Alberta pastors felt that meeting in Saskatoon would prejudice the case against them. They proposed instead that there be separate meetings of the conferences with Pfotenhauer at the two locations being proposed so that each conference could state its case calmly without a heated debate resulting. As secretary of the conference, Schwermann was deeply involved in these negotiations.

In the end, Pfotenhauer and a member of the Board of Directors, Mr. Henry Horst, visited not only Saskatoon and Edmonton but also Winnipeg, Calgary and Regina. The Synodical Board met on December 2-3, 1920, decided on Edmonton as the site for the college, and set in motion the organizational machinery which would enable the college to start operation. On January 25, 1921, *Der Lutheraner* announced that Synod's Board of Directors had appointed the Board of Control for the College. Named to the Board were Eberhardt, Rehwinkel and three area laymen, all of whom had been on the college committee for Alberta. An electoral college as also announced consisting of Herzer, Schwermann and three other pastors from western Canada. At its April 1 meeting, the Synod's Board of Directors authorized Concordia's new Board of Control to rent a vacant hotel near St. Peter's Church and renovate it for college use. It also gave authorization to call a professor so that the institution could open in the fall as projected.

A list of thirteen names was eventually developed by congregations of the Synod as candidates for the position of director and first professor of the college. Among the names proposed were those of Schwermann, Herzer and Rehwinkel. The initial composition of the electoral college now changed as the people who allowed their names to stand for election were prevented from continuing on the committee. When the electoral college met on July 5, 1921 at the founding convention of the Alberta-British Columbia District, John E. Herzer was elected president of the college. He declined the election, and on July 26, the lot fell to Schwermann. Thus, Schwermann, at age thirty, became the founding president of the new Concordia in western Canada.

Although young in years, the constantly changing group of pastors in western Canada made him a comparable veteran. Of the sixty-three pastors serving in western Canada in 1921, only nine had been on the scene when Schwermann arrived in 1913. Of the candidates which had been assigned to the region in 1913, only one other man besides Schwermann continued on the scene in 1921. Schwermann had been elected first vice-president of the District at its founding convention, a position which he relinquished upon accepting the presidency of the college.

Schwermann moved with his family to Edmonton on August 18. The Caledonian Temperance Hotel, about four blocks from St. Peter's Church where Rehwinkel was the pastor, had been leased in anticipation that it would accommodate not only the projected number of students but also the president and his family. When thirty-five students registered, double the number projected, a badly dilapidated boarding house four blocks away was rented to house the president's family and to serve as the kitchen, dining room and infirmary for the college. These were the first buildings occupied by the college.

By October 31, 1921, the college was ready to be opened, and Schwermann was formally installed as president. Thus, Schwermann entered another phase of his Canadian ministry, pioneering as a Lutheran college educator in Western Canada.

Pioneer Lutheran Educator

Concordia was not, strictly speaking, a college in 1921; all of the students were in grade 9. But this was only the first step in the development of this institution; additional class levels were added each successive year thereafter until Concordia became a full-fledged institution in the Missouri Synod's system of higher education for training pastors and teachers.

The curriculum for the college attempted to accommodate two systems: the system of high schools in Western Canada and the standards and goals of the synodical school system in the United States. Schwermann's intent was that the Edmonton school would be a truly Canadian Concordia. The curriculm for the first year thus included the following subjects and class hours: religion (4); German (5); English (5); mathematics (5); Latin (5); history—British (2) and world (1); geography (2); science (3); and music (1). Schwermann's conviction about the value of some musical ability for the pastoral ministry is evident in the standard which he set, i.e., that every student must show before he leaves college that he can play at least the chorales of our church on the organ or a similar instrument.[9]

Students at the college under Schwermann's administration led a structured, spartan existence. While the school occupied its initial quarters, students had to walk to the dining room, a distance of four blocks, three times a day. Students arose daily at 6:00 a.m. and retired at 9:30 p.m. In addition to classes from 8:45 a.m. to 4:00 p.m. (with a 1 3/4 hour break at noon), the daily schedule included study periods from 7-8 a.m. and 7-9 p.m. Although the details of the daily routine changed somewhat after the college moved into permanent quarters in December 1925, structured activities continued to characterize student life throughout the years.

The house rules drawn up for the first years of the college's existence reflect a similarly controlled lifestyle for the students. In addition to the normal rules one would expect for a Christian college, there were rules against attending the theatre; going home or elsewhere without the director's permission; leaving the school premises after 9:00 p.m.; smoking, unless students were eighteen years of age and had their parents' permission in writing; and dating, unless the girl's family was present. Students were also required to attend morning and evening chapel; to keep themselves and their clothing neat and clean; and, to clean their rooms daily.[10] With few modifications, these house rules continued to be enforced throughout Schwermann's presidency. Unannounced bed checks in the dormitory after lights out were a common occurrence even in the early fifties.

That Schwermann should choose to transplant the regimentation of his Fort Wayne college experience to the new Concordia in Edmonton is not surprising. He appreciated that experience in his own life and had no alternate model of college life upon which to draw. Furthermore this kind of regimentation was probably necessary if he was to survive that first year. With no experience in running a high school or college, he was faced with thirty-five ninth grade boys ranging in age from fourteen to twenty-two and no upperclassmen to serve as examples of what was expected. Since many of these boys had not experienced anything except their own rural communities, Schwermann and his wife had to serve as houseparents in addition to caring for all the normal matters which one associates with a boarding school. As the school developed, regimentation became an essential feature of student life.

Student life under Schwermann was disciplined but not harsh. His own bouts of homesickness at college made him sympathetic to similar problems experienced by his students, many of whom had left home at age fourteen. Futhermore, Schwermann's interest in sports and his love of music ensured that these and other non-academic activities would be part of student life at Concordia. In 1929, for example, a Concordia student, Fred Gabert, became champion of the Edmonton district in the Canadian oratorical contest, a feat which not only made the local papers but which was talked about at Concordia for many years.

In addition to his wife, whose openness to pioneering seemed almost to match his, Schwermann's greatest help in getting Concordia off the ground seems to have been Alfred Rehwinkel, the pastor of St. Peter's where the students worshiped. Not only was Rehwinkel on the Board of Control, but he had achieved a good grasp of Canadian education through his contact with the University of Alberta and was prepared to assist with teaching part-time during the first year of Concordia's life. Also assisting in the teaching for part of the first year was H. Seyer, a student from the St. Louis seminary.

In 1922, Rehwinkel accepted the call to become the second professor on the faculty. Other teaching assistance was also forthcoming. That same year another St. Louis seminary student, John H. Herreilers, arrived to assist in the teaching. In 1923, with Herreilers, remaining on at Concordia, Walter A. Baepler arrived to join the faculty. These instructors and others eventually took over most of the teaching responsibilities at Concordia, but Schwermann never relinquished responsibility for teaching in addition to his other duties at the college.

The initial impulse for having a faculty which had achieved recognized Canadian teaching credentials may have stemmed from Rehwinkel. Almost immediately after he arrived in Edmonton in 1914, he began to take classes at the University of Alberta, and by the time he joined the Concordia faculty he had earned an M.A. from the university. But Schwermann supported and carried forward this concept. By the beginning of the 1930s, it was a standard procedure for professors to be involved in university studies, and with the introduction of the provincial high school curriculum in 1939 it was mandatory. Schwermann himself, in spite of his many other duties, set the example. He enrolled in correspondence courses offered by the St. Louis seminary and he attended the University of Alberta, earning his B.Ed. in 1946.

Although the original purpose of the college was to educate boys for the preaching and teaching ministry of the church, girls were also admitted as early as 1925. Co-education was introduced at the request of a Lutheran girl who wanted to become a Christian day school teacher. The following year the Synod sanctioned this action, but stipulated that the number of female students not exceed twenty percent of the total enrollment. For three years the girls who enrolled lived in the homes of the professors. Then two old houses bought with the property in 1925 were joined and converted into a girls' dormitory. The limitations of the pre-seminary program as preparation for teacher training students soon became apparent, but the limited faculty did not permit the introduction of the additional courses needed. Consequently co-education was discontinued in 1931 and was not re-introduced for another decade.

Pioneer Churchman

In addition to his wide-ranging responsibilities as president of Concordia College, Schwermann was called upon again and again to serve the church-at-large, particularly on the Canadian scene. While he relinquished his position as vice-president of the District when he was elected president of Concordia, he continued to serve as chairman of the District School Board. He subsequently also served as chairman of the District Publicity Committee (1933-1936); as chairman of the District Mission Board (1933-42); and as a member of the District Board of Directors (1942-45).

When the District decided in 1924 to issue a church paper under the title, *Unsere Kirche,* it asked the Concordia faculty to edit it. The paper became a casualty of the Great Depression, and in 1936 the two districts in Western Canada decided to publish two joint church papers, one in English and one in German. For the German periodical, entitled *Kirchenblatt,* the choice for editor was Schwermann, who retained this position for the first decade of the paper's life. In addition to serving as co-editor and editor for these two church papers, Schwermann was often called upon to deliver doctrinal essays at pastoral conferences. The focus of many of his essays was church and ministry. In 1934, he delivered an essay in German to the two districts in western Canada on "God-pleasing Unity between the Synods of Western Canada." In the 1950s he delivered essays on "The Call into the Glorious Office of the Holy Ministry," "The

Office of the Keys," and "The Doctrine of the Church" at various district conventions in Canada and the United States. This led to his contribution to *The Abiding Word* and *The Pastor at Work* in 1960.

Schwermann's literary efforts reflect some of the concerns which he faced as he became involved in the struggle of the synod to determine its stand in a setting of growing Lutheran cooperation. An Inter-Lutheran Home Missions Conference of representatives of the National Lutheran Council churches had recommended in 1944 that a Canadian Lutheran Council be established to be patterned after the National Lutheran Council. Although the Synod was not part of the National Lutheran Council, President Behnken was invited to send representatives from the Canadian districts to the meeting to shape the proposed Canadian Lutheran Council. Behnken appointed Schwermann and the three Canadian district presidents to attend. With Schwermann serving as spokesman, the Missouri contingent participated fully and actively, not only in the shaping of the constitution for the proposed Council but also in the devotional periods. Under their influence, the 1945 meeting adopted a purpose for the proposed Council which would have significantly changed the thrust of the organization from that of the National Lutheran Council and made it a vehicle for "promoting free sectional conferences with a view to the achievement of complete doctrinal unity."

The three Canadian districts subsequently elected Committees on Doctrinal Unity. Meeting together as a joint committee with Schwermann as chairman, they consulted with a member of the Synodical Committee on Lutheran Unity to formulate suggestions for further revisions in the constitution of the proposed Council. Ultimately, neither these revisions nor the particular Missouri Synod slant on the 1945 proposed constitution of the Council were acceptable to the other Lutheran bodies, and the Missouri Synod Districts in Canada were unable to become part of the Council. In the process, however, Schwermann emerged as the natural spokesman in theological discussions for the Missouri Synod in Canada.

With the benefit of this inter-Lutheran exposure on the Canadian scene, Behnken saw Schwermann as a natural choice for chairman of the crucial Committee Three on Intersynodical and Doctrinal Matters at the Synod's conventions in 1947 and 1950. Several controversial issues faced the Synod at this time: "A Statement," signed by a number of prominent pastors and professors which questioned the application of passages like Romans 16:17 to other Lutherans; a movement toward fellowship with the American Lutheran Church on the basis of the "Common Confession"; and membership in the National Lutheran Council. Behnken requested that he continue to serve as chairman of this convention committee in 1953, but Schwermann felt that he could not face the pressure of this position for the third time and declined to serve.

By that time also Schwermann was becoming involved in other developments in Canada. World War II had focused the attention of the Canadian church on the need to project a distinctive image in Canada. Already in 1941, a proposal had been adopted by a joint pastoral conference of the two districts in Western Canada which called for the formation of a corporate body bearing a name which would identify it as being Canadian. The proposal was not followed through until 1954 when both of the western districts appointed committees to study the matter. Chairing the committee for the Alberta British Columbia District was Schwermann. He not only identified in detail the points which would require attention but wrote to the districts in Argentina and Brazil for their experience, since they were compelled by language and culture to be national in orientation.

A joint meeting of the three Canadian district committees on national incorporation was held in April 1956 and two *ad hoc* committees were established: an Ontario-based committee to draft a charter and an Alberta-based committee to draw up a constitution. Schwermann was named chairman of the latter. After submitting it to congregations for their input, the constitution was adopted by the three Canadian districts in 1957, and on September 11-12, 1958, a founding convention of The Lutheran Church in Canada (later changed to Lutheran Church—Canada) was held. Elected as the first president was Schwermann. Thus, Schwermann, at age sixty-seven, was again faced with a pioneering venture which would draw on his native creativity and wisdom and require his energy and enthusiasm if it was to succeed.

There was a major challenge in this new pioneering venture in the fact that the new body to which Schwermann was elected in 1958 was not a church in the accepted sense of the word. Nor was it a synod. It was a provisional body organized primarily for the eventual formation of a Canadian synod; until that time the relationship of Canadian congregations and districts to the Missouri Synod would not change. While that eventual goal would not be reached for three decades, to Schwermann and the other architects of Lutheran Church—Canada, it seemed in 1958 to be just around the corner. A committee was authorized to inaugurate procedures for incorporation and a Dominion charter. A Board of Public Relations was appointed. A chairman of the Armed Forces Commission was named and empowered to appoint two others to his Commission. A committee was appointed to study the advantages of a Lutheran seminary in Canada. For more aggressive communication, a three-member Board of Internal Information and Promotion was created on which Schwermann himself served.

Recognizing that involvement of as many people as possible throughout Canada was crucial for building a sense of ownership, the Lutheran Church—Canada Board of Directors under Schwermann's direction established fact-finding committees in each district to investigate fourteen phases of synodical work. The process involved well over one hundred pastors and laymen and did a good deal to encourage input from the grass-roots of the church. In addition, the Board of Internal Information and Promotion provided articles for church papers and issued informational pamphlets for general distribution in congregations. Then, in 1961, Concordia College granted Schwermann a sabbatical to be used in full-time service of Lutheran Church—Canada. After he had relinquished his presidency of Concordia in 1954, Schwermann had continued teaching at the college. In addition to providing him time to give attention to the myriad of details needing attention at this point in the process, this sabbatical provided him with the opportunity to travel across Canada, conducting seminars and making other contacts on behalf of Lutheran Church—Canada. The effect of Schwermann's work was evident in 1961 at the fourth convention of Lutheran Church—Canada at which a time-table for the establishment of an independent Canadian body by 1965 was adopted. Schwermann then handed on responsibility for Lutheran Church—Canada by declining to accept nomination for president for health reasons.[12]

Assessing the Man

Albert Henry Schwermann died on October 10, 1983. For some years before that time, his many contributions had been recognized. King George VI and Queen Elizabeth had, in 1937 and 1953 respectively, awarded him coronation medals in recognition of his contributions to education in Canada. His *alma mater* in St. Louis had in 1946 honoured him with a Doctor of Divinity degree. Concordia College had given its first *Christo et Ecclesiae* award to him in 1977. At the time of his death, Edwin Lehman, president of the Alberta-British Columbia District who in 1988 was to be elected the first president of the autonomous Lutheran Church—Canada, said of

Schwermann, "The one word that immediately comes to mind is that of a giant. . . . He left an imprint on the church that no one else can duplicate. He was the kind of person who does not appear on the scene today."[13]

Notes

[1] Albert H. Schwermann, "Notes for a Biographical Sketch of Albert Henry Schwermann," p. 6 (typewritten), Lutheran Historical Institute, Edmonton, Schwermann biographical file.

[2] *Ibid.*, p. 13.

[3] Albert H. Schwermann, "My Debt of Gratitude to the U.S.A." *Concordia Historical Institute Quarterly* 50 (Spring, 1977): 25-26.

[4] Walter A. Baepler, *A Century of Grace* (St. Louis: Concordia, 1947), pp. 220-221.

[5] Schwermann, "Notes," p. 18.

[6] Carl S. Meyer, *Log Cabin to Luther Tower* (St. Louis: Concordia, 1965), p. 89ff.

[7] Postcard from Schwermann to John E. Herzer, February 4, 1920, Lutheran Historical Institute, Edmonton, Schwermann Collection, Box 1.

[8] Postcard from Schwermann to John E. Herzer, June 24, 1920, *Ibid.*

[9] Mimeographed Letter of Schwermann to the pastors of Western Canada, September 3, 1921, Lutheran Historical Institute, Edmonton, Schwermann Collection, Box 7.

[10] House rules for 1921, *Ibid.*

[11] "Proceedings of the Conference to Draft a Constitution for The Canadian Lutheran Council," April 5-6, 1945, p. 2 (Mimeographed).

[12] Albert H. Schwermann, *The Beginnings of Lutheran Church—Canada* (Edmonton: Lutheran Church—Canada, 1969), pp. 56-69.

[13] "Lutherans Lose a Founding Giant," *The Edmonton Journal,* October 13, 1983, p. D7.

Justification: Crown Jewel
of Faith

KURT E. MARQUART

It is a commonplace to observe that the Second Vatican Council ended the Counter-Reformation. We need not speculate here whether and to what extent this outcome was in fact a result of the self-destruction of the historic churches of the Reformation. What is startling, however, is the claim that Vatican II not only signals the conclusion of the Counter-Reformation, but also "marks the end of the Reformation."[1] This significance is attributed specifically to the "Declaration on the Relation of the Church to Non-Christian Religions," by J. M. Oesterreicher, who was one of the leading spirits behind the Declaration. The grounds cited for the coroner's verdict on the Reformation's alleged demise are by no means trivial: "More exactly: the main concern of the Reformation is no longer of interest to us. Today the pious Christian is no longer worried by the question: How do I obtain a gracious God? The question that concerns him is: How does God accomplish the salvation of all creation?"

It must certainly be granted that if the question about personal justification, or, "How do I obtain a gracious God?" is today beside the point, then the Reformation is beside the point too. It may have served some good purpose in a more guilt-ridden age, but if its central and constitutive article has been rendered pointless by the cultural changes of the intervening centuries, then the Reformation is truly irrelevant now and should be given a decent burial once and for all. Attempts to revive or restore an irrelevant Reformation could yield at best some charming exhibits in a museum of religious oddities.

Now, of course, the issue here is not whether "modern man" as such finds or does not find justification appealing. No sensible person would gauge the value or relevance of basic Christian truth by its standing with the general public. Professor Oesterreicher, too, expressly speaks about today's "pious Christian," not about the views

---

KURT E. MARQUART is Professor of Systematic Theology at Concordia Theological Seminary, Fort Wayne, Indiana.

of the irreligious. He is in fact at pains to refute the suspicion that the new direction "is a symptom of the fact that the Church has lost the conviction of her own identity and has capitulated to the 'world.' " He insists, rather, that the new approach is more Christian than the old and "has nothing in common with the contemporary spiritual malaise nor with the modern passion for indifference."[2] On the other hand, however, Oesterreicher's own account of the history of the text in question amply documents the strong background of secular pressures and passions emanating from the volatile politics of the Middle East and its global ramifications. That aspect is of no further interest here.

Our object here will be twofold: 1) to probe a little beneath the surface of this ostensibly new and modern attack on the Reformation's central theme; and 2) to trace some connecting lines showing how and why justification is everywhere at stake in the Christian faith and church.

I

One is surprised, first of all, at the brusque tone with which the Reformation is dismissed: "the main concern of the Reformation is no longer of interest to us." This in a chapter that urges the utmost respect for all, indeed just after an excursus entitled "The Omnipresence of Grace, "which states that the "non-Christian religions, too, have a certain measure of sanctifying power" and that "no Christian would regard the multitudes of pious Hindus who wash in the sacred river to be cleansed of their sins as merely victims of an illusion."[3]

A posture of openness and magnanimity towards other religions is one of the elementary demands of the modern spirit, also and especially in its religious form. One could hardly point to a better example than the eloquent honesty of Simone Weil. Although attracted to Christianity, indeed in her own mind a Christian already, Simone Weil refused Baptism because that would have implied a move on her part away from "the intersection of Christianity and everything that is not Christianity." Demanding of Christianity an inclusiveness which it did not at present exhibit, Miss Weil wrote:

> But everything is so closely bound up together that Christianity cannot be really incarnated unless it is catholic in the sense that I have just defined. How could it circulate through the flesh of all nations of Europe if it did not contain absolutely everything in itself? Except, of course, falsehood. But in every-

thing that exists there is most of the time more truth than falsehood.[4]

Thirsting for universality, the modern mind recoils instinctively from all that is parochial or sectional, and so "divisive" of global consensus and comprehensiveness. It is not surprising, therefore, that world public opinion, "formed and in many ways guided by the press, " gave strong and decisive support to the Vatican Declaration in its formative stages. Indeed, according to Oesterreicher, it "can be asserted without exaggeration that the efforts made on behalf of the Declaration, as in other Council matters, would have come to nothing, had not the press repeatedly directed the eyes of the world to them."[5]

Now, given the sordid history of "Christian" uses of political power to deny justice, not to speak of charity, to non-Christians and even to dissenting Christians, the public press had every right to demand solid assurances from as global and prestigious an assembly as the Second Vatican Council. Nor should Christians be left in any doubt about the wrongs of inquisitions, pogroms, and persecutions. Had the Declaration limited itself to urging Christians to show proper love and respect to their neighbors, regardless of their religion, it would have earned the gratitude not only of Christian citizens but of all who value civil decency.

Not only Oesterreicher's explanation of the Declaration but the Council's dogmatic constitution on the church, *Lumen gentium*, itself goes far beyond these demands of justice and charity, in granting a salvific significance to non-Christian religions and to natural religion.[6] Oesterreicher asserts, to be sure: "Idolatry is still an abomination. . . . The prophets' and apostles' curse on the worshipers of Baal has not been annulled, nor has the Church, in a fit of indecision, suddenly made peace with godlessness." Instantiations of such idolatry are difficult to imagine, however, in view of the solemn conclusion, two paragraphs later:

> The more we penetrate into the convictions and religious practices of non-biblical origin, the more we shall perceive God's gentle, almost shy action everywhere, even in the jungle, in the mountains and the temples that have not yet been marked with the Cross. It is the greatness of those sections of the Declaration dealing with the various non-Christian religions that they praise the omnipresence of grace.

On an earlier page we read: "Thus the openness of the Council, too, has no other source than Christ's work of reconciliation." Second

Corinthians 5:18 is cited, yet nothing is made of verse 20: "Be reconciled to God!" Instead, the paragraph culminates, true to the Declaration itself, in the goal of making "common cause in fostering justice, peace and freedom among all men."

One might conclude from all this that Oesterreicher and the Declaration are mounting a radically new attack on the absoluteness of Christianity in deference to the *Zeitgeist*. Such a conclusion would, however, be mistaken. That an accommodation to modern thinking is involved, no one would of course deny. No qualitative break with previous Roman Catholic thinking, however, is involved. Oesterreicher cites Thomas Aquinas, Karl Rahner—that Roman Catholic Barth, whose prodigious work both influenced and now reflects Vatican II—and Henri de Lubac, who supplies patristic references.

The views advanced are not essentially new. Substantially similar ideas were in vogue already at Trent, although they were not expressly dogmatized there.[7] Among the "frightening theological opinions" for which Oesterreicher cites solemn papal condemnations, the first is: "All works of non-believers are sin and the virtues of the philosophers are vices."[8]

This cuts to the heart of what the Reformation was all about: "If this is Christian righteousness, what difference is there between philosophy and the teaching of Christ? . . . If we can be justified by reason and its works, what need is there of Christ or of regeneration? On the basis of these opinions, things have come to such a pass that many people ridicule us for teaching that men ought to seek some righteousness beyond the philosophical" (Ap, IV, 12, 13).[9] The lack of interest in "the main concern of the Reformation" then is not a recent development, but was there from the outset!

The Council of Trent consciously rejected the Reformation doctrine of justification. A certain ambiguity and evasiveness, which lend to that Council's formulations almost an air of sleepwalking, must not be mistaken for aimless or inattentive bungling. Hubert Jedin, in his great work on the Council of Trent, has shown that the leaders of the Council were well aware that the "article of justification" was the chief theological challenge and "the most important item" before the Council.[10] He also reports that Trent's decree on justification had in view mainly Luther and the Augsburg Confession, and that the "Reformed doctrines of Zwingli and Calvin were only lightly touched upon in the course of the debate."[11]

Actually the tracks for a decision on justification are set already in the article of original sin. Here the Council "was brought up against the very basis of the Lutheran teaching on justification, and one of the most difficult points of controversy, because Luther's view seemingly found support in St. Paul and St. Augustine."[12] Incredibly, the Council decreed that concupiscence, "which at times the Apostle calls *sin* [Rom. 6:12ff.] . . . the Catholic Church has never understood to be called sin, as truly and properly sin in those born again. . . ."[13] Jedin comments: "The teaching of Canon 5 on concupiscence laid the foundation of the subsequent decree on justification."[14] Not to be overlooked either is Canon 7 on justification, which rejects the teaching that "all works that are done before justification . . . are truly sins" (see note 8 above).

What this adds up to is that the exuberant optimism about fallen human nature which came to such spectacular fruition in the Second Vatican Council's "openness" towards non-Christian religions represents not modernism but the deeply ingrained Pelagianizing cautiously but deliberately dogmatized at Trent. Noble and magnanimous as such flattery of human nature and religiosity may appear today, from a Christian point of view it must bear the reproach of St. Augustine: "Why is so much assumed about the ability of human nature? It has been wounded, hurt, injured, ruined. It has need of a true confession, not of a false defence."[15]

It seems on the face of it laudably self-effacing and altruistic to ask no longer "How do I obtain a gracious God?" but "How does God accomplish the salvation of all creation?" Yet this innocent-seeming switch from the first question to the second is really a flight from faith to reason and from theology to philosophy and speculation. One must bear in mind, of course, the context of these questions, which is the assumption that divine grace is accessible also through non-Christian religions. That is the meaning of Oesterreicher's slogan-heading, "the Omnipresence of Grace." In this context of virtual universalism the grace of God ceases to be a matter of personal urgency. Nor, on these premises, can there really be an urgent concern for the salvation of others. *That* "others" are being saved is already assumed—the question is *"how?"* Attempts to find a plausible rationale for this foregone conclusion, however, arise not from the all-out emergency of standing personally under God's judgement and grace, but from the posture of a "disinterested" and leisurely contemplation of intellectual options, with the aesthetically pleasing harmony and symmetry of one's world view as goal and reward. That, of course, is philosophy, not theology.

It is astonishing how closely this seemingly modern set of problems is anticipated in the exchange between Erasmus and Luther about fallen human nature's spiritual freedom or unfreedom. There,

too, it was a matter of reason against faith, of an optimistic, com-
plimentary view of sinful humanity against the terrors of the divine
Law, of a pale philanthropy against the costly love of God. One need
not agree with Luther on all particulars to see that taken as a whole
his approach corresponds to the nature of the Gospel and of faith,
while Erasmus, for all his good intentions and his appeals to Christ
and the Gospel, really is more concerned with keeping the accounts
balanced, intellectually and socially.

Luther recognizes that human reason is offended by the apparent
contradiction of a merciful God consigning to damnation sinners who
cannot help being sinners. And so, "setting aside faith," reason "wishes
to feel and see and understand how He is good and not cruel." Reason, in the form of religious speculation, hankers after a soft and
non-paradoxical universalism in which God "hardens no one, damns
no one, but has mercy on all, saves all, so that with hell abolished
and the fear of death removed, there would be no future punishment
to be dreaded."[16] It is in these interests that God's clear self-reve-
lation in His Word is twisted with excuses for God which are really
more blasphemous than outright accusations, and with extenuations
for man which minimize his sin.[17] Such philosophizing in effect demands an accounting of God, "much as you might summon a cobbler
or girdle maker to appear in court." Unlike faith, reason cannot
endure the tension between truth and appearance and does not
submit humbly in the face of difficulties. It refuses to "give God such
glory as to believe Him just and good when He speaks and acts above
and beyond what the Code of Justinian has laid down, or the fifth
book of Aristotle's *Ethics*."[18]

We may not of course judge individual hearts, and so usurp the
prerogatives of God. Nor may we excuse rash judgment by pointing
to some obvious conflict of surface meaning or implication with God's
Word. It is always necessary to take account of fallen human nature's
ample capacity for illogical thought and for the accommodation
therefore of all sorts of inconsistent odds and ends prized for one
reason or another. Great verbal flaws and confusions (Matt. 21:28-
32!) may yet turn out to conceal a struggling, faithful heart, or even
a smoldering wick not to be quenched (Matt. 12:20; cf. Is. 42:3).
Nonetheless, at the objective level indefensible language cannot go
unchallenged, lest the weak be offended and misled. It is in this
spirit that we are probing our hypothetical modern "pious Christian's" paradigm shift from personal pre-occupation with a gracious
God to a universalistic thrust wishing to see Christ's salvation of-

fered through all other religions as well. No one denies, of course, that a serious regard for one's own salvation will issue also in a missionary zeal for the salvation of others. The point is, however, that a shift from personal salvation to an anonymous mass-salvation through all religions makes nonsense precisely of the whole missionary outlook and spirit of the New Testament—however soothing such ideas may be for the nerves of our intelligentsia.

Apparent zeal for the salvation of others need not be the fruit of a mature faith and spirituality. Perhaps the most obvious illustration here is the parable—if such it be—of Dives and Lazarus in Luke 16:19-31. Selfless concern for others is clearly not a characteristic of the lost in hell. Dives' apparent interest in his brothers' salvation really has another motive altogether. The man feels he has been unfairly treated but dare not come straight out with it. Instead, he discreetly wraps his resentment in tender solicitude for his brothers: "At least give them the chance I was denied," is the thrust of his importunity. And Abraham obliquely but pointedly refutes the claim of injured innocence: "They have Moses and the Prophets"; and then, anticipating the crowning miracle of the Lord's own resurrection: "If they will not listen to Moses and the Prophets, neither will they be converted if someone were to rise from the dead!"

Just so it is quite possible to evade personal repentance and justification by plunging headlong into "larger questions" and seeking refuge in the anonymity of religious collectivization. It is just the exclusive particularism of the cross which offends religionist and secularist alike (1 Cor. 1:23). But when the all-encompassing splendor and urgency of the justifying mercy of God pale into insignificance or recede to secondary status, it is a sure sign that sinners have become oblivious of their condition. "Those, however, who have not yet experienced the office of the law, and neither recognize sin nor feel death, have no use for the mercy promised by that word."[19] This need not prevent them from discoursing ingeniously if abstractly, like Erasmus, about salvation.

The "pious Christian," however, never outgrows his need for "a gracious God." The treasure of justification never becomes a comfortable relic of the past, to be taken for granted in the present and the future (2 Cor. 2:2; Phil. 3:7-14). That is why "everything in the Christian church is so ordered that we may daily obtain full forgiveness of sins through the Word and through signs appointed to comfort and revive our consciences as long as we live" (*Large Catechism*, Creed, 55).[20]

II

Let us begin with a deliberately restrictive definition of justification. The Formula of Concord, Solid Declaration III, 25, excluding what precedes and what follows faith, puts it like this: "The only essential and necessary elements of justification are the grace of God, the merit of Christ, and faith which accepts these in the promise of the Gospel, whereby the righteousness of Christ is reckoned to us and by which we obtain the forgiveness of sins, reconciliation with God, adoption, and the inheritance of eternal life."[21] This reflects exactly the definition in the Apology IV, 53: "In speaking of justifying faith, therefore, we must remember that these three elements always belong together: the promise itself, the fact that the promise is free [*gratuitam*, from *gratia* = grace], and the merits of Christ as the price and propitiation."[22]

The "grace of God" and "the merit of Christ" already cover virtually the whole Christian faith. The merit of Christ, for instance, embraces the vicarious satisfaction, which in turn rests on the personal union of the Savior's divine and human natures. That truth again presupposes the sublime article of the Holy Trinity, "the greatest mystery in heaven and on earth."[23] W. Maurer was quite right therefore to insist that the ancient Christological and Trinitarian dogma, far from being mere traditional dead-weight imposed on the Reformation by historical inertia, was in fact the dynamic and indispensable foundation for the Reformation's central doctrine of Justification.[24] It is hardly surprising that G. Ebeling enters an energetic protest here, to the point of proclaiming "a fundamental *dissensus* in regard to the understanding of the Reformation" between himself and Maurer.[25] Ebeling's own Christology is an emaciated critical-existentialist spectre.[26] Lutheresque "justification" or "Law/Gospel" rhetoric must, without a genuine Incarnation, remain empty words.

Furthermore, although love and good works do not belong to justification, "they are not excluded as though they did not follow, but trust in the merit of love or works is excluded from justification" (Ap, IV, 74). *Sola gratia* and *sola fide* cannot be explained except within the dialectic grace/works or faith/works. And then the whole inner renewal—love and good works—must be seen as a fruit and outcome of faith, not of the compulsion of the Law (Gal. 3:2ff.; 5:22 ff.).

And then there is the Gospel or the "promise," that most easily overlooked constituent of justification and of justifying faith. It includes, of course, the Sacraments and at once involves also the public ministry and the church. In this way it becomes quite clear why justification cannot be reduced to some isolated, self-sufficient quintessence which is indifferent to the fate of the other "articles of faith."[27] Rather, as *chief* (not *only*!) article, justification binds all other articles of the Christian faith into one organic whole which is in principle indivisible. To attack the Christian faith at any point is to violate and diminish its chief article, which is everywhere involved. Not a single article of faith confessed in the Book of Concord is extraneous or superfluous in respect of that central article on the proper understanding of which "the entire Gospel that we preach depends" (LC, Creed, 33).

"Word and faith are given together in marriage and neither can let itself be divorced from the other." So said Luther in a remarkable sermon on Matthew 9:1-8 for the nineteenth Sunday after Trinity, 1533.[28] Faith without God's express Word is for Luther a mere figment, arrogance, and superstition. Everything faith has, it has only from and through the preceding eternal means of grace. To attack or pervert these is to imperil the salvation of Christians. Here Luther sees his opponents converging. Neither the papacy nor the deniers of Baptism and of the true sacramental presence of Christ's body and blood really value the God-given channels of salvation: both resort ultimately to mysticism. "For the whole papacy rests on this doctrine: grace is poured into man by a secret operation."[29] The fanatics who boast of the Spirit and belittle the Sacraments also "tear the Word away from the forgiveness of sins."[30] (This shrewd assessment of the common ground among Luther's opponents is repeated in the Smalcald Articles.)[31] Against all this we are to remember that the Word and faith are both God's gift and doing, but He gives and does this through men: "Therefore forgiveness of sins is to be sought in the Word, which lies in the mouths of men, and in the sacraments, which are administered through men, and nowhere else; for it is nowhere else to be found."[32]

It may very well be that today the article of justification is most vehemently and concretely controverted precisely at the point of the external Gospel means. This is certainly the case with the type of universalism made popular by Vatican II. There is no question that "Christ alone" is formally maintained there, inasmuch as only Christ is said to have established the salvation which "anonymous Christians" then receive also through non-Christian religions. What is totally missing here is the outward Gospel Word and Sacrament. Therein lies a radical, unbridgeable discontinuity with Holy Scripture and the Reformation—though not with scholastic Pelagianizing.

We all need the salutary reminder, just in this connection, of the distinction between God-hidden and God-revealed: "God does many things that He does not disclose to us in His Word; He also wills many things which He does not disclose Himself as willing in His Word."[33] For this very reason, however, we must cling all the more firmly to His revealed will and scrupulously avoid those unfathomable abysses where He has not bound himself by His word, but has kept Himself free over all things."[34] It is not modesty or faith but the rankest *hubris* to proclaim universal salvation through all religions and none apart from the outward Gospel, when God Himself has solemnly charged us to cherish and proclaim that Gospel to all nations, with the built-in logic: "How shall they believe in Him of whom they have not heard? And how shall they hear without a preacher? And how shall they preach unless they are sent?" (Rom. 10:14-15). Beyond that we know nothing; results and ultimate judgments we leave to Him.

Yet for all its faults, Vatican II, with its sonorous allusions to Biblical and patristic language, seems positively "Lutheran" compared to the frankly secular vacuities urged upon the church from all sides as passports to success and popularity. One scheme wants to re-interpret everything in terms of "self-esteem" and modestly predicts that such a "new reformation" would demote the former one to an outdated "reactionary movement."[35] When faithful preaching, sound doctrine, and sacramental life are increasingly forced to yield their central, constitutive position to mass-appeal, group-dynamics, mood-making, and other emotional and psychological claptrap, then much more is involved than a mere change of "style." To cherish the supreme gift of justification is to prize above all the divine Gospel and Sacraments through which alone that gift is given, and to barter away the means is to lose the content as well.

> See, the streams of living waters,
> Springing from eternal love,
> Well supply your sons and daughters
> And all fears of want remove.
> Who can faint while such a river
> Ever will their thirst assuage—
> Grace which, like the Lord, the giver,
> Never fails from age to age?[36]

Notes

[1] J. M. Oesterreicher, "Introduction and Commentary," in H. Vorgrimler, gen. ed., *Commentary on the Documents of Vatican II* (New York: Herder and Herder, 1969), vol. III, p. 94.

[2] *Ibid.*, p. 92.

[3] *Ibid.*, pp. 92, 91. The Reformation also knew that by the Baptism of His Son God had "consecrated and set apart the Jordan *and all water* as a salutary flood and a rich and full washing away of sins" (*Luther's Works*, Phil. ed., 53, 97). But is it really charitable to suggest that as a cleansing from sin the Ganges without God's Word is anything other than "plain water and no Baptism" [Small Catechism], hence an illusion?

[4] H. T. Kerr and J. M. Mulder, eds., *Conversions: The Christian Experience* (Grand Rapids: Eerdmans, 1983), p. 236.

[5] *Commentary, Vatican II*, p. 45.

[6] "Those also can attain to salvation who through no fault of their own do not know the Gospel of Christ, yet sincerely seek God and moved by grace strive by their deeds to do His will as it is known to them through the dictates of conscience" (*The Sixteen Documents of Vatican II* [Boston: Daughters of St. Paul, n.d.], p. 126).

[7] Martin Chemnitz, *Examination of the Council of Trent*, vol. I (St. Louis: Concordia, 1971), p. 426.

[8] Errors of Michael du Bay, condemned by Pius V in 1567: "25. All works of infidels are sins, and the virtues of philosophers are vices" (H. Denzinger, *The Sources of Catholic Dogma* [New York: Herder, 1957], p. 306, par. 1025). Compare Trent's Canon 7 on Justification: "If anyone shall say that all works that are done before justification, in whatever manner they have been done, are truly sins or deserving of the hatred of God, or that the more earnestly anyone strives to dispose himself for grace, so much the more grievously does he sin: let him be anathema" (Denzinger, pp. 258-59, par. 817).

[9] T. G. Tappert, ed., *The Book of Concord* (Philadelphia: Fortress, 1959), p. 109.

[10] H. Jedin, *A History of the Council of Trent* (London: Thomas Nelson, 1961), vol. II, p. 171.

[11] *Ibid.*, p. 307.

[12] *Ibid.*, p. 145.

[13] Denzinger, par. 792.

[14] Jedin, *A History*, vol. II, p. 162.

[15] *De natura et gratia*, ch. 53, cited in Chemnitz, *Examination*, vol. I, p. 411.

[16] *The Bondage of the Will*, Luther's Works, St. Louis ed., vol. 33, pp. 173-74. (Hereafter cited as LW.)

[17] Erasmus is the victim of the optical illusion that "the precepts of the [pagan] philosophers agree very markedly with the precepts of the gospel," by which he makes himself suspect of "mocking and deriding the dogmas and religion of Christians" (LW, vol. 33, p. 111). Is there any difference between this and the supposed perception of God's salvific action "everywhere, even in the jungle, in the mountains and in the temples that have not yet been marked by the Cross" (*supra*, p. 5)? The trouble in both cases is the same: failure to distinguish the righteousness of the Law and works from that of the Gospel and faith (LW, vol. 33, pp. 263, 270ff.).

[18] LW, vol. 33, p. 206.

[19] *Ibid.*, p. 138.

[20] Tappert, *Book of Concord*, p. 418.

[21] *Ibid.*, p. 543.

[22] *Ibid.*, p. 114.

[23] *Ibid.*, p. 597, FC SD VIII, 33.

[24] Wilhelm Maurer, *Kirche und Geschichte*, eds. E.-W. Kohls and G. Muller (Goettingen: Vandenhoeck and Ruprecht, 1970), vol. I, pp. 20, 26, 32, passim.

[25] G. Ebeling, *Word and Faith*, tr. J. W. Leitch (London: SCM Press, 1963), p. 184.

[26] In *Word and Faith* see particularly the essays "The Significance of the Critical Historical Method for Church and Theology in Protestantism," pp. 17ff., "Jesus and Faith," pp. 201ff., "The Question of the Historical Jesus and the Problem of Christology," pp. 288ff., "Rudimentary Reflexions on Speaking Responsibly of God," pp. 333ff.

[27] See the formidable analysis of just such a reductionism as the driving force behind the Leuenberg Concord, in T. Mannermaa, *Von Preussen Nach Leuenberg* (Hamburg: Lutherisches Verlagshaus, 1981).

[28] *Dr. Martin Luther's Saemmtliche Schriften* (St. Louis: Concordia, 1904) XIII, col. 915.

[29] *Ibid.*, col. 917.

[30] *Ibid.*, col. 921.

[31] SA III, VIII 9, Tappert, *Book of Concord*, p. 313.

[32] *Saemmtliche Schriften*, XIII, col. 920.

[33] *Bondage of the Will*, LW, vol. 33, p. 140.

[34] *Ibid.*

[35] R. Schuller, *Self-Esteem: The New Reformation* (Waco: Word Books, 1982), pp. 174-75.

[36] "Glorious Things of You Are Spoken," Hymn 294, st. 2, *Lutheran Worship*.

Biblical Hermeneutics:
Where Are We Now?
Where Are We Going?

JAMES W. VOELZ

Questions of hermeneutics seem to be the critical questions in Biblical and religious studies today. Not only did the Lutheran Council in U.S.A. (LCUSA) feel compelled to institute hermeneutical discussions among its member churches in the 1970s, issuing in a volume entitled *Essays in Lutheran Hermeneutics,*[1] but numerous books (including textbooks[2]) have been published in recent years from every possible theological/philosophical perspective.[3] Indeed, it must be noted that recent religious hermeneutical discussions have taken place within a larger context of hermeneutical debate which includes not only secular literature[4] but also fields outside of literature as well.[5]

Concordia Seminary, St. Louis, in its history has not been uninterested in questions hermeneutic. C. F. W. Walther's *Die Rechte Unterscheidung von Gesetz und Evangelium*[6] can certainly be seen as an exercise in hermeneutical enquiry. As more of a standard, Ludwig Fuerbringer's *Theological Hermeneutics,*[7] encapsulating Georg Stoeckhardt's approach to Scriptural interpretation, was a formal attempt at hermeneutical formulation. In the 1960s, several professors of the St. Louis faculty contributed to an official volume published by the Lutheran Church—Missouri Synod[8] which explored hermeneutical issues relevant to the day. And anyone who was privileged to sit at the feet of Professors Martin Franzmann and Martin Scharlemann knows full well the devotion of these men to the hermeneutical task. Finally, it can be said without need for explication that the turmoil of the early 1970s at the St. Louis seminary, culminating in the walk-out of the majority of its faculty, was in essence a hermeneutical debate.

It seems appropriate, then, in this contribution to a *Festschrift*

JAMES W. VOELZ is Associate Professor of Exegetical Theology at Concordia Seminary, St. Louis.

for Concordia Seminary, St. Louis, to survey the hermeneutical landscape as it were, and to ask, though all too briefly, "Where are we
now, and where are we going?" We will do so by using a model or
diagram developed by Bernard C. Lategan:[9]

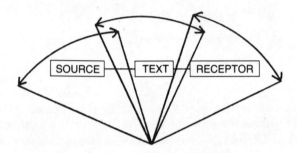

Following this "triptych" model, it may be observed that all interpretation of texts concentrates on one or more of the panels of the
triptych, whether that be text production (left panel), the text itself
(center panel), or text reception (right panel). Concerns with all of
these foci are still in evidence, and to these we now turn.

Left Panel of Triptych: Author/Text Production

A. History

According to Lategan,[10] interpretation has in recent history moved
progressively from the left hand panel of the triptych to the right,
from concern with the author and his world, to concern with the
reader and his world. He is correct. In general, it is proper to say
that interest in historical and/or historical-critical matters has increasingly receded in recent years among Biblical scholars. Though
sections, seminars, and colloquies are still held at scholarly society
meetings[11] and though books are still produced[12] on such subjects,
it is apparent from a glance at society proceedings and at book
catalogues, that interest in literary studies especially has grown.[13]
These studies concentrate either upon the text or more frequently
upon the interaction between reader and text (see below). Indeed,
Edgar McKnight has discussed the decline of interest in the historical area of scholarship specifically.[14]

What may be a significant breakthrough in synoptic studies may
be noted however. The last major work of Bo Reicke[15] has renewed
interest in the synoptic problem by presenting a coherent synoptic
theory based upon oral tradition substrata to the Gospels rather
than upon the manipulation of written documents.

B. Language

Concerns which center upon language and, therefore, the language of the Biblical text have grown in recent years, concerns which are largely two in focus. The first deals with meaning and occupies the area of semantics. The second deals with usage—how language functions—and has been given the name of "pragmatics."

1. Semantics
    a. Modern linguistic analysis of traditional semantics has found much with which to disagree. The basic problem is the Greek substratum of the approach, viz., that:
        (i) anything may be understood as the sum of its parts, so that the meaning of the whole is the sum of the meaning of its parts;
        (ii) we therefore understand a whole by breaking it into its essential parts and obtaining the meaning of those parts;
        (iii) the essential parts are the smallest parts; and
        (iv) therefore the key to the meaning of the whole is the meaning of the smallest parts.

This approach is wrong and must be rethought on several counts:

        (i) Etymology is no key to the meaning of words as used at any given time.[16] Therefore, no essential meaning of words exists but only different, though perhaps historically related, meanings.
        (ii) The meaning of a word depends upon context.[17]
        (iii) However, if context is essential to determine the meaning of a word, then the essential unit of meaning in any communication is not the word but units as large as necessary for the thought.
        (iv) Therefore, we do not get the meaning of any utterance or communication by breaking it down into its smallest units and then getting the meaning of those units. Rather we must see each linguistic usage in its entirety and view smaller units as having meaning only within the context of the larger whole. That is, the meaning of the whole is more than the sum of its parts; it is the meaning of the parts as a whole.[18]
    b. A positive approach taken by modern linguistics would make the following points:[19]
        (i) Modern communication theory is key for a general

understanding of linguistic usage. Such theory is conceived of along the following lines:

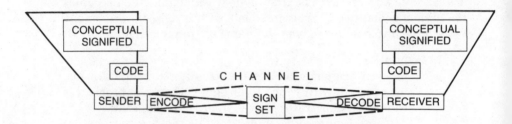

According to this model, a sender puts a message (conceptual signified) into a code (e.g., English) and sends it through a channel (e.g., the printed word) as a set of signs (the actual document). A receiver decodes the sign set using (hopefully!) the same code and from it obtains a conceptual signified.

(ii) As far as the relationship between meaning and signs is concerned, meaning precedes signs. Therefore, meaning precedes words. That is to say, words as signs do not *contain* meaning. On the contrary, they point to meaning which precedes them in time.[20] Thus, words as signs are arbitrary relative to meaning.[21]

(iii) Relationships between the meanings of signs themselves contribute to the meaning of the whole. Thus, grammar is not an afterthought to be considered only after "word studies." The meaning of a whole resides largely in relational factors. Especially problematical are two questions (a) To the meaning of which sign/ group of signs does the meaning of another sign/group of signs relate?, and (b) What sort of relationship between these meanings exists?[22] Indeed, modern "discourse analysis" seeks to understand the relationship between the meanings of very large units of signs (paragraphs, groups of paragraphs, etc.), and understands (properly) that such large components of meaning are only sub-units or subdivisions of a larger whole.[23]

(iv) The semantic components to be interpreted are not signs, forms, configurations, and wholes as they appear but the signs, forms, configurations, and wholes which are implied by them. That is to say, any communication represents hidden semantic components or unexpressed signs, especially those which give a clear indication of the relationship between the meanings of signs or groups of signs. Thus, the phrase "The love of Christ" in 2 Corinthians 5:14[24] represents hidden semantic components which relate love and Christ in some way. In other words, this phrase means either *"We love Christ* (and that act of love constrains/controls us)" or *"Christ loves us* (and that act of love constrains/controls us)." In modern parlance, the ambiguous words (signs) represent a "kernal sentence" (e.g., "Christ loves us") which gives clear expression to the thought. Perhaps better put, we can say that all language usage is shorthand, which means that words (signs) are elided in any utterance/communication, producing an economical but potentially ambiguous utterance/communication, whose full set of signs must be filled in by the receiver from the context. How one fills in the ellipses is, of course, a continuing source of conflict in interpretation, for as one so fills out the shorthand of a given text, one reads, in effect, signs—and, therefore, meanings and relationships of meanings—which, at least physically, are not actually there.[25]

2. Pragmatics

A modern approach to linguistics is increasingly conscious of the use to which language is put. That is to say, language is used to accomplish things. What is accomplished may, of course, be a description of fact. But other functions are also possible. By means of language, one may also express one's feelings, blame another, warn another, paint reality so as to give pleasure to another (cf. poetry), change a situation (cf. pronouncing of forgiveness), etc. Concern with this area has been brought to the fore by "speech-act theory," an approach popularized by J. L. Austin[26] and J. R. Searle.[27] According to the speech-act theory, language has not only a "locutionary force" (= the meaning of the words), but also an "illocutionary force," often defined as "what the words 'count as'." Thus, the question "You are going to do that again, aren't you?", given a certain setting, may "count as" a statement expressing amazement, a question eliciting information, a musing or thinking out loud, a rebuke, and more. This means that the form of an utterance bears no resemblance to its intended function—to what it "counts as"—for an admonition may be given as a statement, a question, a command, an interjection, etc.[28] Concerns with issues of pragmatics have been a motivating force in the modern renewal of interest in rhetoric, and in the rhetorical criticism of Biblical texts.[29]

Center Panel of Triptych: The Text Itself

The center panel of our hermeneutical triptych concerns the text itself and its characteristics, not factors relating to text production or text reception. Work has been done within recent years on the matter of what sorts of meanings a text may convey and how it conveys them, and to these issues we now turn.

A. *Structuralism*

Structuralism is a movement more than a system, encompassing a diverse collection of methods and approaches, which ranges by analogy through a number of loosely related disciplines. Its three characteristics are:

(i) Totalities are explained in terms of the relationship among the parts.

(ii) The structure basic to explanation is not obvious to the naive observer but lies below the surface.

(iii) Synchronic (at a cross-section in time) not diachronic (developmental) analysis is key.[30]

In the words of Anthony Thiselton: "Structuralism concerns the operation of signs within a structured system, how these signs reciprocally condition one another, and how an underlying 'code' . . . determines the range of possibilities within which the signs operate."[31]

Structuralism began in linguistics with the work of Ferdinand de Saussure (1857-1913). Saussure made the following important distinctions between:

(i) synchronic and diachronic views of language,[32]

(ii) *langue* (the total language system)[33] and *parole* (an individual act of speaking),[34] and

(iii) *signifié* (that which is signified) and *signifiant* (that which signifies).[35]

He further determined that:

(iv) signs are arbitrary and contain no natural link to that which they signify,[36] and

(v) all is defined by relationships, either syntagmatic (relating to the linear sequence of signs in actual discourse) or paradigmatic (relating to other signs in the *langue*).[37]

Saussure concluded that all language is a system which operates on several levels simultaneously in which what is hidden (cf. *langue)* determines what is seen (cf. *parole)*.[38] Saussure's concerns have been continued in linguistic studies by several schools,[39] and especially, recently, by Noam Chomsky, who has popularized the distinction between surface (seen) and deep (unseen) structures in the analysis of language[40] (cf. Left Panel, p. 236 above and the concept of "unexpressed signs").

What is especially significant for this panel of the triptych, however, is the movement of Saussure's ideas into other disciplines. Two fields, especially, have been affected. The first is literary studies. Especially among Czech and Russian literary scholars, strong structuralist influences held sway.[41] On the one hand, a structuralist approach gave rise to a very "systemic" and "synchronic" approach to literary interpretation (names such as Jakubinskij and Jakobson are key), which applied the insights of Saussure "metaphorically" with the following results:

(i) Meaning in a literary work is based upon relationships within a structure (cf. systemic principle).
(ii) A literary work's primary purpose is not in providing referential information but is aesthetic (systemic principle).
(iii) A literary work is autonomous as a linguistic entity and independent of production factors such as the author's life, social setting, etc. (synchronic principle).

Which meant that for these men, the concern was not what the work was about but how it was constructed.[42]

On the other hand, Saussure's structuralism gave rise to the very systemic but now "syntagmatic" approach to the analysis of Russian folk-tales, especially that done by Vladimir Propp.[43] Propp saw that in over one-hundred Russian fairy tales only thirty-one actions or "functions" occurred to advance the action of the plot.[44] Such actions are part of a larger system, he discovered, which entailed the actions of seven different character types,[45] with the thirty-one functions distributed invariably among the same character types, so that a tale constitutes a development proceeding from villainy or lack, through intermediate acts, to marriage (or another suitable denouement). He then followed the linear organization of the text as a manifestation of a larger, unseen system. The direction of Propp's work has been continued especially by A. J. Greimas, who has applied his insights to narrative analysis.[46] Greimas has attempted to determine the course which the mind follows as narrative is conceived, and has asserted:

> We can imagine that the human mind, in order to achieve the construction of cultural objects (literary, mythical, pictural, etc.), starts with simple elements and follows a complex course, encountering on its way constraints to which it must submit, as well as choices it can make.[47]

In other words, Greimas has detected a "narrative grammar," i.e., he believes that the mind organizes actions by specific actors into "narrative statements," and that such "statements" are joined into chains or "syntagms."[48] Thus, in the words of Edgar McKnight, "the human mind conceives of and composes meaning in narrative by a logical arrangement of syntagms."[49]

Structuralism has also affected the field of anthropology. The key figure here is Claude Lévi-Strauss. Lévi-Strauss took the principles of Saussure and applied them to culture. Basing his approach upon the insight that culture is a system of signs which conveys meaning, he asked rhetorically:

> Although they belong to *another order of reality,* kinship phenomena are *of the same type* as linguistic phenomena. Can the anthropologist, using a method analogous *in form* (if not in content) to the method used in structural linguistics, achieve the same kind of progress in his own science as that which has taken place in linguistics?[50]

And Lévi-Strauss concluded,[51] drawing upon both linguistic and literary studies before him, that: (i) synchrony is primary; (ii) cultural objects and acts must be viewed relationally; (iii) what appears is not as important as what is below the surface (the "unconscious infrastructure"); (iv) general laws are to be sought which would have an absolute character; and (v) the concept of system is crucial, in which binary oppositions are key.

Lévi-Strauss put these insights into practice in his analysis of culture,[52] and he found that the analysis of myth was an important tool in anthropological investigation.[53] Specifically, Lévi-Strauss discovered that in the myth of various cultures, many binary oppositions occur, e.g., raw/cooked, fresh/decayed, moistened/burned,[54] gods/men, fiber/sinew.[55] Also in these myths, there seemed to be a consistent attempt to mediate these oppositions,[56] i.e., to take a middle ground. From this, Lévi-Strauss concluded that myths in the various cultures of mankind reflect fundamental oppositions in reality (life/death, male/female, nature/culture), that such fundamental oppositions are irreconcilable logically, and that myth is an attempt to reconcile the irreconcilable by substituting surface binary oppositions, which do admit of mediation, for deeper oppositions which do not.[57] Therefore, we find many surface binary oppositions, plus attempts to mediate them. Thus, in the Zuñi system of myths,[58] life and death are represented by the activities of agriculture and warfare, which are themselves mediated by hunting (which provides food, as does agriculture but involves killing, as does welfare). Hunting, in turn, is represented by predator animals, which themselves are in binary opposition to herbivores (= agriculture), and this opposition is mediated by scavengers (which eat flesh but do not kill).

What does this mean? Going beyond Lévi-Strauss, Daniel Patte suggests the following:

> This brief series of oppositions . . . provides therefore a progressive mediation of the fundamental opposition which taken in itself does not admit of a mediation and confronts man with an existential dilemma. The mythical structure unites as a meaningful universe a potentially meaningless and broken existential reality. In the case of this version of the Zuñi myth, death is viewed as sustaining life.[59]

Therefore, Lévi-Strauss concluded, the meaning of myths (which is the key to understanding culture) is not their traditional meaning. Rather the elements of myth, when seen within their structure, provide an insight not so much into a specific culture but into the basic structure of the human mind:

> . . . *myths signify the mind that evolves them* by making use of the world of which it is itself a part. Thus there is simultaneous production of myths themselves, by the mind that generates them and, by the myths, of *an image of the world which is already inherent in the structure of the mind* (emphasis added).[60]

And this mental structure is transcultural, not limited by any specific cultural manifestation.

How is all of this relevant to Biblical studies and Scriptural interpretation? It is significant because structuralism has affected the way modern interpreters approach the sacred Scriptures. First, and by no means least significant, structuralism has affected the way language as such is now viewed. Much of this is reflected in the Left Panel, Section B, above. The emphasis that the whole is more than the sum of its parts, that relationships are key, and that what is unseen is more important than that which is seen—all of these are particularly structuralist emphases.

Second, structural approaches have been applied directly to the Biblical text. Propp's concerns with function and actors has been taken up by Robert Culley, e.g., with the conclusion that the miracle stories of the Old Testament consistently built upon three successive units of action or "motifemes."[61] Lévi-Strauss' structuralist analysis which entails binary oppositions, mediations, and the structure of the human mind has been applied by Edmund Leach to the creation story, with the conclusion that the so-called "myth" of Genesis 1 reflects the fundamental oppositions between "the world of God" and "the world of man."[62] Leach's effort is the clearest example of an attempt to see the mediation of binary opposites in a story. He accomplishes this for each day of the creation and for the entire week.[63] And the syntagmatic approach of Propp/Greimas, plus the paradigmatic approach of Lévi-Strauss, have been continued by Daniel Patte, to produce works which are both theoretical and exegetical.[64] His *What is Structural Exegesis?*[65] is a fine introduction to the entire proceeding, while his recently published *The Gospel According to St. Matthew: A Structural Commentary on Matthew's Faith*[66] brings the concept of oppositions to bear on narrative,[67] producing exegetical insights which are truly helpful.[68]

The problem with structuralism is its anthropocentric, anthropological orientation, which seems to make of religion an entirely human thing, and which tends to view man as creating God in the image of his own mind. It must be said, however, that the concept of binary oppositions may have certain apologetic benefits. Vern Poythress has taken Lévi-Strauss' idea that life and death are binary opposites which admit of no mediation and concluded that: "In fact, Christ has accomplished in history the real 'mediation', corresponding to which the supposed oppositions and mediations in non-Christian myths represent only a groping in darkness in response to general revelation and deepest human needs."[69]

B. *Type/Levels of Meaning: A (Step-) Child of Structuralism*

Structuralism makes the point that the signs of a text convey meaning and that the meaning conveyed is beyond the surface or basic sense of the words as signs. Further, it directs our attention to the deeds described by the words of a text as signs and analyzes their meaning. Finally, it suggests that a, if not the, value of a text may be in its ability to give insight into the maker/speaker of the textual signs. These insights, it seems, can be put to good use in any analysis of text, especially the texts of narrative.

There are, it would seem, at least three types or levels of meaning which texts convey.[70] The first may be called the level of sense, the basic meaning of the words as signs. Thus, Luke 7:14b-15a[71] means: "And he (Jesus) said, 'Young man I say to you, "Arise".' And the dead man sat up and began to speak . . ." not "The disciples went to buy bread and ate it." On this level, we are concerned with the marks on the pages as signs and their denotation (taken, of course, as a matrixed whole, not as a sum of parts).

The second level may be called the level of significance, the meaning of the acts depicted by the words as signs (in the case of narrative; in the case of discourse, we may say: the meaning of the ideas asserted by the words as signs). In the text from Luke above, the activity depicted, i.e., the resurrection of the young boy, has theological significance. What that is is given, in fact, in verse 16b: "God has visited his people" (the crowd could "read" the activity!). On this level, we are concerned with the meaning of the acts depicted (or ideas presented) by the words on the page as signs.

The third level may be called the level of implication. Here we are concerned, as is structuralism, with what the words of the text or what the deeds/ideas described by those words tell us about the maker of the text himself. To continue our example from above, Luke includes this story in his Gospel; indeed; he is the only Gospel writer to do so. Does that fact tell us something about Luke or about his audience? In other words, the fact that Luke deals with this matter may reveal something about him and his time: perhaps the problem of the death of believers was acute, or, perhaps there was a question concerning who Jesus was and what He could do. The fact that something is included in the text at all tends to imply things about the writer and/or his audience.[72] On this level, we are concerned with "reading between the lines" for information regarding the writer and his audience at their place in time.[73]

The analysis here suggested takes seriously a text as a matrix of signs, which matrix signifies a matrix of conceptual signifieds, all of which signifies further matrices of signs and conceptual signifieds.

Right Panel of Triptych: Reader/Text Reception

Structuralists are numerous, and it is well known that structuralists do not agree. The question naturally arises, "Why not?" If structures are objectively present in a text, and if meaning is conveyed by those structures, should not interpretation be a simple task? Increasingly this problem is pushing itself to the fore. And the answer increasingly given is, "Perhaps everything isn't in the text." Different readers read the same text and produce different readings of that text. Perhaps the reader/interpreter is a factor in the matter of the meaning of a text. And this is the concern of the right hand panel of our hermeneutical triptych, text reception. In very recent years, the focus has been upon the reader/hearer/receiver of the Biblical text, with the assertion that the reader is a necessary component in the process by which meaning arises in a text. It is to these developments which we turn in this final major part of our hermeneutical *Forschungsbericht*.

A. *The Role of the Reader in the Interpretation of a Text*

The role of the reader/receptor as it relates to the meaning of a text is raised by the field of semantics itself. For signs convey no meaning unless they are decoded, and such decoding is done only by the recipient(s) of the signs. What is the meaning of a given set or matrix of signs? Increasingly, the answer given is: meaning is apart from a discussion with the author/sender of those signs,[74] that the receiver determines. This is true even on the most basic level of sense. Consider again 2 Corinthians 5:14. Do these words of Paul mean that Christ controls him or do they mean that his love for Christ controls him? Some argue for the former, some for the latter, and some for both. The truth is that the answer lies only in the text. But the text cannot speak for itself—the reader is interpreting the text! And it is of no use appealing to the "intention" of the author, for apart from a special interview with him,[75] the author's intention is detectable only in the text. Indeed, the importance of the receiver for the meaning of a matrix of signs is seen especially on the more complex level of significance, i.e., the meaning of the deeds/ideas depicted or asserted by the words the text assigns. Generally, the receiver finds significance in the acts/ideas depicted or asserted by the text, apart from any explicit guidance from the author of that text. This is especially true in the genre "story." As a reader interprets story, he is left to consider—on the basis of his own knowledge of the times, his own experiences in the world, and his own understanding of the rest of the books of Scripture—what it means, e.g., that the Sanhedrin met at night to try Jesus for murder, or that the workman covered up the treasure which he had discovered in the field.

And it is even more complex than this. Consider how meaning, especially in narrative texts, actually arises; not through a consideration of individual deeds, persons, places, things, events, situations, and so on. Rather, meaning arises through a relational understanding of these things: through the flow of events, through the connection of activities, through the development of situations. But how is this complex detected—the development, the flow, the connections? And how is this complex understood—what is the meaning of it all? That is seldom explored; here there seem to be few rules. Here the interpreter must act, for it is he who relates and connects, and it is he who sees meaning or not.[76] The so-called "structure" and meaning of the text is seen by the receiver alone.[77]

B. Valid Interpreters/Interpretations

Who, then, is a valid interpreter of a text? To this modern scholarship has devoted much attention. It can best be answered by examining a diagram which details the distinction between the reader, the text, the author, and the story of the text:[78]

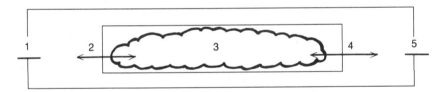

The inner box represents the (physical) text. The actual author (#1) and the actual reader(s) (#5) are concrete entities in the world outside the text, while the action of the story (#3), which constitutes the "world" of the text, is not physically in the text (not as the marks are on the page) but is depicted by the signs of the text itself.[79] What, then, is the relationship between the reader, on the one hand, and the text, author, and story, on the other? The reader (#5) reads the text, and in so doing he "(re)constructs" the author in his own imagination (the "implied author," #2), plus, he brings the story (#3) to life ("actualizes the text") from the marks which he sees on the written page.

But what is on the other side (i.e., opposite) of the implied author (#2) in the scheme: (#4)? The answer is the obverse of, the complement of, the left side: namely, a reader of whom the author is conscious, one who may also be called "implied." And this implied reader stands in the same relationship to the actual reader as the implied author stands to the actual author; he is, again, a construct, not in

the real world, and he is detectable (only) in the text.[80] This implied
reader is a person, a receptor, with that knowledge, those abilities,
that competency, which enables him to actualize the text. He is a
conception of the author—it is for him which the author writes (though
he in no actual fact corresponds to any actual reader of the text).
Who, then, is a valid interpreter of a text? It is he who conforms to
the expectations of the author. It is he who conforms himself to the
given text's assumptions. It is he who becomes the implied reader—
and only such a one—of a given text.

Where does one find the implied reader of the Bible or any other
text? The answer of modern criticism[81] increasingly is: one does not
find him by looking for an individual, for a reader is not alone. A
reader is taught to read. A reader knows facts because he is instructed. A reader develops attitudes by conversation and discussion. That is to say, a reader interprets in a community, with other
readers, with other receptors, with those who are his contemporaries, and with those who have gone before. Therefore, a reader
can become the implied reader only as he is trained to be that implied
reader within a context where the implied reader of a text is appreciated and understood.

A valid interpreter of a text, then, is that person who assumes
the role required by a given text—who becomes the reader implied
by that very text. And such a one is instructed to assume that role
by a community, a community which has assumed that role itself.

What this means for the Scriptures is quite clear. The reader
must know Jewish culture, ancient Mediterranean civilization, the
entirety of Scripture, and much more. All of these things are plain.
But the reader must also believe—he must embrace the faith. St.
Paul writes "to the saints" (cf. Rom. 1:7). St. Mark heads his Gospel
with a reference to the "Son of God" (1:1). And St. Luke says explicitly
to Theophilus: ". . . that you may know the surety of those things in
which you were first instructed" (Luke 1:4). A believer is implied.
And only such a one can read and read correctly. It is for this reason
that St. Paul says in 2 Corinthians 3:15-16: "But until today when-
ever Moses is read, a veil lies on their [the Jews'] hearts. But when
a man turns to the Lord, the veil is taken away." According to Paul's
argument, the Jews do not believe; therefore the Jews cannot be the
implied reader of the sacred text.[82] A veil lies before their understanding.

This entire set of competencies, then, encompassing knowledge,
attitudes, and beliefs, is required of a reader of the sacred Scriptures
and one will find one with this set of competencies in a community

which has assumed the role of implied reader of this given text, i.e., in a baptized and believing community of the people of God.

C. The Reading Experience and Meaning

But a modern hermeneutical approach sees the reader as critical to the meaning of a text, not only as a factor in the process by which meaning arises but also in another important and novel way (again, narrative is often in view). Consider once again the chart presented above. As a reader reads a story, he gets the distinct impression that the (implied) author (#2) is narrating a story (#3) and telling it to him.[83] The reader normally assumes (or tries to assume) the role of the implied reader (#4), i.e., of the one to whom the story is told.[84] In this process there is a definite distinction between the implied reader and the characters in the story, with the characters having knowledge beyond that of the implied reader, and the implied reader knowing things which the characters do not know. The result is that the reader reacts to the characters in the story—he has expectations, disappointments, etc.,—which means that, the reader experiences as he reads. The insight of modern hermeneuticians, especially of those who work in "reader-oriented criticism,"[85] is that the meaning of a text is not simply something that a reader is told or understands. Rather, the meaning of a text is also what a reader experiences as he reads. Robert Fowler expresses it well in his analysis of Jesus' telling of the Parable of the Sower and the Seed in Mark 4:

> The experience of reading Mark 4:11-13 can be summarized briefly. The temptation here is to say that the text tells us that those who "see" often are in fact "blind," and those who "hear" often are in fact "deaf." The text, especially the parenthetical comment in 4:12, does say something like that, but far more important than what the text *says* is what it *does*. We are not merely *told* about those who "see and yet do not see," *we are given the opportunity to experience this for ourselves.* The reader lives through the experience of being shut out of insight and understanding by an opaque veil, followed by the gift of sight and understanding, in a surprising reversal of position with those who had started out on the favored side of the veil.
>
> The experience of reading Mark 4:11-13 is illustrative of the experience of reading Mark's Gospel as a whole in several respects. For one thing, reading Mark's Gospel is less a matter of being informed of certain facts and ideas and more a matter

of being given the opportunity to live through certain kinds
of experiences.[86]

D. Application: A Fourth Type/Level of Meaning

Finally, of course, a reader is active in determining the meaning
of a text on another level, viz., on the level of what the text means
to him. Such meaning is not, of course, meaning in the senses used
in the discussion of meaning in the previous part (Part III, Section
B), but it is, in fact, what might be called "application."[87] Thus, as
a reader decodes a textual set of signs, on the level of sense, significance, and/or implication, he makes application from any one or
more of these three levels to himself in his situation.

But reader-oriented criticism has shown in recent years that in
this area, too, texts are infinitely more complex than they have
heretofore been seen to be. First, we are reminded, readers do not
just draw conclusions as they interpret a text. When they read, they
have the experience of being spoken to by a text: that is, discourse
occurs between the implied author and the reader who assumes the
role of the implied reader of the text. This may be called the "discourse level" of a text. As a result, the implied author "speaks" to
the implied reader on the discourse level, through the medium of
the story level. But, second, we are reminded that it is really much
more complex than this. As a reader decodes on the level of sense,
significance, and/or implication, he may not only hear the implied
author speaking to him on the discourse level. As he actualizes a
text, application may be made to him directly by the text. That is
to say, as a reader reads and the world of the story arises, it is, at
times, discovered that elements of the world of the story speak to
him, directly, apart from the lesson of the story or the "voice" of the
implied author of the text. This occurs, it seems, in the Gospel of
Mark, and that in two ways. Robert Fowler, following J. L. Austin
and speech-act theory, has shown that it occurs at those points in
the story where the characters in the story do not seem to hear or
understand what is going on—when they do not exhibit "uptake" in
the story over against what has just been said (or done).[88] In such
cases, the words are heard by the reader as he reads and they speak
to him, even though they are never taken up by any character on
the level of story in the actualized text. Prime examples are the Son
of Man sayings throughout the Gospel of Mark.[89] The world of the
story also makes application directly to the reader by the actual
effect which the story has upon the reader, regardless of the factor
of uptake on the story level. That is to say, the effect of being spoken

to directly may be experienced vividly at various points by the reader of a text. An example may be in Jesus' discourse before His Passion in Mark 13. Again, in the words of Robert Fowler:

> Mark 13 begins with Jesus and four disciples coming onto . . . the Mountain of Olives, strategically set "opposite the temple." Jesus has just said that the stones of the temple will all be torn down. The disciples ask when this will occur, and what will be the sign pointing to this calamity. Jesus then delivers the chapter-long discourse, full of the veiled, figurative language of apocalyptic. Although the disciples remain on the stage throughout the apocalyptic discourse, we in the audience all but forget their presence, for the entire discourse is spoken over their heads and directly at us.
>
> One linguistic signal of the dramatic and rhetorical nature of Mark 13 is the profusion of second-person plural pronouns in the discourse. In a highly inflected language such as Greek, the use of pronouns, at least in the nominative case, is semantically superfluous. Therefore, the use of such redundant pronouns serves as a way of adding emphasis to one's language. Mark 13 is full of such emphatic, redundant, second-person plural pronouns. . . . Ostensibly these pronouns are designed to engage the four disciples on the stage, but they are too strong, too emphatic, merely to serve that elementary purpose. Rather, they raise the intensity of Jesus' language to such a pitch that the story level is all but transcended. Jesus' words function primarily at the discourse level, the pronouns pointing at the extra-narrative audience. If this were not clear enough in the midst of the chapter, the very last verse of the chapter spells out to whom the discourse is really aimed. . . . "And what I say to you I say to all: Watch . . ." (13:37). What Jesus says to "you"—ostensibly the four disciples—is really aimed at "all"—the audience of the Gospel drama.[90]

The Gospel of John would seem to be an especially promising text to explore for application made to the reader directly by a text, whether through lack of uptake on the story level or by the story's actual effect.[91]

Conclusions

What does all of this mean—all which we have surveyed? The importance of much of what has been reviewed is clear; indeed, lesson/applications have been drawn out as this essay has proceeded. Perhaps it is good to draw two further conclusions, however, before the essay reaches it close.

First, it must be emphasized that interpreting a text—any text, including the Biblical texts—involves many factors, including text production, the actual text itself, and the reception of that text. Simplistic views of textual interpretation will not do. Textual interpretation does not involve, at its most fundamental level, "simply" factors of production (e.g., knowing the historical setting, or seeking to determine the "intention" of the author), "simply" the text itself (e.g., considering the text as autonomous sign without any regard for historical context), or "simply" text reception (the "modern" fallacy, e.g., considering any reader's meaning as a legitimate meaning of the text[92]). Interpretation is hard work, and it is a difficult task.

Second, the role of the reader/receptor must be appreciated in our Lutheran circles, especially in the Lutheran Church-Missouri Synod—and that not only in the matter of application. The receptor is a factor also in the process by which the meaning of a text arises. In this end of the process the community is quite key. But this is no insight or principle to fear. For it promotes a thoroughly confessional stance when it is rightly understood. From the first, the church has said that all interpreters of the sacred text must hold to the church's faith or they cannot treat that text at all. This was the consistent witness of Irenaeus,[93] Tertullian,[94] and a host of other church fathers as well. And now literary studies, as has been shown,[95] suggest that, in principle, this is true. For the Scriptures are the church's book. As a result, those who adhere to her words, those who confess the faith which she has sworn she will confess are they who can interpret these books. Historic Christianity, true "catholic" (i.e., universal) doctrine and belief—this is the womb of our book. And this can only mean that the readers who are among those who believe and who hold this faith are the implied readers of that book which is the foundation of that very faith.

Notes

[1] John Reumann, ed., *Studies in Lutheran Hermeneutics* (Philadelphia: Fortress, 1979).

[2] See, e.g., Henry A. Virkler, *Hermeneutics: Principles and Processes of Biblical Interpretation* (Grand Rapids: Baker, 1981), and Duncan S. Ferguson, *Biblical Hermeneutics: An Introduction* (Atlanta: John Knox Press, 1986).

[3] An excellent introduction to the field is Terence O. Keegan, *Interpreting the Bible: A Popular Introduction to Hermeneutics* (New York: Paulist Press, 1985). Also extremely helpful but more narrowly philosophical is Anthony C. Thiselton, *The Two Horizons: New Testament Hermeneutics and Philosophical Description* (Grand Rapids: Eerdmans, 1980). For an introduction to liberation

and feminist approaches, see Juan L. Segundo, *The Liberation of Theology* (Maryknoll, NY: Orbis Books, 1976), and Mary Ann Tolbert, "Defining the Problem: The Bible and Feminist Hermeneutics," *Semeia* 28 (1983): 113-126. For a very conservative/fundamentalist approach, see Norman L. Geisler, *Explaining Hermeneutics: A Commentary* (Oakland, CA: International Conference on Biblical Inerrancy, 1983). Also of interest in denominational terms is Kenneth Hagen et al., *The Bible in the Churches: How Different Christians Interpret the Scriptures* (New York: Paulist Press, 1985).

[4] A classic work is Richard E. Palmer, *Hermeneutics: Interpretation Theory in Schleiermacher, Dilthey, Heidegger, and Gadamer* (Evanston, IL: Northwestern University Press, 1969). See also Josef Bleicher, *Contemporary Hermeneutics: Hermeneutics as Method, Philosophy and Critique* (London: Routledge and Kegan Paul, 1980); Kurt Mueller-Vollmer, ed., *The Hermeneutics Reader: Texts of the German Tradition from the Enlightenment to the Present* (New York: Continuum Publishing Co., 1985); and Edgar V. McKnight, *Meaning in Texts: The Historical Shaping of a Narrative Hermeneutics* (Philadelphia: Fortress, 1978), as well as Roger Lundin et al., *The Responsibility of Hermeneutics* (Grand Rapids: Eerdmans, 1985). For a fascinating work which interprets the Gospels, especially Mark, against the background of literature in general, see (John) Frank Kermode, *The Genesis of Secrecy: On the Interpretation of Narrative* (Cambridge, MA: Harvard University Press, 1979) (cf. pp. vi-xi).

[5] For the area of science, see Mary Gerhart and Allan Russel, *Metaphoric Process: The Creation of Scientific and Religious Understanding* (Fort Worth, TX: Texas Christian University Press, 1984), and Vern S. Poythress, *Science and Hermeneutics: Implications for Scientific Method for Biblical Interpretation* (Grand Rapids: Zondervan, 1988). For counselling, see Donald Capps, *Pastoral Care and Hermeneutics* (Philadelphia: Fortress, 1984).

[6] C. F. W. Walther, *Die Rechte Unterscheidung von Gesetz und Evangelium* (St. Louis: Concordia, 1897).

[7] Ludwig Fuerbringer, *Theological Hermeneutics: An Outline for the Classroom* (St. Louis: Concordia, 1924).

[8] Richard Jungkuntz, ed., *A Project in Biblical Hermeneutics* (St. Louis: Commission on Theology and Church Relations of the Lutheran Church—Missouri Synod, 1969).

[9] Bernard C. Lategan, "Current Issues in the Hermeneutical Debate," *Neotestamentica* 18 (1984):3.

[10] Lategan, "Current Issues," p. 4.

[11] The 1988 meeting of the Society of Biblical Literature (SBL) included, e.g., Qumran Section, Sociology of the Second Temple Consultation, Historical Jesus Section, as well as the sessions of ASOR.

[12] See, e.g., Wayne A. Meeks, *The First Urban Christians: The Social World of the Apostle Paul* (New Haven, CN: 1983).

[13] The 1988 meeting of the SBL also included many sub-units such as Literary Aspects of the Gospels and Acts Group, Literary Study of Rabbinic Literature Group, Narrative Research on the Bible Group, and Biblical Criticism and Literary Criticism Group. Major publishers are now putting out books such as Bernard C. Lategan and Willem S. Vorster, *Text and Reality: Aspects of Reference in Biblical Texts* (Philadelphia: Fortress, 1985); John P. Heil, *The Letter of Paul to the Romans: A Reader-Response Commentary* (New York: Paulist Press, 1987); Robert Alter and (John) Frank Kermode, eds., *The Literary Guide to the Bible* (Cambridge: Belknap Press of Harvard University Press, 1987); and Stephen D. Moore, *Devouring Our Living with Harlots: Literary Criticism and the Gospels Today* (New Haven, CN: Yale University Press, forthcoming). The volume by Stephen D. Moore will contain the creative and wide ranging unpublished essay "Stories of Reading That Have No Ending: An Introduction to the Postmodern Bible."

[14] Edgar V. McKnight, *The Bible and the Reader: An Introduction to Literary Criticism* (Philadelphia: Fortress, 1985), pp. xv-xix.

[15] Bo Reicke, *The Roots of the Synoptic Problem* (Philadelphia: Fortress, 1986).

[16] Thus, knowing that "post" in the sense of "posting a ledger" comes from "men stationed along a road to go with dispatches" provides no key to the meaning of this word in this context.

[17] "Run" means something different in each of the following sentences: "They run marathons." "The river runs down to New Orleans." "She runs her husband." "They run steam engines on that line." "The door runs from ceiling to floor."

[18] For similar critiques, see Johannes P. Louw, *Semantics of New Testament Greek* (Philadelphia: Fortress, 1982), and Anthony C. Thiselton, "Semantics and New Testament Interpretation" in *New Testament Interpretation: Essays in Principles and Methods*, I. Howard Marshall,

ed., (Grand Rapids: Eerdmans, 1977), pp. 75-104. Of great importance as a landmark work in this area is James Barr, *The Semantics of Biblical Language* (London: Oxford University Press, 1961). Also of value, though written from a somewhat traditional perspective, is George B. Caird, *The Language and Imagery of the Bible* (Philadelphia: Westminster Press, 1980).

[19] An interesting new overview of modern linguistics as applied to the New Testament, though the material which follows is not dependent on it, is David A. Black, *Linguistics for Students of New Testament Greek: A Survey of Basic Concepts and Applications* (Grand Rapids: Baker, 1988).

[20] Following this theory a new Greek-English lexicon for the New Testament has just been released, Johannes P. Louw and Eugene A. Nida, eds., *Greek-English Lexicon of the New Testament Based on Semantic Domains,* 2 vols. (New York: United Bible Societies, 1988). Rather than grouping its entries by signs (i.e., words) and indicating which meanings may be attached to those words as signs, it groups its entries by meanings and details which signs (words) may reflect/point to those meanings.

[21] There is nothing inherently problematical, e.g., in using the word (sign) "gay" to denote (signify) "homosexual," for it does not "really" mean anything.

[22] To what, e.g., does the thought of Col. 3:4 relate (to the thought of which verse or sentence preceding [v.1?, v.4?])? And how is that relationship to be understood (as indicating reason, result or something else)?

[23] See, e.g., Louw, *Semantics,* pp. 91-158, and Robert E. Longacre, *The Grammar of Discourse* (New York: Plenum Press, 1978).

[24] ἡ γὰρ ἀγάπη τοῦ Χριστοῦ συνέχει ἡμᾶς . . .

[25] The phenomenon here discussed stands behind much of the problem surrounding Bible translation technique. Those translations which employ a "dynamic equivalence" approach seek to make the "deep structure" or hidden semantic components explicit in the translation (e.g., NIV, TEV). Traditional translations seek more or less to reproduce the simple "surface structure," i.e., what is seen (e.g., KJV).

[26] John L. Austin, *How to Do Things with Words,* 2nd ed. (Cambridge: Harvard University Press, 1975).

[27] John R. Searle, *Speech Acts: An Essay in the Philosophy of Language* (London: Cambridge University Press, 1969). For a simple introduction to the speech-act approach, see Kevin J. Vanhoozer, "The Semantics of Biblical Literature: Truth and Scripture's Diverse Literary Forms," in *Hermeneutics, Authority, and Canon,* Donald A. Carson and John D. Woodbridge, eds., (Grand Rapids: Zondervan, 1986), pp. 85-92.

[28] See Thiselton, "Semantics," p. 77. A commentary which considers these factors is Wolfgang Schenk, *Die Philipperbriefe* (Stuttgart: W. Kohlhammer, 1984). See page 19 for theory, and, e.g., his treatment of ἀδελφοί and ἐγώ in Philippians 3:13 (p. 259):

> Wie also P[au]l[us] in 3,18 mit dem eingesprengten Relativsatz den imperative-Aspekt zur Warnfunktion einbringt, so hat er auch sonst andere Mittle ais nur imperativ-und Kohortativemorpheme des Verbs, diesen Textpragmatischen Akzent zu verbalisieren: In 3,17 wie 4,1 wurde dies deutilich, als der imperative durch die Anrede ἀδελφοί verstärkt wurde. Diese Anrede findet sich . . . in 3,13. Dort ist diese ἀδελφοί der Addresaten direkt gefolgt von einem redundant verbalisierten ἐγώ des Senders. Dam it wird die Beispiel-und Vorbildhaftigkeit dessen, was Pl von sich selbst sagt, auch für die Andressaten schon signalisiert. Was 3,17 als Mimesis-Aufforderung direkt ausformuliert, ist hier schon gegeben . . . Die ἀδελφοί-Andrede hat also ebenfalls imperativfunktion. . . .

It must also be said, in something of an anticipation of Part IV below, that speech-act theory speaks of language's "per locutionary force" as well. This is intended to say that what an utterance "counts as" for the speaker may not be the same as what it "counts as" for the recipient, i.e., a question uttered as a rebuke may, in fact, be received by the recipient as a cognitive question, in which case a breakdown in communication has occurred—not on the level of meaning (semantics) but on the level of pragmatics.

[29] See, e.g., Wilhelm Wuellner, "Where is Rhetorical Criticism Taking Us?" *The Catholic Biblical Quarterly* 49 (1987):448-463, which contains excellent bibliography. A classic work is George A. Kennedy, *New Testament Interpretation Through Rhetorical Criticism* (Chapel Hill, NC: University of North Carolina Press, 1984).

[30] Michael Lane, ed., *An Introduction to Structuralism* (New York: Basic Books, Inc., 1976), pp. 14-17.

[31] Anthony C. Thiselton, "Keeping up with Recent Studies: II. Structuralism and Biblical Studies: Method or Ideology?" *The Expository Times* 89 (1978):329. Note that sign and code are concepts similar to those of the communications model described above.

[32] Ferdinand de Saussure, *Cours de Linguistique Générale*, (Paris: Payot, 1969), p. 117: "De même *synchronie* et *diachronie* désigneront respectivement un état de langue et une phrase d'evolution."

[33] *Ibid.*, pp. 30-31: "La langue n'est pas une fonction du sujet pariant, elle est le produit que l'individu enregistre passivement. . . . Elle est la partie sociale du language, exterieure à l'individu. . . ."

[34] *Ibid.*, p. 30: "La parole est au contraire un acte individeul de volonté et d'intelligence."

[35] *Ibid.*, p. 99: "Nous proposons de conserver le mot *signe* pour designer le total, et de remplacer *concept* et *image acoustique* respectivement par *signifié* et *signifiant*."

[36] *Ibid.*, p. 100: ". . . le signe linguistique est arbitraire. . . ."

[37] *Ibid.*, p. 171. Saussure calls these relationships "le rapport syntagmatique" and "le rapport associatif." For the basics of Saussure, see also McKnight, *Meaning in Texts*, pp. 97-99, and Thiselton, "Structuralism," p. 330.

[38] See McKnight, *Meaning in Texts*, p. 99 and Thiselton, "Structuralism," p. 330.

[39] Of primary importance are the so-called "Czech School" (especially Troubetzkoy) and the "Copenhagen School" (especially Hjelmsley) in the 1930s, and Leonard Bloomfield (U.S.) in the 1950s. See McKnight, *Meaning in Texts*, pp. 99-103.

[40] Noam Chomsky, *Aspects of the Theory of Syntax* (Cambridge: MIT Press, 1965).

[41] For the treatment of this topic I am indebted to McKnight, *Meaning in Texts*, pp. 104-107.

[42] An excellent example is the analysis of Baudelaire's poem "Les Chats" by Roman Jakobson and Claude Lévi-Strauss in "Charles Baudelaire's 'Les Chats'," in *Introduction to Structuralism*, M. Lane, ed., pp. 204-216. See an extensive treatment of this analysis with response in McKnight, *Meaning in Texts*, pp. 109-116.

[43] McKnight, *Meaning in Texts*, pp. 155-158.

[44] E.g., absenting oneself, reconnaissance, fraud, return, pursuit, exposure, etc. See McKnight, *Meaning in Texts*, p. 156 and n. 42, p. 196; also p. 262.

[45] These comprise villain, donor, helper, princess, her father, dispatcher, hero, and false hero. See McKnight, *Meaning in Texts*, p. 156.

[46] See McKnight, *Meaning in Texts*, pp. 167-179, and n. 119, pp. 200-201.

[47] A. J. Greimas and F. Rastier, "The Interaction of Semiotic Constraints," *Yale French Studies* 41 (1968):86-87.

[48] McKnight, *Meaning in Texts*, p. 260.

[49] *Ibid.*

[50] Claude Lévi-Strauss, *Structural Anthropology*, transl. from the French by Claire Jacobson and Brooke Grundfest Schoepf (New York: Basic Books, Inc., 1963), p. 34. See also p. 71: ". . . we have not been sufficiently aware of the fact that both language and culture are products of activities which are basically similar."

[51] *Ibid.*, pp. 33-35.

[52] I am indebted to Daniel Patte, "Structural Network in Narrative: The Good Samaritan," *Soundings* 58 (1975):232, for the organization of this paragraph.

[53] Claude Lévi-Strauss, *The Raw and the Cooked: Introduction to the Science of Mythology: I*, trans. from the French by John and Doreen Weightman (New York: Harper and Row Publishers, 1969), p. 1, and Lévi-Strauss, *Structural Anthropology*, pp. 206-231.

[54] Lévi-Strauss, *The Raw and the Cooked*, p. 1.

[55] Lévi-Strauss, *Structural Anthropology*, p. 222.

[56] *Ibid.*, p. 224.

[57] *Ibid.*: "If we keep in mind that mythical thought always progresses from the awareness of oppositions to their resolution . . . we need only assume that two opposite terms with no intermediary always tend to be replaced by two equivalent terms which admit of a third one as mediator; then one of the polar terms and the mediator become replaced by a new triad, and so on." See also p. 229: ". . . the purpose of myth is to provide a logical model capable of overcoming a contradiction. . . ."

[58] *Ibid.*, pp. 221-225, especially p. 224.

[59] Daniel Patte, "Structural Network in Narrative," p. 232.

[60] See p. 341. See also p. 10: ". . . when the mind is left to commune with itself and no longer has to come to terms with objects, it is in a sense reduced to imitating itself as object. . . ."

[61] Robert Culley, *Studies in the Structure of Hebrew Narrative* (Philadelphia: Fortress, 1976), p. 92. For specific examples, see especially pp. 73, 81, 82.

[62] Edmund Leach, *Genesis as Myth and Other Essays* (London: Jonathan Cape, 1969), p. 10.

[63] *Ibid.*, pp. 12-18. See especially days 1-3 and 5.

[64] Among the best is his "Structural Network in Narrative," pp. 221-243, referred to above.

[65] Daniel Patte, *What is Structural Exegesis?* (Philadelphia: Fortress, 1976).

[66] Daniel Patte, *The Gospel According to St. Matthew: A Structural Commentary on Matthew's Faith* (Philadelphia: Fortress, 1988).

[67] *Ibid.*, pp. 5-8.

[68] See, e.g., his treatment of 11:1-6 (Patte, *Gospel According to Matthew*) pp. 157-159.

[69] Vern S. Poythress, "Structuralism and Biblical Studies," *Journal of the Evangelical Theological Society* 21 (1978):233.

[70] A fourth level is also possible. See below, Part IV.

[71] . . . καὶ (ὁ Ἰησοῦς) εἶπεν νεανίσκε, σοὶ λέγω, ἐγέρθητι. καὶ ἀνεκάθισεν ὁ νεκρὸς καὶ ἤρξατο λαλεῖν. . . .

[72] Historical-critical investigation, and, traditionally, "Introduction" *(Einleitung)* deal with a text on this level.

[73] For a more complete explication of this analysis, see James W. Voelz, "The Problem of 'Meaning' in Texts," in a forthcoming issue of *Neotestamentica*.

[74] Even this is more problematical than it seems. It is said that Ezra Pound found at least three, if not more, meanings to his own poem "In the Station of the Metro." See Robert Crosman, "Do Readers Make Meaning?" in *The Reader in the Text: Essays on Audience and Interpretation,* Susan R. Suleiman and Inge Crosman, eds. (Princeton, NJ: Princeton University Press, 1980), pp. 151-154, including footnote 7.

[75] But see n. 74 above.

[76] Wolfgang Iser has expressed an idea similar to this with his concept of "gaps" *(Leerstellen)* in a text. A reader fills in what an author does not tell him in a story, not only in somewhat trivial matters such as what the hero looked like, but also and especially in relating events, determining significances, etc. See Iser's programmatic work *The Implied Reader: Patterns in Communication in Prose Fiction from Bunyan to Beckett* (Baltimore: Johns Hopkins University Press, 1974), pp. 274-297.

[77] This problem is complicated by narratives which partake of the genre of history. For history is story, but it is story with a twist. It is not only the author's tale. Here, external occurrences are the key. Here, the story, at least to some extent, precedes the story-teller. It is independent of him, in part. And, therefore, in part, it may be interpreted apart from him. His intention for the "facts" cannot fully control the story which precedes. Thus, we may read that story apart, as it were, from his intention, apart from his conscious meaning, even, beyond his own intention.

[78] The diagram presented is my own variation of a standard diagram (see, e.g., Keegan, *Interpreting the Bible*, p. 94), normally attributed to Seymour Chatman (cf. Seymour Chatman, *Story and Discourse: Narrative Structure in Fiction and Film* [Ithaca, NY: Cornell University Press, 1978], pp. 146-151). See also Robert Fowler, "Who is 'the Reader' of Mark's Gospel?" in *Society of Biblical Literature Seminar Papers*, Kent H. Richards, ed. (Atlanta: Scholars Press, 1983):38-46.

[79] I have made the lines of this somewhat amorphous, because the content of a story will be different when read by different readers or when read repeatedly by the same reader.

[80] It may also be said that the detection of the implied reader is accomplished only by a reader as he reads.

[81] See especially Jonathan Culler, *Structuralist Poetics: Structuralism, Linguistics, and the Study of Literature* (Ithaca, NY: Cornell University Press, 1975), pp. 113-130, and Stanley Fish, "Interpreting the Variorum," *Critical Inquiry* 2 (1976):465-485.

[82] I am indebted to Terence Keegan (*Interpreting the Bible*, pp. 88-89) for this line of argumentation.

[83] Many analysts distinguish between the implied author and the narrator, with the latter being the "voice" one hears narrating and the implied author the one reconstructed as the writer. Normally, there is no difference, but occasionally, as in Mark Twain's *Huckleberry Finn*, the narrator is "naive," and we can tell that he and the implied author are not one and the same. An example from television would be the "voice" over-lay on the "Dukes of Hazzard," who is not as omniscient as an author himself would be! For an important discussion of the relationship between the narrator and the implied author in the Old Testament, which asserts that the

narrator (especially in the Pentateuch) is omniscient as God is omniscient, and, therefore, that he is not distinguishable from God, see Meir Sternberg, *The Poetics of Biblical Narrative: Ideological Literature and the Drama of Reading* (Bloomington, IN: Indiana University Press, 1987), especially pp. 58-128.

[84] See previous note. One could distinguish between the "narratee" and the implied reader in like manner.

[85] Two types (closely related) of reader-oriented approaches exist. The first, essentially Continental and more historically oriented, is "Reception Theory." A fine introduction is given in Robert C. Holub, *Reception Theory: A Critical Introduction* (London: Methuen, 1984). The other, more American and sometimes clinical/psychological, is "Reader-Response Criticism." It receives a fine introduction in Jane P. Tompkins, ed., *Reader-Response Criticism: From Formalism to Post-Structuralism* (Baltimore: Johns Hopkins University Press, 1980). See also Suleiman and Crosman, *The Reader in the Text: Essays on Audience and Interpretation.* In this essay the two will not be distinguished. See also the outstanding bibliography in Stephen D. Moore, "Stories of Reading That Have No Ending."

[86] Robert M. Fowler, "The Rhetoric of Direction and Indirection in the Gospel of Mark," (Unpublished essay), p. 21. This essay will be included in a forthcoming issue of *Semeia* edited by Edgar V. McKnight.

[87] The matter of "application" and its relationship to the "meaning" of a text has been a source of extreme difficulty in recent years, especially in the opposing positions of Hans-Georg Gadamer (*Wahrheit und Methode: Grundzüge einer philosophischen Hermeneutik,* 2nd ed. [Tübingen: J.C.B. Mohr, 1965] and Erich D. Hirsch (*Validity in Interpretation* [New Haven, CN: Yale University Press, 1967]). The position suggested in this paper is similar to Hirsch's but is broader and is not dependent upon it. See James W. Voelz, "The Problem of 'Meaning' in Texts," notes 1-5.

[88] Fowler, "Rhetoric of Direction and Indirection," p. 4.

[89] Fowler says ("Rhetoric of Direction and Indirection," p. 11):

> There is no demonstration of uptake for the Son of man statements in 2:10 and 2:28 at the level of story. Indeed, *no Son of man statement in Mark's Gospel ever receives clear and unmistakable uptake at the level of story.* But if the characters in the story do not hear or understand the Son of man statements, who does? The narratee, obviously. There has never been a recipient of Mark's narrative discourse who has not heard every single Son of man statement in the Gospel and understood them all, at least to some extent.

[90] Robert Fowler, "The Rhetoric of Direction in Mark: Explicit Commentary by the Narrator" (paper presented at the seminar on The Role of the Reader in the Interpretation of the New Testament, of *Studiorum Novi Testamenti Societas,* Trondheim, Norway, August 1986): p. 4. Fowler's observations are true even if one is not reading the Greek. The continual direct address of this discourse, plus the seeming disappearance of the disciples from the scene (as Fowler suggests) makes this direct address to the reader in a translation as well as in the original.

[91] Consider, e.g., the problem of chapters 15-17, which seem to be an intrusion between 14:30-31 and 18:1. Jesus' speech surely functions at the discourse level as well as at the story level. One does not have to see a crude redactional seam here. See R. Alan Culpepper, *Anatomy of the Fourth Gospel: A Study in Literary Design* (Philadelphia: Fortress, 1983) for a reader-oriented treatment of John's Gospel.

[92] A more sophisticated version of this and one that is attaining increasing popularity is the notion that the correctness of readings is basically a matter of power/politics: those groups in power determine what may be done with a text and thereby exclude outsiders. Moore tends heavily toward this viewpoint in "Stories of Reading."

[93] *Adversus Haereses* 1.1.15.

[94] *De Praescriptione Haereticorum* 15-18.

[95] See n. 81 above.